CROSS

C000172852

CROSSFIRE

CROSSFIRE

An Australian Reconnaissance Unit in Vietnam

PETER HARAN
ROBERT KEARNEY

Published in Australia by
New Holland Publishers (Australia) Pty Ltd
Sydney • Auckland • London • Cape Town
14 Aquatic Drive Frenchs Forest NSW 2086 Australia
218 Lake Road Northcote Auckland New Zealand
86 Edgware Road London W2 2EA United Kingdom
80 McKenzie Street Cape Town 8001 South Africa

First published in 2001 and reprinted in 2001.

Copyright © 2001: Peter Haran and Robert Kearney
Copyright © 2001 in photographs: As noted for each photograph
Copyright © 2001 in map: Don Ingram

All rights reserved. No part of this publication may be reproduced,
stored in a retrieval system or transmitted, in any form or by any means,
electronic, mechanical, photocopying, recording or otherwise, without the
prior written permission of the publishers and copyright holders.

National Library of Australia Cataloguing-in-Publication Data:
Haran, Peter, 1948–.
Crossfire: an Australian reconnaissance unit in Vietnam.

ISBN 1 86436 721 0.

1. Vietnamese Conflict, 1961–1975—Reconnaissance operations, Australian.
2. Vietnamese Conflict, 1961–1975—Personal narratives, Australian.
3. Vietnamese Conflict, 1961–1975—Participation, Australian.
4. Vietnamese Conflict, 1961–1975—Veterans—Australia—Interviews.
I. Kearney, Robert, 1946–. II. Title.

959.7043394

Publishing Manager: Anouska Good
Editors: Sean Doyle/Monica Ban
Designer: Karlman Roper
Reproduction: PICA
Printer: Griffin Press

Cover Photo: Canadian freelance war photojournalist Daryl Henry was permitted to travel with the Reconnaissance Platoon during the Long Hais patrol (described in 'Break Contact'). On this operation the platoon was involved in several heavy contacts with the enemy, and during one of these firefights Henry took a series of photos—lying on his side snapping pictures while the bullets were snapping in around him and the Australian diggers. The cover shot captures Platoon Commander Mick Deak, map in hand, preparing to call in mortar and artillery. Henry was respected and admired by the men from Recce. All efforts to find him since the Vietnam War have failed; he was last heard of in El Salvador—with his camera and notebook.

The body copy is set in Bembo, Optima and Courier 10 pt.

FOREWORD

This is a remarkable story. As an older, still-serving soldier, I know the authors, many of the characters and the events they describe, and I have sweated it out in many of the areas in South Vietnam where the story largely takes place.

A considerable amount has been written about Australia's war in Vietnam and quite a bit at this plane—that of personal recollection. To me this account is especially compelling because the authors have a wonderful knack for vivid yet convincing descriptions of operations, battles, moods and the digger vernacular. On many occasions you feel as if you are standing alongside 'Dogs' and his friends. You can laugh and ache with them and feel the unique, breathless, adrenaline rush of close-quarter battle. Like them and me, you feel a great sadness for those lost and damaged souls who still carry the burden of their service for their country in that war, into their middle and ageing years.

All these years later it seems pointless to engage in political dialectic about the whys and wherefores of the Vietnam War. What is undisputed, and from this book unmistakable, is that our young Aussies who went off to that desperate, far-off place, full of hope and apprehension, performed with valour, good humour and stoicism on par with their most illustrious ANZAC predecessors. It was a privilege to stand in their midst.

Read this story. Read about these Australians. They are so ordinary but so extraordinary—they are heroes.

Lieutenant-General Peter Cosgrove, AC, MC
Chief of Army
Canberra
February 2001.

CONTENTS

PREFACE

Crossfire should be titled *Replay,* because that's exactly how I felt when I read it. This is a book that is very much about the digger on the ground during the Vietnam War. It is also about the infantry soldier with his finger on the trigger—that finger, when you inspect it closely, even has dirt under its fingernail, and it's that aspect that makes the book so engaging. In many ways I found the book difficult to read at times, simply because it tends to touch on so many memories and raw nerves. Those nerves in many instances haven't been touched for 30 years . . . and are still quite tender.

As a forward scout in Vietnam between 1966 and 1967, I can identify very closely with every sentiment—from the smell of the maps covered with plastic contact in the wet scrub, to the incident of killing leeches in many different ways. (My favourite method was to impale them on very sharp bamboo thorns and then roll them inside out along the thorn.) Now there we have a case in point—until I read the leech story in *Crossfire,* I had completely forgotten that I used to do that over there. I am so relieved to hear that I was not alone in my perverse sense of entertainment!

However, the book is more than a collection of small stories. It fully recounts the personal confrontations that were part and parcel of that form of warfare—without going into the detail of battle and tactics, and the politics, except where it had its effect on the digger in the field.

To me, *Crossfire* brought back those memories of being a scout, when your every sense was filled with anticipation just prior to action and contact. Once the firing started, it was indeed almost a relief from the tension, and I can once recall describing it as a feeling of 'fearful joy' once the contact began and the bullets started to fly. For many of us, this book may well have come at the right time in our lives, as I suspect it will help many Vietnam vets get that monkey off our backs.

Major (Retired) Les Hiddens, 'The Bush Tucker Man'
Townsville, Queensland, 2001.

ACKNOWLEDGMENTS

This book was written by two Vietnam veterans. It tells of a group of men who went to war—and of those who survived and came back. But it is also the story of many soldiers who served with the Australian Forces in South Vietnam between 1962 and 1972.

Every soldier who ever walked out beyond the wire returned with his personal account of combat and its attendant trauma. Some men will never reveal those circumstances and events that left them deeply scarred for the remainder of their lives. They were men caught in the crossfire of war and its aftermath. But others found, three decades later, that with some encouragement and compassion from other vets they were able to talk about their war experiences—and purge their demons.

The story told here is about the first Australian Reconnaissance Platoon formed in Vietnam. The 'Recon' or 'Recce' story tries to capture a time and a place during the Vietnam conflict, while the other narrative running in tandem reflects on that conflict and its repercussions in personal terms. We have avoided writing an exhaustive historical account, and have changed dialogue only where necessary to maintain fluency and coherence.

The stories could not have been told without the help of former soldiers who sat and talked, and on occasion wept. Much of this took place on what is called 'Trojans' Trek', a self-help program for Vietnam veterans conducted in the South Australian Flinders Ranges over five days. Here vets share their experiences in an effort to heal past hurts, a process enhanced by the natural beauty of the Australian bush. At no time have we broken confidences or identified the men from Trojans' Trek.

We also relied on previously published material by former soldiers. For this we are thankful to former 5th Battalion Intelligence officer, Captain Robert O'Neill, and his excellent account of the battalion's 1966-67 tour of duty in *Vietnam Task* (Cassell

Australia, 1968). Thanks also to Dr Tony White, 5RAR's Regimental Medical Officer, for his account of the Long Hais mine incident (first published in *The Canberra Times*, 22 February 1967). Vietnam veteran Brian Tate researched and discovered the identities of the two missing-in-action American airmen, Captain Charles Stephen Franco and Major John Charles Jacobs (see 'The Secret of Nui Nghe'). Their names can be located at the Vietnam War Memorial in Washington (also known as 'The Wall'), on Panel 08E, lines 17 and 18.

We appreciate the help of former Reconnaissance Platoon members John 'Blue' Mulby, Mick Deak and Trevor 'Taffy' Cheeseman, who gave us advice and encouragement while we were researching for this book. Thanks also to Denise and Liz, who were 'war widows' during the writing process.

To the men and women at New Holland Publishers who had to come to grips with the complexities of Australians at war in Vietnam, we salute you. Thanks to Publishing Manager Anouska Good for her interest in the project and for going in to bat for *Crossfire*. Finally, this book would hardly have been possible without the skills of editor Sean Doyle, who worked tirelessly to make the manuscript hang together and to make the two stories work as one.

Peter Haran
Robert Kearney
Adelaide, 2001.

BACKGROUND BRIEFING

Australia's military involvement in the Vietnam War began in May 1962. The Australian Government eventually withdrew all military forces from the conflict in 1972—the end of this country's longest war, effectively 10 years, and of a commitment which divided this nation, at times, in violent, bloody confrontation between anti-war demonstrators and authorities. Many will recall that the Vietnam experience actually led to blood being spilt on Australian streets.

Here is a brief chronicle of Australian involvement in Vietnam.

- May, 1962—The Australian Army Training Team, a group of 30 officers and senior NCOs, is dispatched to training installations across Vietnam.
- June 1964—The number of advisers is increased to 80. The first Australian, Warrant Officer Kevin Conway, is killed in combat in July.
- November 1964—The Australian Government introduces selective conscription.
- May 1965—1st Battalion Royal Australian Regiment and support units, totalling 1100 men, arrive at Bien Hoa and begin ground operations.
- January 1966—Prime Minister Harold Holt increases the Australian commitment to two infantry battalions, 5RAR and 6RAR, and a Task Force group—4500 men, including 500 conscripts—which arrive in South Vietnam's Phuoc Tuy Province in April 1966.
- December 1966—The Australian Government increases its commitment to the war with another infantry battalion, taking the ground force to about 6500.
- January 1968—Major Australian combat units begin operations in Bien Hoa and Long Kanh provinces.

Communists launch the TET Offensive and the Vietnam War reaches its highest level of intensity—as does opposition to it in the US and Australia.

- November 1968—President Richard Nixon pledges to end the war and negotiate an acceptable peace.
- April 1970—It is announced that one of the Task Force's infantry battalions will be withdrawn. The South Vietnamese Army takes a greater combat role in the war.
- September–October 1971—The last major actions involving Australian troops.
- November 1971—4RAR is the last unit to withdraw from the Task Force base at Nui Dat.
- November 1972—A handful of Australian advisers remain in South Vietnam. All Australian troops are home by Christmas.
- March 1973—Prime Minister Gough Whitlam announces the establishment of diplomatic relations with Hanoi, while still recognising the South Vietnamese Government.
- March 1973—The last US troops leave Vietnam.
- April 1975—The Australian Embassy in Saigon closes and South Vietnam continues to fight the North.
- April 1975—Ten years after Australia's involvement in the war began, South Vietnam falls to Communist forces.

THE ENEMY IN PHUOC TUY PROVINCE IN 1966–67

The North Vietnamese Army (NVA)'s 274 Main Force Regiment—known as the Dong Nai Regiment—moved into Phuoc Tuy's north-western zone in 1965. It comprised two experienced battalions, totalling about 2000 soldiers. The NVA were trained, disciplined and well-armed troops with support units of mortar and heavy machine-gun squads as well as engineers, or sappers, capable of carrying out well-mounted assaults on an Australian or American force of almost any size. In November

1965 the 275 Regiment ambushed and virtually wiped out an elite South Vietnamese Ranger Battalion in central Phuoc Tuy Province—only five kilometres from where the Australian Task Force would be built.

In addition, a Vietcong (VC) mobile battalion, known as D445 Provincial Mobile Battalion, with an estimated 550 soldiers, was active in the province.

All this was supported by 400 guerillas operating in groups ranging from 5 to 60 in number. These VC units were supported and directed by Vietcong infrastructure in villages and hamlets across Phuoc Tuy. This means that at the time 5RAR and 6RAR arrived to establish the first Australian Task Force, there were up to 3000 enemy ready to fight for domination of Phuoc Tuy Province.

COMPOSITION OF AUSTRALIAN COMBAT UNITS

Military units referred to in this book range from section to Task Force and battalion strength. During the war no unit was up to full strength, for a variety of reasons, ranging from sickness and casualties to leave and unit transfers. But generally—on the books—the units were as follows:

- An infantry **section** comprised 10 men with a corporal in command.
- A **platoon** numbered 33, led by a 2nd lieutenant with a sergeant second-in-command.
- An infantry **company**, usually about 120 personnel, comprised three platoons and a company headquarters group, and was led by a major.
- A **battalion**—nine of which were formed and saw active service during the Vietnam War—numbered just over 800 troops, and was made up of four infantry companies (A, B, C,

D), an Administration and Support Company, and a Battalion Headquarters Group. The Support Company included Signallers, Mortars, Assault Pioneers and an Anti-Tank Platoon, which, because of the absence of enemy tanks in the war, carried out infantry platoon tasks. The battalion was commanded by a lieutenant-colonel.

• A **regiment** comprised three infantry battalions and supporting services. Australia did not have a regiment at the start of its involvement in the Vietnam War, so a Task Force of two battalions and support services was assembled. The two battalions in Vietnam were reinforced by a third battalion in late 1967.

The First Australian **Task Force** in 1966 included the two above-mentioned battalions (5RAR and 6RAR), artillery (1st Field Regiment), an armoured component (1st Armoured Personnel Carrier Squadron), engineers from the 1st Field Squadron, 103 Signals Squadron, 3 Squadron Special Air Service (SAS), a Task Force logistics company, and the RAAF's No. 9 Squadron of helicopters and Independent Reconnaissance Flight aircraft.

NATIONAL SERVICE

All 20-year-old males in Australia were required to register for National Service, or conscription. The exceptions were tribal Aborigines, non-naturalised immigrants, employees of a foreign government, and permanent members of the armed forces. There were two registration periods a year: in January for those turning 20 in the first half of the year, and in July for those with birthdays in the second half. In 1965 an annual maximum requirement of 4200 men was set; this figure was raised to 8400 a year from 1966.

Selection by ballot was adopted and conducted each March and September, with marbles representing two dates—one in the first half of the year, one in the second—drawn from a barrel. Males with those birth dates were called up. Those who did not register for conscription, about 12,000 in all, were liable to be fined and conscripted whether or not their birth dates were chosen in the ballot.

VIETNAM WAR FACTS
- Overall casualties: 5.7 million
- Estimated dead: 2.1 million
- Dustoff missions: 500,000
- Estimated South Vietnamese killed: 587,000
- South Vietnam military killed: 220,000
- Defoliants sprayed: 19 million (US) gallons
- Helicopters used: 12,000
- Helicopters shot down: 4865
- Americans killed: 58,169
- Australians killed: 504
- Average age of Australian soldier in Vietnam: 20
- Average age of Australian soldier in World War II: 26
- Number of Australians who registered for National Service: 804,000. Of these 63,735 were called up and 19,450 went to Vietnam.
- Number of National Servicemen who became casualties: 1479, with 200 dead
- Numbers of days Australian combatants spent in the field in one year: 314

Phuoc Tuy Province

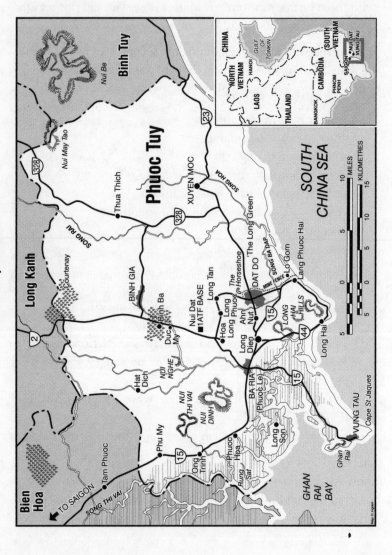

PROLOGUE

Adelaide, 2000

Robert 'Dogs' Kearney tossed me a laminated, rat-chewed, red mud-splattered, musty-stinking Army map. Kearney was a soldier I had served with in Vietnam during my second tour in 1971, and the ex-combat infantry sergeant thought the map would come in handy for a book we were planning to write.

'*Vietnam with Mud in Your Eye*', he suggested for the title. 'Or how about *Stop Whispering*? All we did in Vietnam out in the weeds was whisper. When we got back to the 'Dat we were *still* bloody whispering.'

There were a lot of things about the war, and the two years that Kearney and I spent there, that nearly drove us mad; nearly drove thousands of men mad—things like living a life whispering in the jungle. 'Dogs' Kearney, like me, went through near-meltdown after the Vietnam War. We were told to put the experiences behind us when we came back, but that was absurd: how the hell do you put it *behind* you when every day you rewind and replay thoughts of war and remembrance? I suppose we assumed that as the years drifted away, so would the war: like an old soldier, it would never quite die, just fade away. And those who had never heard of Vietnam, never witnessed—or taken part in—the anti-war moratoriums, wouldn't give a stuff any more anyway. The Vietnam War had passed from an experience to a historical event, so forget the war, digger, everyone else has.

Maybe we could have, but for the fact that a curious thing has happened in recent years: a lot of the next generation *want* to know what happened in Vietnam; how we came to be up to our necks in that foul mess for 10 bloody years. They thirst to know what it was *really* like, and what's happened to those men since.

As for the state of the Vietnam vet today: the truth is, he's not travelling too well. Time hasn't dulled the effects of war neurosis—it's made it worse. After I wrote *Trackers,* about my first year in Vietnam as a 19-year-old soldier with a war dog, the publisher and many readers asked: what's with the men now that the war's over? What's all this post-traumatic stress disorder (PTSD)? Well, PTSD basically means you can't deal with what you saw and what you felt—you are fucked in the head. Excuse the emphatic expletive, but that's exactly what's wrong with thousands of vets today, with varying degrees of severity.

Bob Kearney, an interesting blend of the intense, the abrasive and the compassionate, asked me about writing another war book.

'It has to tell the truth,' he said. 'Include the insanity, the intensity and stink of the Vietnam War, sure, but let's also tell how men have survived, are now living a better life and are coping with the aftermath. Explain how after Vietnam they are warriors, not victims. And let's also tell how the rehabilitation has been managed.'

Bob's idea seemed to be a way to reveal a lot I didn't write about in *Trackers.* A dog called Caesar seems to have hogged that book . . .

We decided to write this one together. Bob would write his story of the Reconnaissance Platoon in the first person, from his viewpoint, and I would add background details based on my experiences in Vietnam: the debris of war that is missed in historical studies, the grunt, the 'Namstalgia', the story of men who went to the edge and clawed their way back with a new perspective. We decided the book would be one with *attitude,* to use a contemporary buzz-word—the attitude of the Vietnam combatant, then and now. After 1000 capuccinos, travelling a lot of dusty roads, exchanging a few thousand words, here is the story of men who were—are—caught in the crossfire . . . and of their redemption.

I still didn't want to look at Kearney's map. The stench of it made me remember a time and a place.

You can replay your past by reading old letters, playing old rock music or standing in the room of a house where you lived as a child, and your past can certainly breathe again when you open a 35-year-old map on a kitchen table.

Run a finger over the plastic contact skin and feel the history, bend and smell the combination of mildew and mustiness. Look closer now and you will see the faint red chinograph pen marks smudged across the plastic skin. The red, ruler-straight lines were compass bearings drawn by a patrol commander in the jungle.

Jump from a hovering Huey or from the back of an armoured personnel carrier at any location on this map and you knew that ahead of you were days—even weeks—of crossing those 1000-metre-wide grid squares, contour lines of brown, jungle greens and swamp blue. You couldn't look at a map of South Vietnam's Phuoc Tuy Province without picturing the soldiers who traversed the terrain; soaked in the Wet, parched in the Dry. Exhausted all day, every day. If voices could rise up from a map and speak, they would drift up from Phuoc Tuy Province in 1966.

Memories are also names, places and images. Here they are now. Run a finger west to Nui Thi Vai and see men fleeing a crashing chopper, beating itself to death on the side of a mountain, pieces of rotor flying like shrapnel. Go south to the Long Hais: an orange flash, black smoke and men trapped in a minefield. South-west, and your finger traces the blue hues of the Rung Sat: a Zippo lighter and a peasant's burning hut. Move 20 grid squares across to Xuyen Moc: soldiers breathing in and breathing out, drenched with sweat under triple jungle canopy.

Every name on this map tells a story, but to really know the stories you need to go back and walk across every grid square, metre by metre . . .

BEACHHEAD AND BAYONETS

Flinders Ranges, 2000

First rays of morning sunlight strike Oratunga Station and a group of men are standing around the cold embers of a camp fire. They are all in their mid-50s, a disparate, dispirited group; many coping with the first cigarette of the day, coughing back at the crows in the nearby gum trees. Stiff joints pop and crack.

Each man straps on a belt with water bottles attached and then hoists a backpack. Some wear old Army bush hats, others Akubras, and there is a sprinkling of sweat-rags and neckerchiefs. One man stands apart from the rest and quietly gives instructions.

'No spitting on the ground—to spit upon the ground is to spit upon your ancestors and mother Earth.'

The men shake out into single file and turn towards the horizon where the Flinders Ranges, jagged and weatherbeaten, shear upwards in a series of crags, folds and ripples. The men have a long trek ahead. Within minutes they collectively slip into old habits and space themselves out—almost like a military patrol . . .

CONFIDENTIAL INTSUM (Intelligence Summary): July 1966—Latest official statistics show the Communists have an estimated armed force of 250,000 in South Vietnam. US Military recently disclosed Hanoi now infiltrating 5500 troops per month and the tempo could conceivably rise. Allied Forces: 700,000 South Vietnamese, 255,000 Americans, 26,500 other Free World Military Assistance Forces.

We could smell Vietnam long before we saw it.

It was that curious Asian mix of fish, rotting vegetables and human faeces. The shit stink was easy to explain—it floated in the

4

waters off Cape St Jacques. The fish and veggie smells drifted across the sea from the port of Vung Tau.

The old aircraft carrier, *Sydney*, had dropped anchor earlier that morning and the Navy set to dropping charges in the water to deter—or kill—any Vietcong divers trying to mine the ship. I thought for a second: *do the VC actually have frogmen?* A few minutes later in came the chopper, drum-beating across the ocean. A group of men alighted after the Huey touched down on the deck, including what we recognised as two of the Military's heavyweights—General William Westmoreland and an Aussie called Brigadier Oliver Jackson. This was the Top Brass: Commander-In-Chief of the Armed Forces in Vietnam and the leader of the Australian Forces in Vietnam. We knew who these men were, we'd seen their pictures. Both the bullshit and the buck stopped with these two: the Power and the Glory.

Westmoreland was jut-jawed, no-one-stuffs-with-me, dressed in green fatigues with creases that would slice bread.

'Gentlemen of the 5th Battalion, I salute you,' he rasped, and he threw a real salute to an amused several hundred men lined up on the flight deck. The digger next to me, Warren 'Wogsy' Burns, farted and grunted.

'That's two firsts for me: being saluted by a four-star Yank general, and being called a bloody gentleman.'

The chopper went back the way it came, the landing craft came alongside, cargo nets were thrown down, and we scrambled for a grip as we went over the side. Even the thickest grunt recognised this as high farce. We wore slouch hats with the sides up and a white ID card with a number stuck in the puggaree. Making the whole landing operation only more absurd was the fact that we lugged old World War II pattern packs on our backs, clutched a rifle in one hand and in the other held a kit bag with all our worldly possessions stuffed inside. The LCMs cleaved a wake towards the Vung Tau beaches, loaded with a bunch of idiot tourists armed for combat.

You'd swear this was D-Day, I thought as we sloshed and rocked towards the land. The smell grew stronger, heightening the belly-wobbling, gut-tightening tension in anticipation of what was waiting when we hit the beach.

'Fix bayonets!'

Tich nudged me. 'He's joking, right? Tell me this bloke is joking.'

Bang! The LCM ramp dropped forward, water poured in and we stumbled, staggered and half-charged onto the beach.

The big fat Yank leaning against the door of the closest truck in the convoy parked on the esplanade gaped at us with his chin on his chest. Momentarily stunned by the hordes of men ready to charge at him, the American wasn't sure whether to shake hands or bolt. He did neither, then shouted at us in panic.

'You goddamned guys get those knives off your rifles before you get in my trucks!'

A young Vietnamese boy squatting nearby waved a greeting with a huge smile, '*Eh, Uc Da Loi!*'

That's what they called us: 'People from the South'. Our first taste of Vietnam—no war, a smiling child and red-faced embarrassment.

Some men landed in the war zone under fire, bums clenched down, heads up. Others got shot on day one, week one. One digger I heard of jumped off a truck on his first day and left part of his finger and wedding ring ripped off, dangling on the tailgate.

I arrived for the war late. I was the commander of Seven Section, Nine Platoon, Charlie Company, 5th Battalion. We had spent a week acclimatising in the sand dunes near Vung Tau, waiting and sweating it out, a collective bag of nervous anticipation, preparing for the push north into Phuoc Tuy Province.

The landing in the LCMs, the fat Yank and the humiliation of the D-Day-style disembarkation was behind us. Now we were rationed up and loaded, waiting for the slicks of choppers from the American 68th Aviation Company. Time to go to war.

But Murphy's Law cut in as soon as the choppers began the airlift. Loaded to bursting with soldiers, the machines struggled, rocked and crabbed sideways, the rotor downwash sandblasting the men who staggered forward before clambering into the passenger bays.

'Too heavy, get the goddamn hell off, *we're too heavy!*" the door gunner was screaming into my face. He lunged with his boot and I sprawled back onto the ground.

'The Big Day', 24 May 1966, the start of Operation Hardihood, and I was flat out, looking up at a sky full of Hueys. My section was clattering northwards and I was left behind like a wounded duck. I was late for the war.

A red-faced Warrant Officer who was coordinating the lift strode up to me and shouted above the roar of incoming aircraft, 'What the bloody hell do you think you're doing, digger? Get over here, there's more where they came from—get on the next lift.'

I should have known at that moment that Vietnam was going to be a catalogue of stuff-ups for me, for all of us—downhill all the way.

I was 20 years old, a lad from Kilburn in Adelaide, and on this day I was—not to put too fine a point on it—shitting myself. I was asking myself, *What the hell did I do wrong in this life to be standing here? Did I upset some bastard in a past life? Is God punishing me . . . again?*

God dealt me His first shitty hand when he gave me two huge ears as a kid. That's how I got the name 'Dogs': 'Hey, Dog's Ears,' five-year-old Trevor Norman used to call me. That was at St Bridget's Primary School in Kilburn, a suburban working class suburb previously known as 'Little Chicago'. I underwent reconstructive surgery later (as a child), which helped camouflage the wing nut look. I escaped the 'Dogs' tag for years, until an old school mate who joined the Army the same time I did in the 1960s recognised me on a train with a bunch of soldier mates and called out, 'Hey Dogs, how are ya?' The nickname was an irresistible attraction to my fellow soldiers, who hung a handle on every name they could. We had 'Wogsy' and 'Bones' and 'Tich'; there was 'Skinny', a 'Butch' and 'Little Mac'. Every unit in the Australian Army had a dozen redheads called 'Blue'; a man called Mills became 'Millsy', and a Page ended up 'Pagey.' If your name was unpronounceable, the Army subculture quickly tagged you 'Wheelbarrow'—indicating, of course, that the moniker was so unwieldy you needed a barrow to lug it about. The Army at war in the 1960s comprised men with simple attitudes, and renaming every grunt had a deformalising, levelling effect. It made life a whole lot easier.

Take Marinko 'Tich' Tomas, my section second-in-command. He was a 20-year-old from a small timber and dairy town in Western Australia called Nannup. If anyone epitomised the National Serviceman (or 'Nasho'), it was Tich: a faceless, nameless bloke from the bush whose life was changed forever when a small marble with his date of birth on it popped up. No way was he going to remain Marinko. 'Tich' sort of fitted his size and demeanour; he looked and acted a 'Tich'.

The Australian Government needed young men—needed them fast for the commitment to the war effort. Some called these thousands of Australians 'cannon fodder'; many Nashos were below the voting age (21 at the time), and most of them would end up as grunts in the infantry. Tich, Wogsy, all those Blues and Little Macs, and hundreds like them were now part of the 5th Battalion, the first major unit since the Big One—World War II—to go to war with a hefty component of National Servicemen in its ranks. I met Tich in an old hut at Holsworthy Army Barracks outside Sydney. He was a little older than me; he was a bloke with a grin, and always a fast quip. We connected straight away.

He slung his pack up on his back in the middle of what had been designated LZ Hudson and listened to my mumbled apology about being late.

'Shit, mate,' he said, 'I thought you'd handed over to me and changed your mind about being here.'

'I *have* changed my bloody mind—how about you?'

The last of the Hueys had swung away back to Vung Tau. 'Too late now, Dogs, they're not taking passengers the other way.'

In the 5th Battalion—the Tiger Battalion—there were other National Servicemen lumped in with regular soldiers. One I had liked straight away was Errol Noack, a Bravo Company digger also from South Australia. We'd met on pre-embarkation leave before the Vietnam tour and I'd chatted with him while we downed a few beers on the train. Easy-going Noack was one of those soldiers who made me appreciate in those pre-Vietnam months that Nashos were no different from us Regulars: we were all going to some dump to fight a shitty war. All but three men in my section, including myself, were Nashos. We all had to make the best of it.

The beginning of our first operation against Charlie, and we—regular soldiers and National Servicemen alike—were all green as the jungle around us, standing in a clearing in a silence that was almost unreal after the chaos of the airlift. That silence gave a moment's break for contemplation. For the months before landing on the beaches at Vung Tau I had felt prickles of concern, self-questioning. Now those uncertainties were coming on in a flood. I stood at LZ Hudson thinking to myself, *I'm no Audie Murphy.*★ I was worried as hell what to do next. Men were looking at me, a bloke who had been promoted to section leader because there was simply a shortage of non-commissioned officers. I was younger than most of these punters, and I had no confidence. I could drink and bullshit around with the best of them, but leadership I didn't have. Self-doubt I now had by the shitload.

Strung out in single file ready to move, Tich whispered confirmation of what I already felt. 'I could have stayed a bit longer in Vung Tau, you know, Dogs.'

A group of American infantry, part of the 173rd Airborne Brigade, who had swept through Phuoc Tuy before the big Australian operation was launched to 'take over' the province, watched us saddle up and push north.

One who was smoking called over to us, 'We had some real shitty fighting, but I reckon you guys are gonna find this place is pretty cleaned up now.' He gave a grin and a knowing wink, then turned away with a mutter, 'Those guys are really going to wear it.'

★ *Audie Murphy was a US military hero during World War II who went on to a successful movie career.*

A HARD RAIN

Flinders Ranges, 2000

A few hours' hiking and the men are puffing. Faces are mopped, and every now and then a man looks up at the sun blazing over the Flinders' ridge lines. No one is talking, just the occasional grunt and quip. We stop and you sit on a rock holding that long stick in your hand—'the snake-killer', you call it.

'Let's talk about the day each of us joined the Army,' you say, 'or the day we were conscripted.'

One man jumps in straight away. 'Well, let's get this straight. I didn't want to join the Army, I wanted to get into the Navy. Then before I went down to the Recruiting Office in Currie Street, I got into a fight with a bloke and was belted around the head with a beer bottle. I was 17, didn't know shit from a sandwich, and the Navy guy tells me a belting in the head sorta rules me out of the Navy. He says all that rocking and rolling on a ship might make me crook. I move to the next counter and the Army bloke says "no worries". I'm in. Not long after I'm in Airborne jumping out of planes. You tell me that didn't rock and roll my head!

'I really remember the Army recruiting bloke—he was a POW in World War II and had won an MID. I can still see him today: he looked like Jack Nicholson in *A Few Good Men*.'

Another man stands up. 'I trotted into the Recruiting Office and this Army sergeant is looking at me, but I'm not looking at him. I can't take my eyes off the poster stuck on the wall behind his head. It read, "A MAN WITH A MISSION—JOIN THE ARMY". It actually ignited adventure in me. I was 17 years and 10 months old at that stage in 1965, and I really wanted to be a man with a mission. It was that or a fitter and turner at Holden. My father was pissed off: he wanted me in the Air Force, so he got really savage when I signed on for the Army for six years. I wanted to be an engineer and build roads, and they told me there were lots of engineers in the infantry. You know the rest of the war story.

'Well, I went to Vietnam and my old man wrote me not a single letter. I did Vietnam a second time and still no bloody letter.

'I came home and all he wanted to do was show me the new wall he built around the front garden, one of those ugly, grey, besser block things. We went over to the pub and I'm in my uniform, and he just looks at me then stares into his beer and says, "I wish you hadn't gone into that dirty war." Well, he goes home and I stand there drinking on and get so angry I want to vomit.

'I get home that night and I kick at his new wall, and I just keep on kicking till most of it is knocked down.'

CONFIDENTIAL INTSUM: June 1966—As the monsoon season progresses and with the introduction of new units into Phuoc Tuy, VC resistance to our patrols is likely to build up.

From LZ Hudson we shook out into single file and headed towards Route 2. It was a dull day with heavy cloud and a sky like pewter; all the main features on the horizon had that washed-out look. Behind us a low mountain range reared up, the Dinh Hills; ahead, a huge rubber plantation, and a low hill designated on the topographical map as Nui Dat. We reached Route 2, a bitumen road that carved Phuoc Tuy Province in half. 'The Highway', as the Vietnamese called it, connected the provincial capital, Phuoc Le (known as Baria) and the huge rubber plantations of Binh Ba and Ngai Giao to the north.

You didn't need a science degree to work out that we had entered a war zone. The stink, the silence seemed to be speaking to us—and images of destruction were now beginning to appear. Only 100 metres away from my forward scout was a blown bridge, a mess of metal and wood lying in the Sui Da Bang River. It looked like someone had stomped on it with a heavy boot then twisted down to make sure it was impassable. A short distance further on, grey smoke rose gently into the sky. I checked the map I was carrying—Ap An Phu was a hamlet on this road, but Ap An Phu was gone. In its place was smouldering timber, a lone squealing pig and an old woman staring at the Australians, who were staring back. Her look was a mixture of resignation, weariness and puzzlement at these unfamiliar men. We dressed differently from the Americans and Vietnamese soldiers; was that why there was no wave or acknowledgment from her?

Charlie Company had split into three platoons, and we gradually moved into the gloom of the unworked rubber plantation, with its knee-high ferns and thorny undergrowth. I knelt and waited while the scouts checked out the ground ahead. Suddenly there were shouts a long way ahead. Thumbs down—*ENEMY!*

We fell onto our stomachs and adopted a fire position. Instructions were whispered back.

Get up, move again.

We inched further into the rubber. I felt a dryness in my mouth and a tightening of my sphincter muscle. The crackle of gunfire, then more shouts.

Get down, get up and move again.

By now men were jumping up and down inside their skins. We were actually being fired at by the enemy.

Who were they? What were they? More important right now, where were they? Move into a defensive perimeter, stay on your guts, Dogs, watch the front.

I needed some water. All I could see were rows of rubber trees, planted with almost geometrical precision: tunnels spiralling out and away from where we lay in the last light of day. It was like a giant deserted cathedral—and a two-way shooting range with dead-straight firing lanes.

This is really bad shit.

Wogsy Burns, my gunner, was lying with the big M60 pulled back into his shoulder. Wiping his forehead with his sleeve, he shot me an anxious look. 'Dogs, *Dogs,* what's going on, can you see any prick out there? Who's bloody firing at us?'

I peered around. All I could see were Australians lying flat, lumps of men and equipment in and among piles of dead rubber leaves.

'Wogsy, look at me and listen, just sit tight and watch your front. Somebody'll clue us up in a minute.'

But I didn't believe my own words. I knew this was a stuff-up. We were taking fire, and the only incoming information was through the crackle of the platoon commander's radio. All of a sudden it seemed like a black shroud was thrown over the Nui Dat plantation, then there was a crash and a brilliant explosion as if a gigantic camera flash had gone off. This was instantly followed by a *whoosh* of wind and a cloudburst. In what seemed like seconds, every man was soaked to the skin.

Welcome to where the action is—an afternoon downpour, monsoon-style, and a disused rubber plantation full of VC.

Another flash of light, another deafening clap of thunder, and the rain was pelting down in sheets, smacking against bare arms and faces. We pulled out our plastic shelters, our hootchies, and wrapped them around us. But it was a useless effort: the rain just sluiced down the plastic in small waterfalls and streamed down inside our shirts and pants.

'Dogs, Dogs, get up, get up.' It was my platoon sergeant, squinting and spitting water in my face. 'Take your section out and do a clearing patrol.' He jabbed his finger into the gloom. 'Quick one, mate. Around the platoon and back and see if there's any Nogs out there.'

I threw the plastic sheet to one side and tried to stand, slipping and falling on my arse in the claggy red mud.

'Go *where*?'

A jab of the arm and more gesticulations. 'Get out there and have a look around. VC, see if there's any VC. Someone heard movement.'

My mouth went dry again.

How does a guy get thirsty in the rain? The idiot's gotta be joking. See if there's any Nogs? Weren't they already firing at us?

I pushed Tich Tomas and gunner Wogsy out as far as I could to form an extended line and still keep the platoon in sight, then eight ghosts with guns began a sweep through the rubber, the rain splashing across our faces making it almost impossible to see. We moved as quietly as we could. *Stop, kneel, stand, move.*

The mottled rubber trees combined with our increasing night blindness as the last shards of light retreated from the plantation.

We're gonna get brassed up any fuckin' minute.

I leaned against a tree, and what I saw caused a constriction in my chest: latex, raw rubber juice, was bleeding from the trunk where bullets had torn through it. Wogsy moved up closer to me, eyes spinning in all directions.

This place is scaring the living shit out of me, I thought, looking around the section. I motioned the men to follow me back inside the perimeter where the others were still huddled under hootchie sheets, eyes peering out as if staring out of tiny caves.

As suddenly as it started the rain stopped, as if someone had turned off a tap. *Drip, drip, drip.* Huge drops fell like stones from the rubber trees. Then another flash and bang.

Stuff it, that's not thunder!

Braaat, braaat! Automatic gunfire and shouts from across the plantation. Every man swore and rolled from under his sheet into

15

a fire position. Hushed words came down to us. 'Company HQ has been rocketed.'

In the dark I could see red tracer bullets going out. Tich Tomas crawled up next to me. My 2IC's eyes were white and wide.

'Stuff it, Dogs, they never told us it'd be as bad as this. Did you think it'd be this bad? It's only bloody day one!'

What could I say? 'I'm shitting blue lights, Tich. Piss off and watch your front.'

I watched Tich huddle up next to a tree and point his rifle to the front. He was a top bloke, the youngest of four brothers, and someone who'd never wanted war. Tich's dad, Ivan, came to Australia from Yugoslavia after World War II. It was a war Ivan would never speak about, said Tich.

The family was appalled when one of their own was called up for service. They battled to get a deferment, but that didn't work, so like thousands of others, farmer Tich Tomas became a soldier with a number. If he wasn't behind the rubber tree in Nui Dat, I figured, he would be making his way on the Nannup farm. He'd excelled at Agricultural College, and he'd excelled as a young grunt. I saw goodness and a solidity in Tich—that's why he was my 2IC.

Silence and darkness completely engulfed us. I couldn't believe darkness could be so absolute. Coal-pit black. Only when I moved my arm did I see a glimmer—my luminous watch. And now so silent there was only my breathing and the occasional rustle of men in the leaves a few feet away.

More news came back down the line: Company HQ hadn't been hit by rockets, it was just God reminding us he could still scare the hell out of us with a late flash of thunder and lightning.

Shortly after, the next piece of news had me slumped against a rubber tree, struggling with the words.

'Errol Noack's been shot. He's dead.'

I was staring into the dark as the soldier moved on to make sure everyone got the bad news. How many meanings can bad news have? For the Australian Government back home, the nation had just lost its first National Serviceman in Vietnam, and the political shit was really going to hit the fan. For us, we had lost a digger and a mate. I felt numb, depressed, alone.

I'm not going to make this.

Several days into the feet-blistering, soul-destroying, always-wet-and-hot inaugural operation called Hardihood, we shrugged off our packs and set an ambush. The location was the Sui Da Bang River, the waterway with the bombed bridge we had passed coming in on day one.

The linear ambush used two machine-guns to cover the track and fire into the killing ground. A section of men lay down in the bush between the two guns, while another section of men and another machine-gun protected the rear of the ambush party. Claymore mines were detonated to trigger the ambush. The idea of the ambush was to kill as many enemy as possible, carry out a quick body search, then bug out to the rear as fast as possible in anticipation of a counter-assault.

We took the left flank of the track, which was the killing ground. Terry Tomassi, my forward scout, dropped alongside me. I made sure I was close to the machine-gun group, which is an old soldier's trick: stay with the gun and you get one-third more sleep than everyone else. In an ambush, with men in pairs, one had to stay awake all the time. The gun group, with three men, meant one in three would stay awake.

You selfish bastard, Dogs, I thought as I cut some banana leaves to lie on to keep dry. But wise guys always get some sort of payback, and mine came when the moon rose and I noticed to my horror that the banana leaves shone like glass under the bright moon. I was perfectly silhouetted—the ideal target.

After no more than an hour or so I shot bolt upright to the deafening sound of a *crack* as Terry fired. Then Wogsy the gunner opened up. The M60 machine-gun chewed through a half-belt of link ammunition at nine rounds a second, a racing thump that sent a stream of red tracer bullets flicking, bouncing across the killing ground.

The surviving Vietcong, trapped by the wall of fire, turned on us and fired back. The first overpowering sensation was of terror. The second was of survival, and I crawled backwards on my elbows away from the track.

What the fuck am I doing? Am I really pissing off?

I crawled back next to Wogsy, who grabbed me by my arm with a sarcastic, 'Nice of you to join us, Dogs.'

'Get rooted!' I answered. 'I was asleep, and how was I to know Terry was going to be on the ball all night?'

There is a silence after an ambush in the jungle at night. The darkness holds its breath, every soldier holds his breath, and waits.

What next?

But now, after the blast of gunfire, the silence was broken by a gurgling sound, like water bubbling down a drain. It was the sound of a life ending agonisingly. Somewhere out front was a VC soldier, gut-shot and dying. I felt a sudden stab of pity, but then thought, *Fuck 'em, they were going to kill us anyway.*

I could make out some scraping and dragging sounds, then I heard something whoosh through the air into the bush. An orange flash, then a bang.

'Grenades!' I screamed. 'They're throwing grenades!'

My fear was replaced by anger and action, and I sprayed the track in front of me with a burst from the Owen submachine-gun. The gun chewed through 30 rounds, then silence fell again. After a few minutes, which dragged like an hour, the platoon commander called for illumination flares from the Fire Support Base. The flares lobbed over us and burst with a white–orange flash before swinging down beneath their parachutes. The empty carrier shells clattered down through the trees, whose silhouettes were now twisting and changing shape under the artificial light. There was a yell.

'Get under a tree—those bloody shell cases will kill you!'

Morning light and an AK–47 enemy assault rifle lay on the track, dented by a 9mm round from an Owen gun; alongside it, a blood-covered backpack. Charlie had taken his dead and wounded.

The bullet-riddled backpack was full of blood and a pair of women's panties made from parachute silk.

I've killed a woman.

It was a flash thought of guilt. Then I tried to console myself by sharing the guilt.

No, we've *killed a woman.*

My mind raced again, another attempt at self-justification.

She was a bloody VC soldier and she was trying like buggery to kill us all.

DINKUM AND THE DOG

Flinders Ranges, 2000

On a shelf at home we've got a collection of books on the Vietnam War. Many of us go out and buy everything published on Vietnam. We ask ourselves why; it's maybe because we want to understand . . . WHY?

There are the dry historical analyses of how it all began, who deposed who, and how there were 'commitments' and treaties to 'honour', and how big industry began to fuel the war. There's also the political bullshit, like the Domino Theory (God help us): if Vietnam went communist, we'd soon have Reds coming in the back door. There are the ramblings about the political-economic ramifications of South-east Asian conflicts. And let's not forget the leaders of the Australian troops, who penned their memoirs about how they led men into battle—the 'Gung-hos' who still go to RSLs and blab to anyone who'll listen.

All this meant bugger all to the Australian whose marble came up in the draft: he was handed a slouch hat, greens, a pack and his webbing.

Most grunts' perspective on the war was about 50 metres to his immediate front—and out in the bush, that's the only perspective he gave a stuff about. To the combatant, Vietnam was about staying alive; getting out with your balls intact.

Some soldiers were prepared for the war in Vietnam; others stalked through their 12-month tour terrified. Then there were those who stumbled through a year in the jungle, came home and went back to car detailing, carpentry, banking, retailing—the war rolled over them and it seems they never even noticed.

CONFIDENTIAL INTSUM: 29 June 1966—Conduct in ambush sites and at patrol bases—NO fires or Hexamine; NO cooking; NO noise; NO movement; NO

shaving; NO use of soap; NO urinating or
crapping in ambush sites.

Patrolling to the north-west of the big rubber plantation called
Nui Dat a couple of weeks into Hardihood, and the monsoon
came cruising by in mid-afternoon. The rain came down in
sheets; it hammered you, hurt you. It was a drumbeat on the tall
foliage; the double canopy of trees that rose above us shuddered
while the leaves bent and buckled and whipped in the rain.

C Company crept forward like a line of ants, trying to keep
alert, covering our arcs. But it was hard keeping your face up
when the water streamed down into your eyes. I loved the rain—
not the constant soaking, but the way it changed the jungle. It
was cleansing. Dry country looked dirty, but when it was wet you
could almost smell a newness. The jungle dripped for hours after
the monsoon; shining and refreshed. I also looked forward to
those downpours because they cleaned me. All the muck on
my skin was washed away. You could hold your arm out and
watch the rain sluicing down it, taking away the dirt and sweat
and stink.

After the rain came the humidity, when the sweat came back
and you almost felt you were submerged under water. The air you
sucked in seemed thick, saturated.

I heard a wheeze and a grunt behind me. Dinkum was doing it
hard . . . again. I had noticed after we shoved Dinkum down the
back of the patrol file that he was having trouble as tail-end
Charlie. He was a problem child from day one.

The first time I saw Dinkum, he was being bawled out by the
Company Sergeant Major (CSM) for strolling across the parade
ground back at Holsworthy.

' . . . an idle, shiftless, slovenly individual' was part of the CSM's
vocabulary that day. 'Get the hell out of my sight!' he'd gone on.

'Never walk across my parade ground again. Don't you know that's what marching is for?' The CSM blew his gasket and vented himself on Dinkum, who shrugged with a 'Yes, sir' and almost tripped over his own feet. Dinkum looked at me with a smirk that turned into a grin. I could see Dinkum didn't give a stuff.

I think Dinkum's intelligence was akin to that of a rocket scientist, but he had some physical coordination problems. He also had an absence of what we in the regular Army called CDF— 'common dog fuck', the basic necessities of survival. And Dinkum the National Serviceman wasn't unlike all the other Nashos who were in lead-up training to go to Vietnam. He was big, and had a huge round face with a permanent world-weary grin. I found out as I got to know him that he was a mental gymnast with facts and figures, but a mental pygmy when it came to wrapping camouflage scrim around his helmet.

I asked Dinkum one day if he liked the Army.

'Yeah, but I don't think the Army likes me,' he answered. Then: 'Are we going to Vietnam with you, Dogs?'

'Of course you are, Dinkum. I'm your section commander. Who'd you think you were going with?'

Dinkum thought deeply. 'Well, the Sarge said we were getting someone from Airborne, and you're an Army bloke.'

I was getting annoyed at the conversation. Dinkum hadn't been in the Army long enough to know that we had an Airborne platoon. 'Yeah, I'm in the fucking Army—see!' I pointed to my shirt and trousers. 'Jungle green clothes, the green baggy skin, right? What the fuck's with you, Dinkum?'

There was puzzlement all over Dinkum's face, like he was trying to split the atom. 'Well, if you're from Airborne, how come you're not an RAAF bloke?'

Every section had one, and Dinkum was mine. But he was no idiot, he was a highly intelligent 20-year-old. He came from a good home, and had wanted for nothing—his parents had guided him to a potentially successful career in agriculture. Then life dealt a shitty hand and Dinkum was conscripted. How was this poor stumblebum going to handle a war zone?

I looked back at him now. He was sweating and struggling to keep up and I had to halt the section and walk back to him.

Dinkum was panting and could hardly stand with the weight on his back. He slumped in the mud while I pulled his pack off. *Jesus, it was heavy.*

'What the hell's in here, Dinkum?' I pulled out the necessary gear: shelter, rations, pyjamas—'*Pyjamas?* Geez, Dinkum!' Writing pad, thongs and a tin of Johnson's Baby Powder.

I squatted next to the still panting soldier. 'Dinkum, didn't I explain in the Orders Group we'd be out walking in the weeds for Christ knows how long. What is this shit? *Thongs*, for fuck's sake!'

Dinkum looked part embarrassed, part indignant. 'Yeah, you said that, Dogs. But I thought if we were going to be out here that long I'd need a few basics. Well, until we got back to civilisation . . . '

I grabbed his 'necessities' and buried them under a fallen tree.

'You'll be a bit better now, mate. Up, and let's go.'

Dinkum went on as the section's reluctant buffoon: he fell into weapon pits, kicked your brew over accidentally, and in the 'j' he was constantly struggling with the frustration of being snagged on wait-a-while vines. Dinkum was one of the few men I could recall in Vietnam who got chased by a pissed-off water buffalo.

We sloshed on through Hardihood, taking some heart that we would soon be sloshing around a permanent base camp at Nui Dat. In the daily monsoon we ate cold biscuits and cheese, spooned cold turkey loaf from American ration packs, and pork and beans from Australian one-man packs. The luxury, the lift to the whole miserable day, was a hot brew—coffee or chocolate, heated over a small Hexamine tablet and savoured with a smoke.

I smoked Marlboro, Ted smoked menthol. Ted was short for Shit-Head, another of the six Nashos in my eight-man section. Ted would have gone on to a good life in banking if he hadn't got called up. By all accounts he was a good bank clerk. He had also been a good Mormon.

One night before stand-to I found myself talking quietly to Ted about subjects beyond gun piquet rosters and ammo checks. He was just another young bloke who found himself in a dump he had probably not even heard about in school geography classes. Like Dinkum, he was a National Serviceman who took war service on the chin, head down, arse up—do it. I asked him what he was going to do when he got out of this hole of a place.

'Don't know, Dogs. I can't go back to my parents like this, mate, they wouldn't have a bar of me . . . I don't think I want to go back to the way I was before I got called up, anyway.'

I felt a twinge of sadness looking at a man who was a bit older than me and had somehow lost something—his innocence.

'It's not your fault you're over here . . . ' I said, but Ted cut me off with a long stare. I knew he was going to unload.

'Dogs, before I got called up I was a Mormon, went out with a nice girl, held a steady job in a shit-boring town bank, and never smoked or drank. Hell, I was in bed before midnight. Now I'm on the grog every opportunity, I smoke anything I can lay my hands on—bloody menthols out of the ration packs, same as what the Nogs smoke, and when we ever get to Vungas, I'm going to dip my wick as many times as I can.' He grinned. 'Probably only chance I'll get for a shag in this life.'

Ted stood up, hoisting his rifle. 'How do you think I could go home and tell my old man about the bloke I shot the other week? He'd go on about how I should have become a conscientious objector, become a cook, a medic—anything but a grunt. I've already shit in my own nest, Dogs. My life's down the gurgler, I can't go home.'

I sat that night in the bush and thought about Ted and Dinkum. Conscripts . . . I'd never yet met one that didn't do it hard, but still did it without a bloody grumble. They had bonded like men in other wars, I figured. They were reluctant warriors, but warriors nevertheless.

DUSTOFF AND DIGGING IN

Flinders Ranges, 2000

There are many Vets who haven't moved outside their home for years. Some moved into the garden shed or garage; established a perimeter in their own back yard. When they did go out, they'd break their necks trying to get back home. They had serious anxiety attacks about getting 'back behind the wire'. There are many reasons they've become hopeless hermits: one of them has a lot to do with clinging to something permanent.

Walking around the Flinders during the day reminded a few of us of our early days in Vietnam, when you could almost have called us the Legion of the Lost. Homeless men, displaced persons we were back then in '66. We're not much different now: the clothes we're standing in are all we brought up here. And there's been some groaning along the way—sore feet and stumbles for those still a bit unsteady in boots not worn since Army days.

Jesus, we're not Spiderman any more.

Last night was tough for a few blokes, buggering around with their swags. The swags have changed, haven't they? Back there in the Funny Farm they called Vietnam we sacked out in a blanket or single sheet of silk, wrapped up around us, sometimes pulling the thing over our head so we could sort of blot out the war. Now take the modern-day swag—how the hell are you supposed to get in it? How do you lay the bloody thing out? This is embarrassing, mate.

Jesus, you reckon you can snore? Embarrassment again: we didn't think we did snore, but we sure did last night. One bloke was saying that the whole time in Vietnam, he never once heard a soldier snoring in the jungle at night. But back in the base at Nui Dat it sounded like a dozen chainsaws on full throttle in the tents late at night.

CONFIDENTIAL INTSUM: November 1966—RULES OF ENGAGEMENT: Fire will only be opened under following conditions: (a) When a Vietnamese is carrying a weapon; (b) When fired at; (c) When a hostile act is about to be committed. If in doubt, don't shoot.

On a topographical map of Phuoc Tuy Province, run you finger up north from Nui Dat's Task Force Base five grid squares, then roll across west another four grid squares. Your finger settles on a feature with tight contour lines—like lines chocked closely on a weather chart to indicate a cyclone. This blip on the horizon that you could see from Nui Dat is called Nui Nghe. It is six hundred feet, a finger jutting upwards wrapped in a mat of thick bush and bamboo. The enemy used it for observation, and we were going to kick his arse off it.

Just weeks before we set out for Nui Nghe, Bravo Company of the 1st/503rd Battalion, part of the American 173rd Airborne Brigade, were chopped up in a box ambush on the side of the hill. A Vietcong mortar attack and a crossfire killed 8 Americans and wounded 23. Now we were going in.

We'd had weeks on end of wandering through the jungle, over paddy, fighting through bamboo. One foot down in front of the other, study the back of the man in front of you. He turns and motions a field signal with his hands: *creek ahead, track to the front, stop.* Two fingers to the upper arm: *section commander come forward.* Fingers to the mouth in puffing action: *stop for a smoke.*

After an hour of silent movement we sat and lit up cigarettes. The smoke spirals ever so slowly upwards through the light under the jungle canopy. It keeps the mosquitoes away from your face; it can also be smelt by any Vietcong within a hundred yards. But that doesn't matter: we've got to have that fag.

Later that night I lay on my back in the jungle, the sky a magnificent black vault. Vietnam was a country of such contrasts—the beauty above with the stars all upside down compared with Australia . . . and the chomper ants crunching and gnawing away at the plastic sheet I was lying on.

No one talked out there. If we did have to speak, we whispered. The result of this semi-muteness was that when we could talk normally, we didn't: we continued whispering.

'For God's sake, stop bloody whispering!' Tich yelled at me one day after we'd stopped in a secure area. I thought he'd gone mad, but he hadn't: we were all whispering like at kindergarten during nap-time.

I was beginning to notice that a lot of blokes in the platoon were suffering some sort of displaced person syndrome. It was early days in the tour and we still had no home, no base, no permanency. No cot to collapse in, no structure to sit under, no plate to eat food off like a human being, no proper toilet with any sort of privacy. Masturbation was performed quietly at night in the blackness of the jungle; furtive relief in the dark that was called the 'mozzie-net wank'.

Our world was on our back: 60–80 backbreaking pounds of rations, ammunition, and a hootchie that was supposed to keep the rain off but didn't. Life in the wet season was lived in rotting, saturated clothes and boots so sloshing full, that we cut the backs out to let the water drain—and to relieve the heel blisters as big as balloons.

This misery went on day after wearying day, until I thought I'd go mad. Quite often I thought of putting a bullet through the fleshy part of my arse, or my foot—a Million-Dollar Wound to get you out of this place. But I changed my mind about all that in the next contact. It was then that the mouth went dry again; we peered through the bush looking for the VC with such intensity, we thought our eyes would pop out. My tongue caked to the top of my mouth so I couldn't scream even if I wanted to. I would pull myself up, signal back for a break and another smoke, and think, *Get your head together, Dogs, or you'll get the damn thing shot off.*

Out here somewhere was the NVA's entire 274 Regiment— hard-core troops probably slopping through the muddy, black creeks that snaked around the base of Nui Nghe.

Walking at the end of the company as the tail-end Charlie was the pits. You stand, walk 10 paces, then sit, wait 10 minutes, stand, walk 10 more paces, and so on. Ahead of the main body, the scout would stop to cut away thick growth, so we'd all have to stop. But at least someone else had cut the scrub away. Further ahead, nearly 100 men had already churned the soft, black creek banks into a pig swill that sucked the men's boots, ankles and shins down like quicksand.

Tich Tomas squatted next to me during a smoke break. 'I'm wet as a shag and still I'm sweating like a friggin' Clydesdale,' I said.

Tich sat up and became his perky self. 'You know, Dogs, when we get back to Australia you'll have to come and stay with me and the family for a while. My dad's got a small cattle property outside of Nannup in WA. I reckon you'd like my family, and we'd have a helluva good time.'

I listened to Tich and was touched by his genuine offer, more so when he talked about how he loved the farm and his family life and how he was missing it.

'Thanks, Tich, I'll hold you to that. I've never stayed on a farm.'

Crack, crack, crack. Shots suddenly rang out from Nui Nghe. We quickly saddled up and moved up towards the main company position. I had my section moving up behind me when we found the others in Charlie Company, but I couldn't figure out where we were to link into the company harbour position.

I turned back to Tich. 'Wait here while I find out what's going on. Back in a minute.'

Fatigued, my men stood, leaning forward to ease the pain where their packs cut in their shoulders.

The detonation came eight steps later. The explosion picked me up and hurled me to the ground. Rolling on my back I saw men wide-eyed with fear as branches and dirt fell back down through the trees. then a shout. *'What the fuck was that?'*

My mind was spinning, my mouth was dry as sand and a numbness spread through me while my heart was pounding its way out my chest. I heard a yell.

'Check fire, check fire!'

I rolled over and saw Tich slumped over the M60 groaning faintly.

I yanked his pack from his back. 'Tich, Tich, for Christ's sake, *can you hear me?'*

The medics were next to me in a moment, desperately trying to stem the flow of blood frothing out of the Digger's back. The next hour was a frantic rush to get my wounded mate out. A chopper pad was hacked out of the bush and the dustoff came clattering in. Tich was lifted on board, barely conscious, his eyes glazed.

Surgical teams can work miracles, I told myself. *As soon as he gets on that operating table he'll be all right.*

The shots we had heard were from the VC on Nui Nghe. Our commanders had called in artillery to blow them off the hill. One round skimmed the hill and dropped down on my seven-man section on the other side of the feature. There was red-hot shrapnel everywhere, including in Tich's back—one hell of a Class A balls-up.

I sat against a log after stand-to and stared out at nothing. Grief was as paralysing as the blackness on the slopes of Nui Nghe.

Fuck this useless piece of shit they call a hill. Let the friggin' Nogs have it. Nuke the fucking thing.

The platoon commander found me in the dark.

'We've just been informed over the radio Dogs, our dustoff was a fatal.'

'Tich is dead then, that's what you're saying? Why the fuck didn't I tell them to get down when I walked forward . . . '

'S'okay, Dogs, they were tired, we were all rooted. Tich's gone and there's no bringing him back. He didn't make the operating table.'

The lieutenant moved away and for a moment I felt sympathy for him. Like Tich, he was from the land, and a Nasho with the right stuff to make an officer. I bet they didn't tell him at Officer Cadet Training Unit that there'd be days like this. Come to think of it, being a National Serviceman and an officer was a real bastard: the regular soldiers put shit on you, and your fellow Nashos gave you a hard time for being an officer—for having birdshit on your shoulders.

At this early stage in the build-up of forces at Nui Dat, everything was in short supply. Every piece of equipment replacement we requested was halved; from toilet rolls to food condiments, from new greens to new water bottles and boots, we either didn't have any or it was on its way from Australia 'on the ship'.

Tich's gear had to be reissued to other men who sorely needed it. Combat soldiering has its tough jobs, but this was one of the worst.

One of the blokes sidled up to me and said, 'I don't think this is right, passing his gear around.'

I turned on him. 'Shut the fuck up. I need your sentiment like I need a hole in the head right now. If Tich was here do you reckon he'd want to burn it, or reissue it to the blokes? Guys are gonna need this stuff in a few days, so just take what you need and get on with it so I can send his personal gear home.'

I tried to put my friend's death into some small compartment in my brain. He was dead and gone, a casualty of war, a victim of a bloody mistake, and we'd have a few more mistakes yet, sure as hell.

It was the same with the other guys in the section. It was early days and one of our number had been killed. Humour was part of the section's general behaviour—a digger would see a laugh in a heart attack—but now it was tinged with the sobriety of war and death.

Sure, we could all still find a laugh in this dump, but some things in Vietnam were just not funny. On a patrol a week later we came to a disused banana plantation. Willy, the forward scout, called to the rest of us. He had his hand over his nose and mouth and was pointing at a knee that protruded from the Earth. A corpse had been shoved into a hastily dug pit of red, boggy clay that stuck to it, making the gender impossible to determine. We dug a little more and saw that it was a woman.

I called the platoon sergeant to come up; to my surprise he pulled a handful of small cigars from his top pocket and handed them out. We lit up and I figured out why the old campaigner had the evil-smelling smokes: they immediately smothered the stench of death. Two men, Vil and Willy, scraped lightly over the corpse's face with an entrenching tool. The nose came away, exposing red and green flesh crawling with maggots. We scraped across the chest and saw what remained of a breast, and also what resembled black bubbles.

Willy spat out his cigar. 'Fuck this,' he said, 'I'm outta here. I didn't expect to be digging up dead people.'

While Willy threw up his breakfast we dug on, and concluded that the bubbles were bullet holes. I wanted to finish this, fast.

'I reckon she's had three rounds in the guts and we can safely assume she's dead,' I commented. 'Bury her and let's get out of this friggin' place.'

MEETING THE NATIVES

Flinders Ranges, 2000

From day one in the Army the emphasis was on teamwork: work as a tight cohesive group, sleep, run, drill, train, shit, shower, shave, drink, even bloody fight—together. This morning we cover a couple of hundred metres and sit down for a smoko. Someone gets the firewood, another guy clears the fire spot, some blokes go and get the tucker out of the Land Rover—and some of us sit and watch. Well, every unit had his Jackman who did stuff-all, right?

Teamwork is what gets the ex-tank driver up the cliff face so we can abseil down it. He's carrying a bit of weight, the old turret head, but he wants to get up there. This is shit-hot, you know: at first a bit of grunting and straining and then away over the edge with a rope trailing behind—like big kids again, you say. Sure, why the hell not. You also notice how a group of vets becomes a team again . . . so fast. Like in the Funny Farm over there, we worked as a team. It got so that in Vietnam we were bound up so tight we knew what each other was thinking, and that's no shit. And we'd always help some bastard who was doing it tough.

CONFIDENTIAL INTSUM: 13 November 1966—Translation from captured enemy documents: 'Each comrade should kill four enemy, every four children kill one enemy, each village should capture four weapons. Establish suicide cells in each village. District suicide squads are to penetrate deep into enemy areas.'

There were several options open to the Aussie grunt when he went looking for Charlie. There was 'Search and Destroy', where you prowled through the jungle, wet and fatigued, set ambushes, chased the enemy, shot the buggers or they shot you. 'Search and

Destroy' was one of those wonderful Vietnam War buzz phrases where we expended maximum energy and effort for little in the way of return—other than a dose of the shits, foot-rot or malaria. 'S and D' did, however, secure large chunks of the province by simply denying the enemy the freedom to move at will.

Then there was 'Cordon and Search', involving less effort than 'Search and Destroy': a better return in terms of captured enemy and a lot easier on the back and the butt. With 'C and S' you simply surrounded a village, took the locals by surprise and turned them over, looking for Nigel the Nog or any of his re-supplies ferreted away by sympathetic locals. But sometimes 'C and S' was nothing but a joke.

The place was Duc My, a backwater hamlet supposedly housing Vietcong operatives and agents. The military minds behind the search first launched a deception plan, employing choppers flying across the province with diggers sitting bolt upright next to the open doors.

Look, Tran, the Uc Da Loi are going out on operations, said Charlie in the bush. In fact there was only a handful of soldiers in the aircraft, and they lay flat on the floor on the way back.

Look, Tran, Uc Da Loi is out on operations now.

The usually cunning VC actually fell for the full-chopper-empty-chopper deception, unaware that his village was quietly surrounded by lots of grunts later that night.

Gotcha, Tran, you're as sharp as a bowling ball.

I sat with the other section commanders, Bernie Smith and Terry Tuneo, at the Orders Group for the Duc My search. We were trying to get our heads around potentially The Biggest Balls-Up of the War. The platoon commander seemed unfazed when I hit him with the execution of the brilliant plan.

'Let's just get this straight: we tie ourselves together with toggle ropes and creep up on the village at midnight? We keep an eye on each other's luminous watch so we don't end up down some fucking well. Don't you think this is taking bondage a bit far?'

Terry and Bernie were fighting to keep straight faces—imagine the whole rifle company tied together with ropes walking through the jungle to surprise the Duc My population, who were either zonked out or having a bit of late-night fun.

'They're gonna think the bloody Indian Pacific's making a stop at their shitty little village,' protested Terry. 'What about if we get ambushed or some bastard just falls down, he'll drag every poor bastard with him . . . '

The platoon commander shot a look around. 'This is serious—make sure your diggers know how serious this is.'

19 July 1966: 120 men hooked up like Roman slaves with nylon toggle ropes wound their way out from the Fire Support Base. They stumbled and fell, they cursed, spat, knocked each other over in the blackness. The Company HQ Group walked smack into a herd of pigs with tusks big enough to rip your insides out. As predicted, one man went down a well, others stumbled into pools of human shit outside Duc My. And sure enough, Charlie made a run for it in the morning. He was shot or he was captured.

The Duc My village search wasn't unlike the 'C and S' we threw up around the village of Ngai Giao. We were about to exit a hut where a group of papasans was playing cards, but Willy was adamant I look in the thatched roof.

'It's bamboo thatch, there's no-one up there,' I said, keen to get out of the hut. Willy motioned up again. He wasn't conned by the older men, who kept gibbering and offering us some French beer. I pushed a table over and pulled up the bamboo matting. He was sitting astride a strong bamboo beam. He was trembling with fear, I was shaking with the adrenaline rush and pointed my rifle at his head. He was military age and likely VC. The old men continued playing cards as we dragged him out.

I was still shaking when I found the entrance to a tunnel. I crawled nervously into the blackness with just a torch and a bayonet. Just my own breathing and 15 feet ahead a T-junction.

What the hell am I doing here?

Now I could smell fish, rotting fish. Should I go forward to that junction or not?

There's a hundred Nogs down here, I know it—and all I've got is a friggin' bayonet and torch.

Fear won out. I somersaulted backwards and made my way out, gasping for air.

'Anything down there, Dogs?' asked Wogsy, chain-smoking his favourite—Pall Mall.

'No, just a blank wall,' I lied. 'Probably where they keep the women and kids.'

Do I lack courage? 'No Guts Kearney'? I don't care, I'm not going down in a tunnel again as long as my freckle points to the ground. I'll leave that to the tunnel rats—the engineers.

Another village 'C and S', and an old papasan sat squatting on the floor with three terrified children clinging to him. My rifle was pointed at his head and I was looking at the old wooden cabinet against the wall with its padlock.

'Tomassi, you've done a Vietnamese language course, ask this bloke what's in that cabinet. It's locked. He's got maps or some shit in there. Ask the old bastard to open it. Tell him, *now!*'

Old wrinkled hands pulled the key from around his neck, and he trembled as he unlocked his beloved cabinet.

He's shitting himself, something big's in there, I thought.

I yanked it open—and saw a perfectly ironed and spotlessly clean white shirt.

I left the hut immediately, intensely embarrassed. I felt like a Nazi war criminal. The old man, our interpreter later explained, was a reader at the Binh Ba Catholic Church on Sundays. His life was his devotion to the faith. His one and only white shirt was his most valuable possession; it was a sign of his standing in his community and before God. I left behind my whole week's rations and cigarettes, but even that didn't wash away the guilt, or the image of an old man with his grandchildren clutching him in terror.

An old man, so easy to love; an Australian soldier with his rifle, so easy to hate.

It was early days in the war, but there were long, exhausting days in the field as operations ground on. 'Nigel the Nog'—some clown had already found a tag for 'Nog', to add to 'Charlie'—had gone to ground. He was squatting in the 'j' or hunkered down in his bunker, still out there but wary of the Australian forces that had moved into Phuoc Tuy Province. Nigel also had been a little surprised by the Australian method of fighting jungle warfare: the Aussies were just as adept at creeping through the bush and striking without warning as the VC were. The digger did not follow tracks; he utilised deception plans to cover future activities, he moved quietly with the aid of field signals. Most worrying of all, so far as the enemy was concerned, the Australians would ambush day and night. The VC used the cover of darkness to move quickly along familiar foot tracks, but now he knew he could trigger an ambush by doing that. When he switched tactics and tried to move during the day, he could easily run into an Australian patrol.

The arrival of the 5th Battalion in Phuoc Tuy had definitely upped the ante on Charlie's local patch. The Australians still did not have a permanent Task Force base, and it is difficult to explain how we felt about having no anchor in this bizarre and dangerous world. We had to patrol, dig weapon pits, sleep in the bush, wake up, fill weapon pits, patrol, and ambush day and night for days on end. Then those days became weeks, which led to debilitation, which in turn led to tension and silly confrontations with mates. An argument could start over a packet of biscuits. The soldier had to make a conscious effort to hold on to personal discipline as small cracks and flaws in character started to become apparent. The rumours that some day, any day, we would stop and set up a permanent Task Force Base were spreading like plague. One furphy even had us being posted to Hawaii.

Night Orders Group in the jungle, and the platoon commander called his three section commanders in for a quick briefing. He'd tell us what he'd been told by the company commander, and we'd then pass that on to the men in our section. This was the way the Army worked—a drip feed that went down the line with all the important stuff filtered out so that the grunt suffered a largely uninformed existence.

I sat and smoked while the skipper and the platoon sergeant sipped coffee and forced down the last of a cold tea. The skipper was a man who went straight to the bottom line: 'You can tell your blokes that within a week we'll be moving into an area around Nui Dat hill—that's where we're going to set up a permanent battalion camp.'

We knew of Nui Dat; we'd seen and patrolled around it, a pimple of dirt and scrub near a huge rubber plantation. It was smack in the centre of Phuoc Tuy Province, seven clicks northwest of the province capital, Xa Phuoc Le (Baria). The huge Task Force base would be home to us, 5RAR, and 6RAR, which had recently arrived from Australia—all up, more than 2000 grunts and support units.

At last, permanence—a place with toilets, mess halls, a tent, a cot. God, a hot shower! We had been eating combat rations since we began Hardihood, and we weren't feeling or looking too flash. In fact many men had dropped in physical condition because of the relentless patrol–ambush schedule. We were losing our edge. I was the first to greet the news.

'Thank hell for that, I was getting pretty tired of walking around in circles all day long.'

The platoon sergeant gave me a nudge. 'If you knew how to read a map, Dogs, you wouldn't be roaming around in circles all day. Now shut up and let the Skip finish the O Group.'

We squatted in the gloom and listened to how life would change: food, real food, prepared by cooks, mail drops from home, soft drinks, beer . . .

The other two section commanders, Bernie Smith and Terry Tuneo, listened with bemusement—this was classic Army bullshit.

'Just because it's prepared by cooks doesn't mean it's real food,' Bernie chipped in.

As we stood to leave, the Skipper gave a final word. 'You can tell your blokes this won't be a bloody holiday—plenty of patrolling, wiring, digging weapon pits . . . and we'll still be ambushing.'

Just as we'd expected.

THE EYES OF THE TIGER

Flinders Ranges, 2000

A camp fire burning in the Outback. There are few things that bring on silence, reflection and an intimate mood in the bush more than a night camp fire. Why do we all look into a camp fire, gazing into its bluish-yellow centre, listening to the splutter and crackle and hiss of the wood? Are we thinking? Thinking about mateship, maybe, how at times we put such little value on friendship. We let mates and friends—old war buddies—just drift away.

One thing about a Vietnam veteran: he will always recognise another vet—the conversation, the phraseology, particular words that carry loaded meanings from those days at war. In a second you know if someone calling himself a Vietnam vet really did go to war. Why would anybody be mad enough to pretend to be a Vietnam veteran? For whatever reason, many do fake it, which is annoying and disrespectful to the men who died in Vietnam. It gets a few old soldiers quite cranky.

Take a bloke like Blue, a guy we knew in the war. Blue was a sergeant who fought like hell; a thrashing machine in a blue was our Blue. And a very close mate. He went on to become the Regimental Sergeant Major of the Special Air Service (SAS), which by any token is top of the tree in our man's Army. Anyway, we're in the Blinman Hotel—not far down the road from here—having a quiet beer at the bar. The publican hears us talking and asks if we're Vietnam vets. We nod and he nods over to the end of the bar where a bloke is going on about how he was in Vietnam with the SAS. Blue pricks up and listens more closely to the conversation drifting over—and realises in a minute that it's pure, unadulterated crap. The bloke's a fake, never been to Vietnam, never even in the bloody Army. He's what we all know as a 'wannabe'.

Blue cocks an eye and downs his ale, and we know the thrashing machine is getting oiled up. But he calms himself. We sit down to dinner in the dining room and wannabe comes in with his audience, still blabbing on. Blue cocks his eye again, then tucks into his steak. 'Why bloody bother?' On the other hand, another wannabe in a pub in Melbourne didn't fare too well: a vet hit him so hard he went down the stairs and straight through the bass drum a Salvation Army guy was banging near the front entrance. We've put a few bucks in the Salvos' bag ever since, to pay for the drum.

CONFIDENTIAL INTSUM: October 1966—The village of Hoa Long is known to be engaged in numerous activities which support the Vietcong, such as terrorism, propaganda and dissemination and harbouring of guerillas . . . several persons friendly to the government have been abducted, killed and mutilated.

I met Mick Deak in 1963 in the 1st Battalion, where we were both in the same platoon in E Company. I liked him immediately and we became good friends. Then he was promoted to Lance-Corporal. You could have picked him for a soldier who was going places—six months after he got his first stripe he was accepted for training at Officer Cadet School and graduated a Second Lieutenant. In Vietnam we met again.

German born, Michael Gunther Deak arrived in Australia as a six-year-old in 1950. His father, Baron Gunther von Berg, and his mother divorced prior to coming to Australia. She remarried (Deak) and, caught in the crossfire of the acrimonious divorce, Michael as a minor travelling on his mother's passport arrived in Australia as Michael Deak. After their divorce, he took his mother's name and his father's title. He had blue blood running through him, which maybe contributed to his leadership skills, but he sounded more Australian than most Aussies, if that was possible. He certainly looked Aussie—blonde hair, stocky build, physically tough as jarrah, accomplished rugby player, keen swimmer, big-time punter. 'Baron' Mick Deak was a no-nonsense, competently packaged infantry commander.

After his first few months in Vietnam as 2 Platoon, A Company and now Anti-Tank Platoon Commander, he'd had a gutful of the war—not so much the isolation of leadership, more the sights, sounds and smells of jungle fighting. Deak had already done what many other soldiers and officers in the Tiger Battalion did: subconsciously developed their own preservation and survival mechanisms. He was confident and an excellent leader; he was good at navigation and tactics, and he managed men very skil-fully. But Deak knew he needed more; he *had* to have more in order to maintain the edge.

One such device was to devalue the standing of the enemy. In general, the attitude of all the Australian diggers in combat towards the enemy was one of ambivalence—didn't hate them, didn't care for them, had no respect for what they stood for or what they believed in. If we see 'em, we shoot 'em. But Australian soldiers who were exposed to the less appealing results of enemy action and atrocities—the revolting side of war—took from that some measure of their own belief and self-discipline: the amorality that surrounded the diggers often reinforced their own attitudes towards decency and fair play in war, if there was such a thing.

Platoon commander Mick Deak's months in-country so far had also given him time to consider that sudden death in a fire-fight was well down his 'Worst Things That Can Happen To Me In Vietnam' list. Losing a leg or arm or—God forbid—your eyes was worse than a clean shot in the head, he said. He wouldn't be able to play rugby again, or drive that British racing green MGB he was going to buy after the war.

Apart from permanent disability, Deak's other recurring bad dream was the frustration and guilt he felt at losing men. He wasn't one for bravado: he didn't need to go up the guts with plenty of smoke. Rather, he felt that the way to win this war, in this place, was by stealth and cunning. And if he got in the shit, as he knew he would, his team would work as one to get out of it. He believed that every man would help anyone who was wounded, get him Casevaced (Casualty Evacuation) out. There would be no exception, and he would use everything in his power to protect his platoon. That was why Mick Deak had a propensity to use maximum firepower support when he got into trouble: maximum bang and bugger the bucks.

After patrolling week after punishing week, Deak also began to reflect on the nature of fear. He wondered if a man could really smell fear—or was that smell merely some poor bastard who had soiled his pants during a contact? Deak often said that fear slowed everything down. Or was it due to blasts of adrenaline? Everything happening around you was in slow motion; seconds became drawn-out minutes.

Living the life of a grunt, he had come to hate many other things about combat in Vietnam: the unbearable heat, the mosquitoes that drove you mad at night in Nui Dat—so mad you downed a litre and a half of Bacardi and just let them bite. Lying in the scrub at night during 'The Wet', you eventually gave up trying to sleep. You just lay there, soaked, until it was time to get up. Then you learnt to ignore the misery of being continually hot and wet, all day every day.

The 23-year-old 'baron' found it almost funny how fast he woke up to the reality of being shot at in war—if that wasn't a cliché. He walked around the place fairly casually after his first contact with the enemy—until he noticed how cleanly a bullet had taken away the whole back of an enemy's head. At that moment he figured he'd been watching too many Western movies, where the bullet nicked the good guy in the white hat, who then emptied his six-gun with barely a flinch.

Then, in late October 1966, with the first months of survival in Vietnam behind him, Mick Deak was summoned to a meeting with the Commanding Officer of the 5th Battalion. Lieutenant-Colonel John Warr wanted his own special team, a Reconnaissance Platoon: an independent group of volunteers from within 5RAR who would be specially trained to scout up to two hours or a few thousand metres ahead of the main Australian infantry units. This platoon's task would be to gather intelligence and report back to HQ with any important information; and to close with and engage the enemy, but only if such contact was either unavoidable, or the enemy force was relatively small.

About 40 volunteers were needed; of those, 28 would be selected after a gruelling training course with assistance from the Special Air Service (SAS) 3 Squadron. It was Warr's desire that the Reconnaissance Platoon—also called 'Recce' or 'Recon'—become the eyes of the Tiger Battalion. Mick Deak had been selected to pull this group together, so shortly after the briefing Deak sent word to other companies in 5RAR seeking men who thought they had the right stuff to join Recce.

The basic unit of an infantry battalion is the fighting section, usually numbering 10 men. In training, these individuals become as one. There may be an enormous difference in character, physical competence and temperament, but eventually all become as one; in many ways the differences become comple-mentary. The men in the fighting section think as one, move as one entity, and support each other in combat—to the extent that one man in the section may lay down his life for another. This remarkable facet of war has been attested to in military citations thousands of times. It can be easily observed in the way a good sporting team works together, but on the battlefield this concept is extended and multiplied many times over, and is considerably more complex. In war the bond between men is literally forged by fire.

The October call for men to form the Reconnaissance unit brought a bunch of voluntary mavericks from all over the 5th Battalion who wanted to form the three close-knit fighting sections of the Reconnaissance Platoon. I wanted to get into Recce because I knew Deak: I wanted to work with him and be under his command in a unit that promised something different. I also knew another guy who had volunteered, 'Blue' Mulby.

John Thomas Mulby was a career soldier. He came to Australia from Britain as a teenager and lived in Doveton, Victoria, a working class suburb where Blue, as the only son in a family full of daughters, lived with his mother and ex-RAF father. Blue Mulby went into the Army with the aim of getting to the top of his profession, and becoming part of the Airborne Platoon in 1RAR in the early 1960s was certainly some sort of leg-up. The man was bloody huge, well over six foot, with arms that hung down like cords of thick rope. The pencil-thin moustache, red hair and ramrod-straight back only enhanced his take-no-prisoners-take-no-bullshit character. You wouldn't give this man lip.

So the first time I saw him, I did. He was walking past my hut with his maroon-coloured Airborne beret cocked to one side, in the company of another Airborne soldier. I spotted the pair and gave them a big hooray through the open door.

'G'day, you pair of dickheads.'

If you could catch words and shove them back down your throat the instant you'd uttered them, I would have. Too late. Mulby strode into the hut and right up to me like a gunslinger entering a saloon. At the same time I winced with the realisation that I'd made a life-threatening mistake. Mick Deak, close on hand, was instantly between us, preparing himself for a potential murder scene as the man–gorilla Mulby advanced on me. 'S'okay, s'okay, Blue,' Deak said gently. 'That's just dickhead Dogs for you. No problem, mate.'

Mulby's eyes burned into me and I knew I was looking at a human thrashing machine waiting to be switched on. I was certain I was going to be dismantled—painfully.

Mulby shot me a dismissive look, then turned to a sheepishly grinning Deak. 'Tell him to keep his bloody mouth shut in future, right?'

I went to Airborne myself later. I learnt to jump out of planes, and found myself sharing a room with Blue Mulby. He was a soft, humorous man at heart, I later discovered. But I warned myself about making any John Thomas 'penis' jokes.

The other section commander from my old platoon in C Company, Bernie Smith, had also put his hand up to be part of Recce. He had served in Malaya, was regarded as an old campaigner, and brought with him a valuable knowledge of jungle soldiering, including an ability to navigate. Bernie was one of the best map-readers I knew. Married with two children, Bernie loved the bush as much as he loved a cold beer on a warm day. He had a shock of thick, black hair that flopped forward under his bush hat, which in turn complemented a thick, black Pancho Villa moustache. The section commander was noticeably mild-mannered, but what attracted people to him was his infectious laugh. I went out of my way to try and make him laugh— easy enough to do after a few cans of beer.

William 'Suave Harve' Harvey was a friend of Blue Mulby's from Airborne Platoon. Like Deak and Mulby, Harve played rugby in the Army. He lived in Paddington, Sydney with his sister before joining up. What set Harve aside from most other grunts was his immaculate grooming and his love of expensive, fashionable civilian clothes. He was a natural to be tagged 'Suave Harve'.

Bob 'Searley' Searle was a quietly spoken, thoughtful man with a maturity not often seen in a grunt. He was hoping he'd make the grade and get accepted into Reconnaissance like the rest of us because he was a devoted and loyal friend to Mulby and Mick Deak.

Looking around at the 40 who were to undergo training and selection, it was clear that competition was going to be tough. The 28 who finally made it would be a pretty competent bunch.

DOPES AND ROPES

Flinders Ranges, 2000

Nuccaleena Mine. They crawled about on their arses in here 100 years ago. We sit and drop our packs and water bottles.

Silence.

The Ranges up here are so quiet you can hear the blood rushing through your ears. This was—is—pioneer country, a place where you can squat with a billy of tea and imagine for a moment how hard they did it here. We had stress in Vietnam, they had stress here, scraping a living off the marginal land or on their butts down that bloody mine. The stress killed them—along with every disease you could name, not to mention sheer hard work and a broken heart. See here—just down from the mine site is a small cemetery. These are the loneliest graves in the outback, 13 souls and a headstone to one Anson Fry, who died aged 48.

We stand: two minutes' silence.

We decide to go into the mine, but one man hangs back. He won't go: he's been in tunnels before, and they were rigged with grenades, or had snakes tied to the ceiling waiting for the unsuspecting tunnel rat with his torch and 9mm to walk into them.

Fair enough, we say to him. Have a smoke, we won't be long.

In the afternoon we get to talking again about some good times. Good times? In Vietnam? Hell, yeah, remember Vung Tau, Backbeach, the Beachcomber Club and a jukebox with Frankie Valli's 'Can't Take My Eyes Off Of You' played to death or until a Yank threatened to shoot the machine to pieces if we didn't stop playing it?

We recall a Vietnamese who rode on a hand-made trolley up and down outside the street bars. He propelled himself along by pushing on his knuckles while he knelt on his knees. He had no lower legs and we called him Claymore. That was an appropriate name because a Claymore anti-personnel mine likely blew his legs off. That was one of our mines, we hope, because he was a former Vietcong soldier. We all got on well with Claymore and tossed him a dollar every now and then.

He worked the same side of the Vung Tau street as Snake Man. This guy was a born entrepreneur. He also had a trolley on four wheels, and coiled on the small wooden platform was a huge reticulated python. The snake was drugged, or else had been kept in a fridge at home for a while before he brought it onto the streets at night and took pictures of you with the doped serpent coiled around your neck.

Claymore and Snake Man, real characters. But Claymore couldn't understand the joke when we tried to 'skateboard' him at high speed with a friendly push. And Snake Man? He protested and screamed for the Military Police when we kicked his snake to put some bloody life into it before he snapped his picture.

That was Vung Tau—sad, bad and mad.

CONFIDENTIAL INTSUM: 29 August 1966—Report from Radio Hanoi: The Australian mercenaries, who are no less husky and beefy than their Allies, the US aggressors, have proved as good flesh targets for the South Vietnamese Liberation fighters. In two days the Liberation Armed Forces wiped out over 500 Australian mercenaries in Baria (Phuoc Tuy) Province.

The Special Air Service (or the SAS) was both admired and reviled by others in the Army. The ordinary digger—if there is such a creature—considered the highly trained men of the SAS to be stuck-up 'super-soldiers'. The reason for this attitude is probably that healthy Aussie disrespect towards elitism—and the SAS were seen to be elite. I probably held this view before

Vietnam, but it was one I quickly changed after the formation of the Reconnaissance Platoon.

The infantry soldier in the battalion was *highly* trained. The men of the SAS were *specialist* trained. Each individual—infantryman or SAS—was prepared for his role in the Vietnam War in accordance with the needs of the overall military effort. Consequently, the grunt went bush with the express purpose of closing with and destroying the enemy. The Special Air Service was in Vietnam to observe, gather intelligence, collect information and report back. Contrary to myth—and wherever the SAS went, myth followed—the SAS man did not rise up in the dead of night and slit throats, he didn't collect victims' ears and he never launched a six-man patrol attack on an enemy regiment. He prowled like a cat, quietly studying the movements and preparations of the Vietcong or NVA, and reported back so that there was an informed basis upon which to launch battalion-size operations. He also often got into some heavy situations after deep insertion and had to be pulled out in a hot extraction by a hastily summoned Huey. There were always elements of fact and fiction surrounding SAS operations, but there really was no myth or mystery.

The Special Air Service, which was under Task Force Headquarters' control, often operated out of the range of artillery gun support. They carried high-grade, high-protein rations, and were equipped with special packs and weapons. They also specialised in specific infantry tactics, which they adapted to suit the task at hand. Small-group patrols working in remote territory needed special equipment and tactics—useful on most occasions when they 'had their arses hanging out'. All this specific SOP (standard operating procedure) and equipment was necessary, considering the job the SAS men were doing.

Reconnaissance Platoon would, under Colonel Warr's brief, also operate in small groups. But Recon was *not* SAS. We would operate within gun range and were at all times under the command of 5RAR. But we were the first Australian Recon group formed in Vietnam, so there was some anticipation mixed with anxiety when we met our SAS instructors at Vung Tau and the assessment training began.

The first thing to appreciate about battle training is that it can kill you just as surely as the real thing. I came to this conclusion while lying on my back in Vung Tau's 36th Evacuation Hospital. A surgeon was pulling a sliver of shrapnel out of my head with what looked suspiciously like a pair of workshop pliers.

The reason for all this blood and pain was Mick Deak, who part-way through Recce training had nearly killed me because he was thinking about sex while I was watching a hand grenade 'cook' only a few metres away. During grenade-throwing practice, the thrower ducked behind sandbags after lobbing a grenade into a car tyre—which was doubling as an enemy bunker entrance. I had tossed the grenade and was waiting the few seconds it would take for practice supervisor Deak in his sand-bagged control tower to give me the 'Down!' command. I watched the grenade—and him—with mounting alarm while he gazed towards the horizon.

Shit, it's going to cook, it's a blind, and we're going to have to blow it with a slab of C4, I thought, when suddenly there was an orange flash and *bang!*

I picked myself up with blood streaming down my forehead at the same time as Deak yelled across to me, 'Sorry about that, Dogs, I was thinking about Janine—you okay?'

'Okay? Fuckin' *okay*? You're thinking about your sheila and I get grenade shrap in my head.'

Deak tried to staunch the trickle of blood and checked my hat for fragment holes while I ranted on. 'You're supposed to tell me to get down, fuck it.'

'Stop harping, Dogs. Hey, I reckon there's a piece of grenade spring stuck in your skull . . . '

Training was gruelling and thorough. We patrolled as six-man teams up and down the Ganh Rai hills while the SAS soldiers studied, advised, instructed and assessed us. My impression was that the Ganh Rais, close to the port of Vung Tau, was another range of low hills where men could easily get killed by accident. It was on these very slopes months before that Wogsy had an accidental discharge with his M60 machine-gun. I was three metres in front of him and the crack of bullet striking rock caused me to nearly shit myself. It was cold comfort to me that the gunner beat a charge report by maintaining that an M60 could not fire just one bullet—certainly it could not be done by *accidentally* pulling the trigger.

The Recce course toughened up and we got down to specifics as the SAS men from 3 Squadron showed different methods of reconnaissance and patrolling as small, compact infantry groups, and how to lay an ambush using special 'beehive' charges. I was mightily impressed by the SAS men, who gave their information freely and with obvious enthusiasm. A collection of commissioned officers, sergeants and diggers, the SAS training contingent carefully explained and demonstrated how to lay up in the bush during night stops. We all lay with our feet touching to form the spokes of a wheel. By simply lifting your head you could look across to the area behind the opposite man's head; it kept us close and compact and we could all sleep at once in almost total safety. During a lay-up or rest by day, it was almost the same thing: sit back-to-back to form the same wheel, all look out towards the undergrowth. Silent and simple.

Casualty evacuation, or dustoff, was also part of the program. We used the Australian 9 Squadron RAAF helicopter unit—which was almost exclusively used by the SAS—to practise dustoff, swift insertion and hot extraction. Insertion by chopper involved going in fast and low, and leaping from the aircraft at low hover. Extraction, where the patrol was being pursued by enemy and had to get out fast, was the reverse procedure. We practised and rehearsed these techniques by day and night, while fitness freak Mick Deak had us up in the morning and pounding across every sand dune he could find before running through the sea. I was no jockstrapper, and it was not physical fitness that kept me up with the bunch but more youth and the dogged determination to be accepted.

The SAS men got down to the business end of reconnaissance in the final days: what to carry on Recce patrol, how to use it, how to lay ambush, and the use of anti-personnel mines—Claymores. We were taught ways of manufacturing explosive charges in order to cause maximum impact against the enemy when we were making a run for it. There was also 'break contact', or hit and run, just like Charlie. This was a contact method not used by the regular infantryman, who closed with and engaged the VC until there was an outcome.

The SAS men watched us closely and occasionally had a few quiet words with Mick Deak. I knew they were measuring us up, making recommendations on our performance. My main worry was navigation: I wasn't much of a map-reader and I thought that may let me down.

In central Vung Tau—'Vungas'—was a line of flagpoles. Atop each pole flew the colours of a particular Allied nation involved in supporting the Republic of South Vietnam in its fight against the communists. More significantly to us, this line of flagpoles was a rendezvous point where soldiers met after a night of drunkenness in Vung Tau.

'Meet you at the flags' was the catch-cry before men prowled off looking for sex, beer and trouble—not necessarily in that order. The flags were central to everywhere we wanted to go: the Blue Angel and the Washington bars, starting places for a bar crawl that should end by 2300 hours, curfew time; Bob the Tailor, an Indian businessman who changed money at blackmarket rates; and the Central Market. Also at the flags was a Lamboretta taxi stand: if you didn't want to walk, you climbed aboard and held on for dear life as the Vietnamese driver charged through the narrow streets.

Cities and towns at war have a certain smell, sound and taste about them. They repel and attract at the same time. They exude the sweetness of fast sex, and an exhaust fume-filled exhilaration and anticipation of freedom even when they are under siege. Maybe it's got something to do with a cocktail of danger and normality on every sidewalk, in each bar and brothel. We had a few days Rest and Convalescence (R and C) in Vung Tau, but so, apparently, did the Vietcong. Charlie used 'Vungas' to take a break from trying to kill us, and to pick up some local intelligence. We took a break from trying to kill him and picked up his sister—or his mother. In war you share the same debauched fleshpots.

I breathed in deeply and for a few minutes watched the town's madness: narrow streets where garbage seemed to actually grow; beggars and working girls in skirts that were desperately '60s, humming out of tune to the Fifth Dimension and The Supremes. Kids ran their hands gently over your arm while they lifted your wallet or tried to sell you their sister with a 'Uc Da Loi number one.' Barbers changed bucks to Vietnamese piastres, women massaged your favourite muscle, and mamasan bar owners had girls who could take every buck out of your pocket by simply sitting on your lap and pouring weak, expensive Saigon Tea down their throats. There were Lamborettas so overloaded with soldiers that the rear dragged on the dirty ground while the front freewheeled in the air. Shoeshine boys begged for business, beggars clung to every pedestrian, and drunks raced carts pulled by miniature horses. Vung Tau existed at frenzy level . . . it was at war and loving every dollar-making minute.

Mick Deak was issuing a warning. 'If you're on the streets after curfew, you'll be charged. If you get into trouble after curfew with the White Mice, you'll be dead. Those little pricks don't think twice about shooting any bastard giving them the shits.'

The White Mice were the provincial police, who wore white shirts and .45s on their belts. A law unto themselves, they would not hesitate to draw and fire on an Australian, an American or even a Republic of Korea serviceman, the three main groups of Allied soldiers who used Vung Tau for their four-day Rest and Convalescence leave.

Men at war go mad when they get a break, and the Recce group was ready for a break. We needed the company of women, alcohol, a haircut and a good time, which would launch off with a huge dinner followed by stirring the locals and the Yanks. Blue Mulby and Suave Harve took off with Deak in one direction, while I teamed up with the two Smiths—Bernie and Recce platoon sergeant John Lea-Smith—and headed off in the other.

Mick Deak's parting words were both a caution and an advice to play hard: 'Don't forget I know you blokes by now better than you know yourselves. I reckon I'll be busy keeping everyone out of the clag tonight . . . see you in the Sydney Bar at 7 o'clock.'

It was stretching things a bit to call the *Faviora* a restaurant. It had the cleanest white tablecloths in Vung Tau and the Vietnamese table staff spoke fluent French, but the establishment sat above a massage parlour, which sort of lowered the tone as you struggled to find the stairs and a couple of soldiers slipped by, tucking their shirts back in. But *Faviora* must have done something right—there were three American nurses eating opposite us as Bernie pulled his chair out with a whisper.

'Must be a good joint, they wouldn't eat here if it wasn't up to scratch.'

I was a Philistine when it came to manners and taste, and decided to order fish and chips. John rolled his eyes.

'No, Dogs, this is up-market. Order off the menu, proper-like, and keep your bloody voice down, you dag.'

Lobster Thermidor seemed a combination of the rich and the exotic, and I put on a smart-arse act while I ordered. Bernie and John went for two steaks. I chuckled and said, 'Bet you get water buffalo—there's not too many head of beef cattle in Vietnam.'

Less than half an hour later I was eating my words. The Smiths cut into their delicious steaks while I stared down gagging at a crustacean covered in dripping hot cheese. I told the waiter I wasn't happy with the mess and would like 'those French-style fries instead, please'.

The waiter returned with chips, struggling to keep a straight face, and said there'd be no extra charge for swapping the meal before scuttling back to the kitchen to join the rest of his crew tucking into my lobster.

I compensated for the lack of substantial food with a salad roll bought on the street—commonly known as the Hepatitis Roll—and sucked in the smell and sights of dusk in Vung Tau.

'This is better than a sideshow at Luna Park,' I grunted at Bernie. 'The Army can kiss my arse tonight, let me at it.'

Two of life's great levellers: sex and grog . . . Eight hours later I was lying face down on an Army cot, covered in beach sand and cursing the hyena that had used my mouth as a toilet. On my shirt was a name-tag with letters printed in yellow, CHEAP

CHARLIE. The angry little man inside my head was jack-hammering a breakout and my legs were all but numb. They barely supported me while I navigated out into the early morning sun. Blue Mulby sat on his bed holding his head in his hands. The big man, despite an endless capacity for alcoholic beverages, was gagging and struggling to speak when he looked up at me.

'You're still alive then?' he mumbled. 'We carried you back, but really thought you'd die from alcoholic poisoning.'

Mulby pointed to a lump under his bed, 'That's Harve . . . I think. Deak got into a fight with the MPs. The bastards arseholed us out of town with a pretty serious warning not to come back.'

I bent to examine the prostrate man under Mulby's bed, fighting back a retching sensation. The figure looked dead, but then its eyes suddenly sprang open. They were brilliant red, like a pair of crushed Jaffas.

'What about Bernie?' I asked.

'Came back early in a taxi. Said Vung Tau was no place for a married man. Sensible prick.'

Not everyone was going to make the new Reconnaissance Platoon. The course had not yet been completed, but we got the word from Mick Deak as we walked into his tent one at a time. I made it, along with Mulby, Suave Harve and Bernie. John Lea-Smith would be our sergeant. Deak told us Battalion Commander Warr wanted us back for a forthcoming operation. I watched the men who had unsuccessfully tried out for Recce file away. It was a pity: they had the commitment, the enthusiasm and the guts to go for it, but only a set number of us were required.

For a few short and sobering moments I wondered about what I'd done—volunteered. You *never* volunteered in the Army. Certainly not to head out into the unknown with a bunch of original wild men.

ZIPPO AND THE TEMPLE OF BOOM

Flinders Ranges, 2000

Midday heat, dry and comforting in the Australian bush. Sitting, smoking, talking. The conversation gets around to what's-his-name.

'You know, what's-his-name? For God's sake, blokes, everyone remembers what's-his-name.'

Silence.

Another man scratches his jaw then says, 'You mean what's-his-face, you know, the gunner, Schmidty?'

'Yeah, yeah, you remember Schmidty? What happened to that big bastard? He nearly shot the CSM with his M60 when he got pissed one night.'

Only one man laughs, the others exchange looks then stare at the ground. Silence under the huge river gum that now throws an arc of shade over the dry bed of Breakfast Time Creek.

Eventually one man stands up and fiddles uncomfortably with his backpack. 'Schmidty's dead. The port got him.'

Silence, and another exchange of looks all round.

'He never really got over shooting his mate in Vietnam. It was an accident—when his 2IC came back from a shit in the bush Schmidty thought he was a Nog and gave him half a belt of M60. He got back to the 'Dat a day or two later and just lay on his cot looking up at the tent flap, then back at the '60 resting on the sandbags. Schmidty was an easy bloke, a really good bloke from Queensland who never really hit the piss hard—till then. He was soon knocking back Bacardi, Scotch and a shit-load of grog. He got up one night, wobbled down to the CSM's tent and cut loose with his gun. But he trod on the belt and the M60 jammed up. CSM talked to Schmidty really nice like for a few minutes, then the RPs escorted him away.'

We've heard the Schmidty story before: the shooting accident, the dead digger and the aftermath. The big Queenslander was psych-tested, and put on the next plane back to Australia. Medically discharged, he hit the grog again. Inside a year he was finishing a bottle of port before breakfast.

They found Schmidty two years later in his single-room unit on the floor, dead in his own vomit.

It wasn't the port that got Schmidty—it was the bloody war that killed him.

You stand and walk over to the man who didn't know the Schmidty story's tragic finale. You talk for a few minutes about alcohol, your own 20-year battle with the booze and the decision to save your life with a twelve-step program. Vets by the truckload are suffering the effects of booze. It buries the past, wipes away the bad dreams for a while, but in the end you'll probably go mad. Certainly every war neurosis you suffer will be made a hundred times worse.

Out here in the Flinders there's no grog permitted. How do you feel today . . . ?

CONFIDENTIAL INTSUM: Warning Order, 2145 hrs, 6 November 1966—Operation Yass. The area of flat ground to the WEST and SOUTH WEST of Phuoc Tuy is of considerable importance to the VC. Enemy activity is concentrated in the area of Phu My, Phuoc Hoa, Long Son Island. The island is situated near the junction of several sea routes leading into landing points. The most direct route into Phuoc Tuy is Phuoc Hoa. Long Son Island has offered refuge, communication and staging facilities to the VC for several years. Any VC force on the island is expected to fight hard.

In war, any war, there are never enough men to go around. Every unit is—always has been, always will be—under strength. Soldiers get sick, they are wounded, they are even thrown in the cooler for a serious offence. They also get killed and are not replaced.

In the Vietnam War men also went on leave: four days on 'Rest and Convalescence' in Vung Tau or a flight to an Asian capital like Taipei, Hong Kong, Singapore or Bangkok on 'Rest and Recreation' (R and R). And we needed those breaks, a chance to get trashed after days, weeks and months of bush work.

Recce Platoon was no different: our numbers were continually down for one reason or another. The most we could muster would be 24 to 26 men from a full platoon strength of 30. Many infantry platoons were well below that number on occasion. In keeping with his brief to utilise us as small groups, Mick Deak split the Recce unit into four six-man patrols, comprising a commander, a second-in-command, a machine-gunner, a signaller, a medic and a scout. We were by design an under-strength 10-man infantry section. But we had a lot in common with the standard infantry section. We carried the same ridiculous weight on our backs and lugged the same heavy equipment and firepower: grenades and grenade launchers, Claymores, endless belts of M60 ammunition, smoke canisters, machetes, bayonets, shovels and, of course, our personal weapon, rifle or machine-gun.

For the forthcoming operation out to Phuoc Hoa and Long Son Island, Deak briefed us on what we would carry. Outside his tent in the Recon lines we lounged and smoked as he gave his Orders Group—*Situation, Mission, Execution, Administration and Log, Command and Signals.* Every operation followed a protocol; the Army always did things by numbers and regulations. We listened then began to pack.

I stripped and cleaned my rifle. After months in the war zone I thought I'd seen some dopey examples of Army procedure, but now, stripping down the 7.62 L1A1 Self Loading Rifle (SLR)—the standard Australian infantry rifle—I recalled a day in the bush with C Company when I still carried the old World War II Owen machine carbine, the 9mm weapon that had achieved fame on the jungle trails of Kokoda. Despite its awkward 30-round magazines and limited punch power, the Owen had served me well, and would, I thought, do so until the end of my tour. Suddenly across a dry paddy came an armoured personnel carrier with a soldier leaning from the open hatch. He pointed to me and shouted as the APC got closer.

'Hey, you! Yeah, you with the Owen, come here.'

I sauntered over. 'What's with you?'

'The Owen, gimme the Owen. We're withdrawing 'em. You got this now.' He tossed me a plastic-covered parcel. It was a rifle and two boxes of ammunition. The APC thundered away with my old Owen and I clutched the plastic bag. For a second I thought I was on *Candid Camera*.

For the remainder of that afternoon and into the night I struggled to read the instruction brochure for my new Armalite, the 'plastic' 5.56mm fully automatic rifle which was becoming standard US military issue. I sweated out that night and the next day, hoping Charlie wouldn't choose that moment to have a crack at a soldier who was more like a kid struggling to work a new toy.

In Recce we had a choice of weapon, and I went back to the SLR, but made a few adjustments. I replaced the safety catch with one from a L1A2 heavy-barrelled SLR, and filed down the trigger sear and the pin designed to stop the safety catch going onto 'auto'. With a 30-round instead of a 20-round magazine I now had the weapon I wanted in the bush—a 'Slaughtermatic', I called it: in essence a fully automatic 7.62mm machine-gun without a belt-feed, a lightweight rifle with maximum punch when on automatic fire. I considered that too many magazines going through without a break were likely to melt the barrel, but if it ever came to that sort of fight I probably wouldn't be coming home anyway.

Early morning on a small knoll near Route 15, the main road that snaked up from Vung Tau to Saigon. A flight of 10 American choppers came around the small hill as if they were practising for the Indy 500. There was no let-up in their airspeed as they dropped towards the LZ (Landing Zone), and the result was a 'brownout': swirling, choking dust mixed with clouds of green marker smoke. Gaseous, sickening kerosene fumes only added to the confusion and chaos as groups of men stumbled and staggered towards the choppers while air marshals in red jackets screamed instructions, shielding their faces against sheets of grit and sand.

I waved to my section and we jogged forward, bent double to avoid the rotors which dipped and rose, threatening decapitation. The chopper door gunners hung out on the skids, screaming at us and into their radios. We lifted three feet, then dropped back to the deck. We lifted and hovered, then dropped and tilted.

I turned and yelled at the door gunner, 'We got a problem here? We're not with a bloody learner, are we?'

The gunner tapped his helmet radio and grinned. I yelled again, 'Will you tell the silly bastard to get this thing into the bloody air, *please*!'

There was a lurch, the aircraft tilted and we started to lift. The dust dropped away and I suddenly saw how close the nearest aircraft was—I swear I could have reached across and touched the guy in the next Huey. Now it was all cool air and the curious shudder and bounce of a helicopter in flight. There was a welcome sense of peace gazing out across the countryside.

I patted my trouser legs to make sure I had my maps, and

straightened my pack, a Vietnamese Army-type design which I'd chosen to carry in Recce. Other men had scrounged or stolen US Army backpacks, or British-style Bergens, which Mick Deak had. Deak and others had also opted for American fatigues with bundles of pockets to stick all sorts of stuff in. There was a sprinkling of US Army canvas-sided boots with special drainage holes and Australian General Purpose boots, and basic pouches on the pistol webbed belt came in all shapes and sizes, from British '37 pattern (designed in 1937) to Aussie issue. We were a scruffy-looking unit, and I'd heard that the Army of the Republic of Vietnam (ARVN) already considered us mercenaries.

Ahead lay Long Son Island, a gash of brown in a sea of dark blue and almost iridescent green. The island was situated in an area known as the Rung Sat, a serpentine swirl of marshes, swamps and waterways. We weren't there yet, but just looking out at it you knew the whole zone stank of VC. My mind went back to the briefing and the previous 24 hours, when 5RAR had pulled another deception plan. Colonel Warr had dispatched a number of his best beer drinkers to the bars of Vung Tau to tell all the bar girls—many of whom had VC connections—that our next operation would take place in the Dinh and Nui Thi Vai Hills. Disinformation like this was giving the Australians some sort of an edge in the battle to take Phuoc Tuy Province.

The real plan was to Cordon and Search Phuoc Hoa, a fishing village of 700 souls on the banks of the massive Rung Sat. Behind Phuoc Hoa were the Dinh Hills, and to give the deception plan credibility, on day one of our operation 5RAR charged up Route 15 in APCs and swung into the jungle at the base of the low mountain range. It worked: the VC were sure an operation was to be launched into the hills zone. Next morning we started the heli-lift while other 5RAR units, including three sections of

Recce, threw a cordon around Phuoc Hoa. The locals weren't even out of bed when the diggers moved in.

I was section commander controlling the Recce component flying out to Long Son Island. Back in Phuoc Hoa, Blue Mulby and Bob Searle had started the drinking and disinformation deception again. Soon after the Cordon and Search they were challenged by suspected VC sympathisers to a game of pool and a drinking competition. Despite their best efforts, the VC could only extract more lies from one of the most hardened drinkers and one of the best eight-ball players in the battalion.

But the dirty side of the war had now started on Long Son Island. The first rifle company in was the luckless Bravo. Under fire from the top of the hill on Long Son, a Huey wobbled and its rotor hit some rocks on the LZ. The machine shuddered and the rotor fragmented, but all the soldiers and crew managed to escape from the wreck and return fire. Soon after, Bravo lost its first soldier on the operation, felled by a VC sniper.

I watched the waterways of the Rung Sat glide by as we headed for our LZ at a cool 100 knots. The terrain beneath winked back—sampans on the water, the startling green of trees along the river's edge broken by the white flashes of Vietnamese homes.

What a beautiful country this is, and we're fucking it up hour by hour. One day I will come back and holiday here . . . after we win this war.

We patrolled west over the island of Long Son, clearing and relocating people who had probably been here for 100 years. We had to do this, claimed high command, as the area was going to be hit later with occasional artillery fire to keep the Nogs out. It was called 'Harassment and Interdiction', or H and I—a Vietnam War innovation whereby, any hour of the night, our big guns would let loose a salvo into a predetermined location in the jungle, or even into little Long Son. The enemy could never rest at night;

could never be sure when the whistle of 105 shells might come his way. In fact, he would never know when he was going to die, because those killed never heard the telltale whistle behind the shell. The first time I heard the expression 'H and I', I thought it meant 'Help the Infantry'; the war was a bizarre learning curve of jargon and acronyms.

I walked up to a vacated thatched hut and prepared to do my duty. I wasn't comfortable with this; none of us was—it had to be done.

'Give us a match, Taffy,' I said.

Taffy, my section second-in-command, tried to lighten the mood. 'Your dick and a jellybean. Piss off, Dogs, you know I don't smoke.'

'Yeah, well what the hell do you use to light that C4 every day when you brew up?'

Taffy was of Welsh extraction, but you'd never believe it looking at him. A shade under six foot, he looked like that great American Indian, Cochise. He was swarthy, with flat features and jet black hair. He was also a tattoo freak: almost every square inch of skin on his arms was covered in a montage of snakes, anchors and roses. Chains swirled in and out and there were huge eagles, wings spread and beaks beckoning. Appearances apart, what stood out about the softly spoken lance-corporal was the way he stood up. Taffy didn't just stand from a sitting or squatting position, he unfolded like a marionette with a string attached to its head. One moment he was sitting, the next he was fully erect with his chest out and huge arms hanging at his side. Sometimes it seemed Taffy Cheeseman just appeared next to you out of nowhere.

I scratched in my pocket for my Zippo, flicked it and lit the thatch on the hut. Some peasant had put his life into this and we were 'Zippo-ing' it. Within minutes the hut was nothing but charred posts and ashes. I looked down at my stainless steel lighter, noticing again the engraving the street vendor had put on it before I bought it: 'Let me win your heart and mind or I'll burn your goddamned hut down.'

We moved down towards the mangroves and stumbled on a beautiful piece of architecture—a Buddhist temple. The diggers were looking at me.

'What we gonna do about this?' someone asked. 'We can't burn it.'

'Orders are take out everything on this side of the island,' I answered. 'Anything Nogs'll use as hiding spots. We'll have to blow it.'

I consulted one of the engineers attached to us for the ground search and he confirmed it.

'I reckon blowing it's the safest way to do it, mate. But it's your call, you're in charge. Do you want to check with anyone first?'

I gave the sappers the go-ahead: they placed slabs of C4 around the building and fitted up three-minute fuses. 'Fire's on, piss off!'

We scrambled towards any cover we could find and pulled our heads in. The explosion would be massive, I thought, looking across at the gracious old structure. Suddenly I heard the drone and thump of an approaching chopper.

'Fuck me drunk, don't tell me he's heading in *here*?'

The group of faces around me was a picture of disbelief as the Huey droned closer. I could actually see the door gunner giving me the thumbs up with a grin. Frantically I waved back, motioning for him to head port or starboard. The smoke from the shortening fuse was now visible and the engineer next to me was holding his head in his hands.

'Too late, mate, she's going up.'

The chopper passed over the temple and the gunner looked down again, still smiling.

Christ, Deaky's going to be totally rapt in me—sends me over to help out and I'm about to blow up their resupply chopper!

Next moment the gracious old building erupted in a flash, hurling masonry and ornamental trappings just past the tail of the moving chopper. Struck by the shock wave, the aircraft wobbled and tilted, then straightened up and flew on undamaged. I caught one last look at the door gunner, his face blanched and mouth wide open.

The engineer next to me had his hand over his mouth as if he was about to be sick.

'Do you reckon he noticed anything?' I said.

The following day Blue and Bernie were lounging in the sun outside their hootchie when I led my section back into Phuoc Hoa. I was still smarting at the Bravo Company Commander's spray over the temple incident. His mouth was so full of froth he could hardly speak. But I got the message: seek approval from a Higher Authority before blowing up anything, particularly religious buildings. I decided to put on a Joe Cool act and keep dead silent over my explosive decision.

'The warriors return—how was it, Dogs?' Blue started to brew up.

I shot back with as much bravado as I could muster: 'I got in more shit than Ned Kelly over on that island while you've been hanging out here like a pack of Poges.'

'Come on, Dogs, we've been working our arses off day and night, getting no sleep, always worrying about you fellers. We've been ambushing, patrolling, up to our ears in RPGs (Rocket Propelled Grenades) . . . '

'Got the shits, have you Mulby, 'cause you know we've been in the real action?'

I was sure someone would blurt out something about blowing up helicopters, but the moment passed as Mick Deak strode up. He had been already briefed on our next operation, and had a serious look on his face.

'We're heading back into the Warburton Mountains,' he said flatly. 'On our own.'

NIGHT WITH THE ATOMIC KID

Flinders Ranges, 2000

From where we are sitting we can look over to the low range of mountains. At times they are hazy, at others they shine with hues of brilliant green and a deep chocolate brown. Always benevolent.

But there are other mountains, hills we have seen—where men walked and died—that caused a constriction in our chests. Always malevolent.

We walk through the narrow ravine, climbing over rocks, hop-scotching along stones protruding from the creekwater. It is strange how something as simple and innocent as crossing a creek, arms outstretched for balance, can make everyone feel . . . liberated. Stop and bend and scoop up the water in your hands, splash your face. More liberation. Also strange—well, you say it's not so strange really, in fact it's normal—how you can walk through these hills and feel safe, secure.

You tell one man to stop looking for firing positions. Another you tell to stop leading—aiming your imaginary rifle—a foot in front of the wild goats as if he is ready to drop a VC. S'okay, though—just bad habits, right?

Sharp ochre cliffs are on both sides of us now. We are penetrating deeper into the main gorge, where you promise there's something special.

We arrive, stop and drink it in: a clear blue sky that goes on forever, a wedge-tailed eagle circling and dipping. To the front, stretching for 100 metres, drooping river red gums are lined up like sentinels. Look up to the right cliff face, where yellow-footed rock wallabies stand perfectly still. All this beauty around us— doubled upon itself by its reflection in one of the most beautiful rockpools we've ever seen.

We sit in total silence for half an hour or more, and finally you say we really have to make a move. One man stands and asks, 'Just a bit longer . . . please?'

CONFIDENTIAL INTSUM: October 1966—The area of operations comprises the western of two large steep hills approximately equal in size, over 1500 feet and 1700 metres apart. Their average gradient is one in three, but some faces on the NW slopes of both hills have a steepness of one in two overall. There are some precipitous drops of dangerous height. The western hill is Nui Thi Vai.

Nui Thi Vai, Nui Toc Tien and the Dinh Hills dominated the horizon when you looked west from Nui Dat. It was six clicks—6000 metres—in a straight line from the barbed wire fence at the end of Luscombe airstrip at the Australian Task Force (ATF) base to the foot of the hills. They were called 'hills', but in anyone's book they were low mountains; certainly to every poor digger who had ever lugged up and down them. Nui Thi Vai and Nui Toc Tien were separated by a valley, along which a small road meandered down to the fishing port of Phuoc Hoa and the swamps and riverways of the Rung Sat. Between the mountains and the ATF base were paddys, low scrub and a small river called Song Sai.

On the map spread before him, Mick Deak indicated where we would be going, and gave a general outline of the operation. Like two cow pats on the predominantly green Army map, the Nuis showed up as tight, brown contour lines, indicating height. This made soldiers spit chips: it meant straight *up* or straight *down*.

There were layers of jungle at the base, tall trees that gave way to boulders the size of trucks, which eventually reared up to a razorback spur punctuated by scrubby foliage. Anyone in the ATF at Nui Dat could see these hills to the west, as could those who walked outside the wire on Search and Destroy or other pain-in-the-arse patrols across Phuoc Tuy. And the mountains—with their washed-out jagged browns and greens, pockmarked by a thousand bomb craters or splattered with napalm that clung in clumps to the rocks like dried honeycomb—were watching us back.

Every assault on the summit maimed and killed. Every time someone went up, they encountered a new, creative form of death. We hated the mountains as much as the Vietcong loved them. They used the Nui Thi Vais as observation posts, they burrowed into the shale and rock like moles, they strung booby traps and dug punji pits—sharpened bamboo stakes that sliced into the side of the leg, or jagged through the stomach as you fell on them. The VC pushed them into the ground, point up, then urinated on them, even rubbed faeces on the things. You were wounded something awful, not killed—you may die a horrible death later by poisoning. Charlie also laid mines that sprang from the ground and wiped out whole sections of men.

I remember the faces of the Australian diggers as they stopped for a break and a brew when I last went up there. There was serious anxiety every second on the slopes, even when we were having a nerve-calming smoke: no frigging around, no chiacking. Humour evaporated into thin air up there. The mountains were affectionately called 'the Warburtons' by the Australian diggers— not that they deserved any affection. It was a bastardisation of some old country and western song that warned not to go up on Wolverton Mountain.

The description was so well accepted that even Intelligence briefs and INTSUM referred to them as 'the Warburtons' or 'the Warbies'. Some of us went up them time and again. And every step on the Warbies came at a price: death, a wounding, or just the fact that the climb drained away years of your life in a single day's sweat. You could actually hate those mountains by just bloody well looking at them.

Mick Deak sipped the coffee I had just made for myself while he turned and rotated the map and gave his brief.

'There's a large convoy of Americans coming up from a ship in Vung Tau. They've just arrived in-country so they'll be as green as Irish grass.'

'Not Irish grass in bumpacks, though,' snorted Mulby.

Deak went on, still slurping my coffee: 'The Yanks will have their own artillery in support as they move up Route 15 towards Saigon and their big base at Long Binh. They don't want a whole bunch of their reos [reinforcements] ambushed and zapped en route, because apparently there's a swag of Yanks at Long Binh waiting for reinforcements so's they can go back to good ol' US of A.'

I understood the new op: from the Hills and swamps of the Rung Sat the enemy could move up close to Route 15 and cut a road convoy to pieces.

'So where does Recce fit in?' I asked.

Deak finished my coffee and shook the last drop out of the mug before passing it back to me. 'Ta, Dogs, that was a very nice brew. Okay, the battalion will spread itself pretty thin along Route 15 from Phuoc Hoa to Phuy My.'

He jabbed a finger at a small collection of dots 12 clicks north of Phuoc Hoa. 'That's where an American brigade will pick up protection and take over.' Then he looked at us. 'Our job is to go into the mountains and make sure the Yanks don't get mortared or shelled by the Nogs positioned on the sides of the Warbies.'

Bernie, Blue and I looked at each other, trying to envision the rock climbing in store for the next few days.

'Besides SAS, nothing smaller than an Aussie rifle company has been up Nui Thi Vai, and most have copped a fair stick,' Blue said, confirming what we all knew.

'You're right, of course, Blue,' said Bernie. 'The VC'll expect a whole battalion to clear the hills, which is fortunate for us.'

I turned to Bernie. 'Fortunate? What's so bloody *fortunate* about it? If anyone wants my fortune they can have it, and I'll go on R and C to Vung Tau.'

As we approached the jungle-clad slopes of Nui Thi Vai, I recalled that over the last few months each member of the Recce team had been up here, with different units. And in every case they had copped it heavy. I wasn't looking forward to this. Medic Peter Fraser walked near me as we moved upwards. 'You've heard that song, haven't you, Dogs?'

'What song's that?'

He hummed softly and whispered the words, '*They say don't go on Warburton Mountain if you're looking for a . . .*'

Recce patrolled on during the day, and I cast my mind back to when I was with C Company and we'd hit the 274 Regiment—fully tooled-up North Vietnamese Army regulars. The lead Aussie platoon had worked its way up the ridge line when they were hit by snipers. The enemy had booby-trapped every spot the diggers would have dived for to take cover. The platoon commander and several soldiers were taken out in the detonations. With C Company we moved up to start the evacuation of wounded while B Company encircled up to 40 enemy who were moving down to wipe out any wounded Australians. Shits were trumps on the Warbies: intelligence had warned that one of the NVA heavies, 274 deputy commander Nguyen Nam Hung, was hiding his slimy little arse further up the mountain, with possibly an entire regiment.

Battalion Commander, Lt. Colonel Warr, opted not to lose more men and called for support—and the firepower brought down on the Warbies that afternoon took our breath away. Gunships clattered in and loosed a salvo of rockets then opened up with mini-guns spraying bursts of lead into the rocky re-entrants where the VC scuttled like rabbits back into their bunkers.

It was quiet for several minutes, an eerie silence, then came the howl of fighter jets. The pilots of the F100s commenced their dive with a howl that became a scream. From beneath the Phantoms two 500lb bombs spiralled down into the VC bunkers. The jets climbed, circled and flashed in the late afternoon sun. On the return the pilots released a clutch of cluster bomb units (CBUs) that burst open above the ground, scattering small canisters throughout the jungle like firecrackers on Guy Fawkes' Day.

Remind yourself, we thought, *watch for unexploded CBUs tomorrow. Kick one and you're dead.*

Artillery joined in soon after the jets and gunships departed, along with 1000 rounds of mortar bombs. But the grand finale on Nui Thi Vai came just on dusk, when the Phantoms returned with napalm canisters. The purpose of this horrific petroleum-jelly bomb—invented specifically for the Vietnam War—was to suck all the oxygen out of enemy tunnels, caves and bunker systems. It also sucked the air out of everyone's lungs within striking distance. It stuck to skin and burnt its unfortunate victims to death. We watched in silence as huge crimson balls rose into the air after the canisters exploded and flaming yellow blobs of jelly sucked in every atom of oxygen.

The VC stronghold on Nui Thi Vai was an eye-opener. It gave an insight into how the enemy lived and fought and died, such as the VC's endless capacity to conceal and camouflage—like the thou-sands of leaves that were sewn together to make enormous quilts, which were then thrown over every building in the complex. And that complex was a maze of tunnels that led off left and right, plunging into a subterranean city of workshops, a hospital, training and lecture rooms, and an arsenal. A huge Russian flag was displayed where medicines, weapons and ammo were stacked. The VC could have held a small ground army off for years, but against the might of air power they had to retreat: they melted away into the mountains and down to the Rung Sat.

I remembered now, while sitting and having a smoke with the men from Recon, that when I was last up here with Charlie Company, I'd experienced one of my most terrifying—and embarrassing—moments of the war, just a few hundred metres from this spot. It was a pitch black night and we had harboured up near the bombed-out VC complex. The jungle was thick around here; it climbed and closed above you and around you. I tried to sleep, and maybe I did for a few minutes, but then my eyes sprang open. Just 10 feet from me was a brilliant glow—it shone with the intensity of a fluorescent light, in the shape of a man. It seemed to advance and retreat but was not moving at all. I choked on the fear: I was literally frozen to the spot, and I swear every hair on my body shot upright. My mouth instantly went dry. I couldn't have called out if I'd wanted to.

Jesus, is it a Vietcong ghost back from the dead to get me?

A moment later I was aware of a man moving towards me from a different angle. 'Halt! Who's that?' I fought to get the words out.

'It's me.'

'Who's me?' I was nervous and angry.

'Just me.'

'It's me here too, wanker! Tell me who "me" is or you get a third eye.'

'Dogs, it's me, Bones. I'm coming off sentry. What the bloody hell's the matter with you?

I kept one eye on the thing, the other I switched over to Bones. 'Come here, *come bloody here.* Get a look at this, for God's sake.'

Bones crashed down next to me and peered into the black. 'Wassamatter, you having a nightmare?'

'This whole bloody dump's a nightmare . . . what do you reckon that is?'

'Yeah, I saw it going on gun sentry, and told Jack. He told Butch to have a look at it and Butch told Vil . . . '

I went boonta. 'Well what the fuck is it, *for God's sake*? You gonna run through the whole bloody gun roster before I get an answer?'

Bones nodded his head towards the glow, which was now intensifying. 'It's the Atomic Kid, Dogs. We all reckon it's the Atomic Kid.'

I sat stunned, wondering if I should shoot Bones before he rose into the air and flew away. But Bones, a six-footer with buck teeth and glasses as thick as the bottom of Coke bottles, was winding up to his subject.

'That tree stump's really, really old, Dogs, and over the years a rare luminous moss grows on it. During the day it's like any other tree, at night it shines like the Atomic Kid.'

I pushed my face up close to the other man. He had a slight grin on his face and was waiting for an answer, but I was too dumbfounded to discuss it.

'Thanks, Bones, you can go and hit the farter now.'

I lay down and looked at the glowing 'Atomic Kid', a radio-active character from a 1954 Mickey Rooney movie, for an hour. A Vietcong soldier had possibly lain here once and stared at the same apparition . . .

Reconnaissance Platoon continued to prowl around the mountain ridges and slipped under the jungle canopy. There was little talk, and I could not get my head around the current patrol—I kept sliding back to the days when I was up here with Charlie Company. Every gully or large rock I recognised, every track or trail I knew I'd previously walked, brought back those earlier operations.

During a smoke break I went looking for a tree. Not just any bloody tree, but a tree that had wreaked havoc up here months ago during the big bunker attack. Engineers were flown in to demolish the bunker system, but that tree got in the way. Now, on Recce patrol, I saw it and remembered it. It seemed to grow straight out of a rock. I knew that that single straggly trunk and branches and a Huey rotor blade were just made for each other. The chopper came in with engineers. The pilot saw the tree and tried to swing around it; instead, the aircraft flew straight into a cliff.

I recalled now the sight and sound of a Huey beating itself to death, blades breaking and flying at us like shrapnel while at the same time the chopper tried to turn itself inside out—orange and yellow flames, and men staggering, stumbling away from the wreck.

There is an image of a Flight Sergeant covered in blood, mouth open in shock. He'd battled to get his men off the machine before the ammunition went up. Then the dustoff chopper came in with the crew chief hanging off the skid, shouting instructions to his pilot. It was nothing short of brave and brilliant: the dustoff reversed into a landing spot to the cheers of the wounded men.

All this happened simply because a tree was in the wrong place on the wrong day.

MONKEYING WITH THE ENEMY

Flinders Ranges, 2000

Gum trees and huge chunks of shining red rock. There's a creek with bushes growing close to the water, the trickle and tinkle of a clear stream running. Look up and around: the hot sun is bouncing off the cliffs that rise both sides of the creek.

There is silence, peaceful and absolute, not a squeak or an animal rustle. No galah to scream, no parrot with that throaty cackle here . . . just silence.

Sit for a minute and have a smoke. We come up into these hills for the silence, and because we can talk as men who have been in other places where there was also a silence, but one that was always menacing and lethal.

We can't get out of that habit we got into in the war—always casting an eye around for cover from fire and cover from view. We were switched on all the time, and that's what took the energy out of us as much as hauling up the spur line with all that bloody weight on our backs. It makes us wonder if we'll ever be able to relax in a place as wonderful and beautiful as this. Will we ever switch off?

CONFIDENTIAL INTSUM: October 1966—Groups of enemy may seek to escape but a healthy respect for their marksmanship must be allowed. Snipers may lie in wait for individual Australians as in recent operations and small groups may be ambushed by local VC.

'Well, Dogs, do you want me to follow them, or shall I wait till you've got your head out of your arse and come back from wherever you are right now?'

My forward scout, Little Mac, was looking at me as if I was

Above: Ready for action. The 5th Battalion Reconnaissance Platoon. This was the first Australian Reconnaissance unit formed in Vietnam in 1966. The picture was taken at the Australian Task Force base at Nui Dat. (R Kearney)

Top: Faces of war. A familiar sight on the streets of Vung Tau, these children of war became firm friends with the Uc Da Loi (Australians), on leave in the city on the coast of the South China Sea. Children as young as 8 or 9 smoked cigarettes. (R. Kearney)

Above: Taking care of business. Bob's tailor shop at Vung Tau became a 'business centre' for Australian soldiers where money would be exchanged, clothes made to order and other shadowy bartering carried out. (J. Mulby)

Top: Home at last. Reconnaissance Platoon four-man tent at Nui Dat. This was the typical 'accommodation' for all the soldiers at the 1ATF base in the Nui Dat rubber plantation. (J. Mulby)
Above: The eyes of the tiger. Members of the Reconnaissance Platoon during a brief moment's rest inside Nui Dat. (J. Mulby)

Above: The Skipper. Mick Deak (Von Berg) M.C. was given the task of forming and leading the Reconnaissance Platoon with 5th Battalion. He was awarded the Military Cross for valour and later joined the Special Air Service (SAS). (R. Kearney)

Left: Portrait of a Digger.
Reconnaissance Platoon section commander Bernard 'Bernie' Smith, who was killed in a mine explosion during his second tour of Vietnam with 5RAR. (Daryl Henry)

Left: Letters from home.
Recce Platoon's 'Suave Harve' Harvey and a lap full of letters from home in his tent at Nui Dat. (M. Deak)

Top: Testing time. As was the case in other Australian units, Recce Platoon
weapons were test fired into pits before men went on operations.
In the background are the tents occupied by the men of the Reconnaissance.
(J. Mulby)
Above: Shutting up house. Reconnaissance Platoon member Ken Scaysbrook
is packed and ready to go on operations. His pack and basic webbing are
on the sandbags. Ken's Armalite rifle and radio pack are in the background.
(R. Kearney)

Above: Paper warfare. Recce Platoon acting sergeant John 'Blue' Mulby fills out post-operation reports in the Platoon's 'office' at Nui Dat. (M. Deak)

Top: War weary. The strain of weeks of patrolling shows on the faces of Reconnaissance Platoon members Wayne Page (R) and Max Campbell (L).
Above: Grim discovery. Reconnaissance Platoon finds a US Forward Air Controller aircraft which had been shot down by the enemy. Two American pilots died in the crash. At the time of the find the jungle was already growing over the wreck. (5RAR Association)

away with the fairies. He was trying to tell me the platoon had moved on.

'Sorry, Mac, I was thinking about last time I was up on these bloody mountains.'

The scout shrugged his pack higher on his back and looked up and down the slopes. 'I was with Bravo Company last time up here, and we got the stuffing knocked out of us. I wish I was back down there with Bravo rather than up here again—this place gives me the creeps.'

We laid an ambush that night on an ox cart track. It was a non-event. Did Charlie know we were up here and had shot through, or was he waiting for us to get higher; waiting till the time and place was to his advantage, like he always did?

Any soldier fears wandering into the unknown, but patrolling into a place you know is full of horrible things is worse: the devil you know is not a great thing in a war zone, and I knew I was now getting close to a very Bad Place. The chopper incident I'd witnessed on the Nui Thi Vai was suitably horrific, but ahead, I knew, were punji pits. That's how the VC operated: terrorise you, keep you on edge, force a mistake, then take you down. And at the same time, tie up the men and machinery that were trying to get you out. They were terrorists, guerrillas, soldiers—cunning bastards who frequently adopted a policy of 'hugging the belt', I had once been told at a briefing: close with the opposition, and stay so close that he couldn't use air or artillery power. If we pulled back, they pulled back. Hug the belt.

I passed a message back through the platoon for a halt. We were proceeding carefully, but everything here felt wrong.

Follow your gut feeling, I told myself.

Mick Deak came forward, looking up and down the ridge line. 'What's going on, Dogs?'

I pointed forward with my rifle, 'We'd better stay switched on from here on up. We're going to hit a track shortly that's got punjis on both sides. They may be hard to see, but they're there, concealed in the bloody bamboo.'

Deak looked around. 'How do you know that?'

'I've been here before . . . and there's something else. Can you hear anything?'

Deak strained and peered forward into the thickets. 'Can't hear a friggin' thing. You all right, Dogs?'

I was getting annoyed. 'Right, there's not a sound, not a fucking bird, animal, lizard. Nothing. This is a bad place. Ask Bernie—he came through here with me last time.'

Bernie and Blue Mulby came up and squatted near us. Mulby looked around with a sigh and then smiled at me. 'Just checking, Dogs, you know your map-reading—you use the shotgun method.'

'Fuck your boot, Mulby. At the top of this ridge there's a pile of rocks cemented together, a fire position with cover straight down the track.'

Bernie nodded agreement.

'S'right, Skipper. I was with Dogs, bloody lucky we didn't get zapped.'

Mick Deak thought this over, and worked out a patrol pattern with two groups on the high ground and one sweeping down. He planned to cover the cement-rocks with grenade launchers.

'If it gets bigger than Ben Hur, break contact and we'll get artillery in,' Deak said, waving us forward.

We found the punji stakes and the rocky formation. It was covered in old, dry napalm residue, which took on the appearance of honeycomb when it cooled. Turning around and looking across the province, I realised how strategically critical this place was: we were looking straight down at the ATF base and Luscombe airstrip. A man sitting here could observe our every movement in and out of Nui Dat.

We worked our way towards the top of the mountain, where the late afternoon sun threw its last rays onto a magnificent old Buddhist temple. It was a picture from one of those *National Geographics* where the photographer has spent hours, days trying to get the right shot. We were looking at it. Its spirituality was obvious: it was akin to a religious painting where the light of heaven shone down on Madonna and Child. The stonework held a light, soft glow; the building was in the throes of a final battle against creepers and vines, which slithered and clung to the structure like thin green tree snakes.

It seemed, as we stood there, that this was the place from which the silence had emanated. Each man in Recce used his machismo to show he really didn't care about all this stuff, but we also thought of a time lost, an era—maybe as recently as when the French were here—when the Nui Thi Vai were a place of peace, and venerable Buddhist monks climbed them to meditate.

We quietly spread out and prepared for night harbour around the temple. Walking on stone pavings covered in thin spider webs, with columns of ants busy at work, I strained to hear any sound coming from the nearby forest.

Nothing.

The sun had fallen away, with the last shards of light flaming the crumbling masonry, when the first shrieks started. Trees shook, then there were screams.

'They're out to my front!' Suave Harve was the first to yell out. 'Faces, I see faces.'

'Dogs, on the left, they're coming up on the left!' called Wayne Page.

I dropped to a fire position and peered into the gloom.

Smart pricks, they've bottled us up and they'll use snipers to get us tonight from the trees.

Looking around for cover from fire, I had a flash thought: *would they mortar their own temple?*

I wanted to grab my knife and cut the buttons off my shirt to get me closer to the ground. It took jungle veteran John Lea-Smith to give us the good news.

'It's monkeys, you panic merchants! They're curious monkeys, checking out you monkeys.'

I whispered to Bernie and Blue, 'Jesus, don't let this get around, particularly with 6RAR. We won't be Tiger Battalion, we'll be Monkey Battalion and Recce The Monkey Killers.'

I lay awake for some time studying the profile of the temple, my thoughts drifting back to suburban Kilburn and life as a 10-year-old, shoeless in the streets with all the Kilburn kids. We would run laughing down to the slaughterhouse, a place stinking of cattle dung and blood. I loved it, loved helping them get the animals off the trucks, big terrified eyes staring at me. Then away from the stockyards and down to Kilburn Railway Station. It was here, at night, that we put eight-inch nails on the rail tracks and watched the locos crush them flat, producing almost perfect knives.

Kilburn at night again, and we fashioned homemade slingshots from fencing wire and bike inner tubes and popped out every streetlight.

Days of youth were days of collecting mushrooms and wading in stormwater dams with their salt-topped islands. It was out of one of those lakes that they pulled the lifeless body of John Arnold. I knew John, even though he was 18—a lot older than me. He was retarded, and never should have been swimming in a stormwater dam. A dead boy, and someone we knew, was a shock to us young kids. We talked about it for months.

Teen years and fit as hell, I was. I polished pots and pans in a factory, boring as batshit. Then I got the job I really loved—a Coke deliveryman's assistant. How good was that! Lugging Coke crates developed my arms and legs, beefed up strong calves and biceps.

I dreamt of getting on a ship and sailing the world. As kids we could dream of anything, do anything. Young, invincible. Not John Arnold, though . . .

I left the Coke job and decided to join the Navy or the Army. My brother was in the Navy, so was my cousin. My uncle had been in the Navy, on the HMAS *Shropshire* during World War II, and he couldn't even swim. I wanted a clean job in the service, like a cook—plenty of good tucker all the time. The Army Recruiting Sergeant gave me the look up and down and the thumbs up. Sure, he said, I could be in Catering Corps. I never made it as a 'Tucker Fucker' (a cook), but I made it as a grunt—crap food and buggered and wet, or buggered and dry, all the time.

I drifted back to this place and time. Vietnam. Vietnam. The word was beautiful when you really thought about it, but the place was insane. We'd nearly brassed up a herd of monkeys, for God's sake. On the edge, wound up like a coil of wire, silence, not a bloody sound, then a monkey attack. I rolled over and stared into nothing. The jungle was beautiful—and horrible. Neutral but lethal. *If we could switch off for a while*, I thought, *we'd all feel better*.

But we were never going to be able to switch off. Back at Nui Dat we'd relax; come down off that jag we were riding on all the time in the weeds. But even then, not really. Drink grog, pack and get ready for another of Deak's briefings with his bloody map, drinking my brew and telling us we've got another mountain to go up looking for the shit. And I was still dealing with feelings of incompetence.

When I got here, I'd wished that maybe I'd go through a year and not see a Vietcong. Well, I hadn't seen too many Vietcong, but they'd bloody seen me. I felt so alone. I was with the best bunch of soldiers in the Army, but I was alone and my guts were churning around, screaming with more than just the lack of proper food.

There was a way out of all this: kill every Noggie we saw. Shoot the bloody lot. Or just get out of the place, give it back to the VC.

My last thought before dropping into the usual night's coma was: *how long can we put up with this country, this war, before going mad? I started out with 364 and a wake-up. How many days have I done?*

The arithmetic was too hard. I fell asleep.

Next morning we set off in silence, and had gone just a short way from the major spur line when scout John Scales spotted two VC. They were moving fast, and were out of small arms fire range. Mick Deak grabbed the radio handset and called for gunships—armed choppers that were protecting the road convoy on Route 15. He figured we had to kill these two quickly in case they were spotting in order to bring mortar fire onto the Americans.

No sooner had Deak completed his request than two 'Gunslingers'—American-armed Hueys—came thundering in. They did one sweep over the enemy to try and attract fire, wheeled and came up from behind us, pouring streams of fire into the target area. The doorgunners stood out on the skids, blazing down with M60 machine-guns. Deak had popped purple smoke canisters in front of us, indicating our position, and the gunships returned—this time with rockets. Pieces of granite exploded and trees were shredded on each run. Deak politely thanked the pilots and then, not one to be shy about overkill, called in artillery.

Later, we moved through the wreckage. No man could have survived that mincing; and although we found nothing, I was sure that two VC ceased to exist that morning.

HEROES AND VILLAINS

Flinders Ranges, 2000

We work our way towards a Flinders sunset, illuminating gum trees and red rock. On day two of walking through the Ranges, a feeling of peace is coming over us all. On day three we realise there are many good reasons to be here, and to be talking to each other. Coming to the Flinders has washed away a lot of Bad Thoughts. It's also saving some of us from a lot of Bad Things we just may have done.

There were those who self-inflicted a wound—blew a toe or finger off to get out of the bush. It's rare but we've heard about it. We stand, arms folded, and say to ourselves, 'Today remember the bloke who shot himself to get out of Vietnam. Then years later he shot himself to get Vietnam out of him.'

We all go a bit quiet.

A man stands up and hums to himself, then speaks as if he's simply commenting on the weather. 'I was going to kill myself a few years ago.'

No one says a word.

He goes on, a bit sheepishly, grasping for words. 'Maybe it was guilt and shame, but maybe it was because when I came out of Vietnam I was a total bloody wreck, I mean I was a shell of a man, all sort of hollow. I had not a single emotional feeling towards my wife and kids. Nothing. No-one can under-stand what it's like to feel absolutely bloody nothing. I figured I'd top myself . . . '

We mumble to each other while we put a billy on for a group brew. Someone says: 'Yeah, and you'd leave your wife and kids behind, dealing with all the embarrassment and humiliation of you doin' yourself . . . '

'No, hell no,' the man answers. 'I'd thought of that. I was going to kill them too.'

CONFIDENTIAL INTSUM: 25 August 1966—Peking Radio reported the following as facts (after the battle at Long Tan): 'In this battle (the NVA) put out of action 400 Australian mercenaries, thus annihilating two full-sized companies, heavily decimated another, set fire to three M-113 armoured cars, downed one US aircraft and captured a great quantity of arms and ammunition.'

Reconnaissance Platoon occupied six tents in the south-west corner of the 5th Battalion's position at the ATF base. A short walk from our tents, and you could look out across Luscombe airstrip, where Caribou aircraft on the 'Wallaby Run' landed daily, shunting stores and men in, taking out others on leave or going home. The planes droned in from the west where the Warburtons rose up, then suddenly dropped like a stone before thumping down and wobbling to a reverse-engine roar. The reason for the sudden descent was to avoid gunfire from any brave VC who had positioned himself in the bush outside the Task Force. It was a brave Nog who would do that, and braver pilots still who zipped in and out of Nui Dat daily.

The 'Dat hill itself was just a few hundred metres from the strip, and to the east of its tree-covered slopes were the 6th Battalion's lines and headquarters. Looking out to the rubber which concealed the 6RAR lines, all seemed quiet, but just a few months ago 'The Babes'—as the newly formed battalion was known—had endured a baptism of fire. Delta Company 6RAR had taken on 1000 Nogs and fought for its life just a few clicks from 1ATF in a scrubby patch of rubber called Long Tan.

This was packing death Big Time. I sat and smoked, looking over towards 6RAR's position. The Babes—with a heavy contingent of Nashos—were a brand new Australian unit formed to honour our commitment to the war, and they had copped one hell of a battle.

It was 17 August, I recalled, and I was up in Binh Ba, an Army outpost 6000 metres north of Nui Dat. There was supposed to be a huge enemy unit around there—jokingly referred to as the 'Binh Ba 1000'— that was going to hit the hamlet. We laid wire and dug in, we patrolled and ambushed . . . and we waited.

Meanwhile, to the south and east of the ATF base, 1000 NVA and local VC were advancing on Nui Dat; and on the night of 17 August they hit the ATF with mortars and recoilless rifle fire. I heard the attack on the radio at Binh Ba and forgot my sore back and exhaustion: under the circumstances, a small Vietnamese outstation wasn't such a bad spot after all.

Late on the afternoon of the 18th, I crawled inside an armoured personnel carrier and brewed up with the crew commander. We talked while I cast an eye over the big .50 calibre machine-gun mounted on top of his APC. I always had respect for those who drove 'Tracks'—'turret heads', as we grunts called them. APCs bucked and bounced around, attracted rocket fire and land mines like flies to dogshit. The drivers were gutsy bastards, no question.

I hated riding in APCs—the racket, the fumes and the rocket-in-the-side-any-minute sensation. Riding on top of them wasn't too hot, either—branches in the face and red ants that went down the shirt, stinging like boiling water. There was an upside, though: carrier blokes never ran short of rations, and were always good for bludging a coffee and having a chat.

I made myself as comfortable as I could on the bench seat.

'You know how you blokes have the .50 up on top—ever been hit by fire yet?' I asked the crew commander.

He had made me a coffee with loads of condensed milk, and

we were sipping his hot brew. 'Not yet, but if you think about it, who's going to fire back when a .50 gets going?'

'Well, that's right, but if I were you I'd feel a lot safer with some sort of protection, like a shield, around the gun.'

Before the crew chief could reply, the radio crackled to life. It was an alert to stand by: Delta Company 6RAR had run into something big. The small talk between us stopped dead. More radio transmissions. This was looking Deep Serious. The APC commander shook his coffee out and grabbed his maps. 'You ever been through Long Tan, Dogs?'

'No, not yet, but tonight might not be the best time to go.'

'Well it sounds like tonight we might be going.'

I shot a look at the carrier commander. 'With or without us?'

'No, we're on our own. You blokes might go if it gets real big, but this 6RAR thing might just be a ploy.'

The radio transmission fired up again. This was no ploy: the battalion attack on 6RAR might now be a regiment-size assault, warned ATF headquarters.

'Grab your coffee, Dogs, we're pissing off.' The soldier scrambled from the back of the carrier and shouted, 'Start up!'

The APC troop rumbled away from Binh Ba in the dark to a waiting and desperate 6RAR. The Babes were caught in the single biggest fight the Aussies would face in South Vietnam.

Morning, 19 August, Long Tan rubber: 245 VC dead by body count, 18 Australians killed in action, the birth of a military legend called The Battle of Long Tan.

We could glean little of what had happened: the bush telegraph carried a few fragments of information over to us after we got back from Binh Ba. The 5th Battalion had sent a company out to the fight in the rubber where 6RAR's Delta Company diggers had fought in the twilight, and where the artillery had launched salvo after salvo to break up enemy human wave assaults against Delta. The APCs had rolled in during a monsoonal downpour: maybe that, along with a few thousand arty rounds, saved what was left of D Company. But we figured it was a decisive battle that left the enemy with heavy losses: Charlie would now think twice about another strike at the Task Force.

There was a load of work to be done around the Recce lines: 'administration' downtime when grunts had a chance to make and mend. Mould and mildew had crept into the tents, covering our slouch hats with a blue fungus, invading bedding and boots. Leaves from the rubber trees had fallen and blown through the tents; they lay in the flysheets and even in our cots, under mosquito nets that now stank.

Also on the nose were the 'piss-a-phones': tubes protruding from the ground into which we urinated. Just as bad were the three-seat toilets, infested with flies. A week or two or three away from home and the place was a pigsty.

I lined up for the 0700 pill parade. Platoon sergeant John Lea-Smith handed out the foul-tasting, anti-malarial Paludrine pills and ticked our names off on a nominal roll. He was a thick-set Victorian, a shade below six-foot. He was a larrikin with an acutely honed sense of humour—sometimes black, always cutting—and he wore his bush hat with the front brim cut away in order to see better. The three-striper was a no-bullshit infantry sergeant who, to the annoyance of other senior NCOs, grew long sideburns to match one of the hairiest torsos I'd ever seen.

I'd no sooner washed the taste of the pill out of my mouth and was wondering what rubbish to hide first in my tent when Suave Harve strode in, sat down on my cot and lit up a smoke. His body language told me there was a serious whinge coming on, or some other kind of paranoid complaint. Harve was a lance-corporal, a 'lance jack', second-in-command to Bernie Smith—and he was pissed off.

'Is John always such a conscientious prick, Dogs?'

Easy-going Harve wasn't easily upset. I carried on fiddling. 'Stuffed if I know.'

Harve was warming to his whinge 'Well you were in C Company with him, weren't you? I thought you and him were good mates?'

'What's the problem, Harve, giving you the shits, is he? Anyway, he wasn't my platoon sergeant, he was Ray Ferrier's—go an' ask him.'

'I have. Ray reckons he's a good bloke.' Harve started to stand up.

I knew the debate hadn't yet started. I had known Harve since Airborne days; it took a lot to bother him.

'Sit down, Harve. John's no different to other snakes in the battalion. In fact, he's better than most, and if the problem is him asking you to clean up the joint, you've got to admit we've got the messiest lines in the battalion . . . '

'Look, Dogs, I don't want you to say anything about this, but I came to Recce to be a patrol commander, not a 2IC. If I wanted to do that, I'd have stayed in Bravo Company.' Harve's face took on a look of indignation, as if he was dressed in his best threads and he'd just been chatted about his style. 'John's just called all the 2ICs in and given us a rundown of what he expects of us while we're in the Dat. He's allocated my blokes to clean the shithouse! Does he think we're the blowfly police?'

So that was it. Scrubbing the toilet was below Suave Harve.

'Tell me, Harve, do you shit?'

''Course I shit, what are you ramblin' on about?'

'Well, if you shit in the dunnies, what's the problem getting your blokes to clean up after you? Would you prefer me to ask

Wingy Warr or the Task Force commander to sort it out? For God's sake, just get on with it. You'll have plenty of time to be patrol commander when we get back into the weeds.'

Harve was preparing a retort when John himself strode into the tent, grinning. I wondered if he'd heard Harve's whine about the crappers.

'Well, fellers,' John announced, 'soon as we get this garbage tip cleaned up, we're off to Vungas for two days' R and C!'

Harve's face lightened. For a moment I thought he was going to kiss his platoon sergeant, but instead he dove out of the tent. Problem solved by the mere mention of a couple of days on the grog.

It wasn't unreasonable for a bloke to want to wear a clean red shirt after wearing a filthy, crud-covered green one for weeks. This urge led me to Bob's Tailor Shop in downtown Vung Tau. I was surrounded by US Marines bartering for new clothes when there was a commotion outside the shop. Next moment, the enormous bulk of Blue Mulby filled the doorway. He sprang across at me, bent me over his hip and gave me a deep tongue kiss. Pushing me away, he smiled and winked, and said, 'Goodbye, sweetheart, I'll see you down at the Sydney Bar.' Mulby ran from the shop and jumped back into his horse-drawn cart beside Suave Harve—and was gone. A strange silence settled over Bob's Tailor Shop and a dozen pair of eyes were locked on the odd Aussie in his brand new bright red shirt.

I burned for revenge against Mulby but later, at Vung Tau Back Beach, I forgot all about the incident in an ocean of Budweiser beer. The beer was courtesy of a group of Americans, who were dragging on a joint held by a hair clip while we sucked down their booze.

Full as a butcher's pup, I was staring at Blue, Suave Harve and

Mick Deak while they debated the war with an American redneck. Through my boozy haze I could just make out that the big American was running down blacks. I couldn't figure out the Yank's reasoning, as some of the best Australian soldiers I knew were Aborigines. I decided to shut this moron up with a lie. 'You know something, mate, my grandmother's black, so knock off that bullshit, eh?'

The Yank rocked back and forward on his feet. 'Well, if she's black, I s'pose that makes you a half-nigger . . . '

Mulby was instantly on his feet, both hands locked around the man's throat. The American was a lot bigger, but Blue dragged him down to the sea. We quietly drank on, with the thump of meat striking meat and groans coming from the water's edge. In a little while Blue came back, picked up my beer and drank on without a word.

Eventually one of the Yanks, a part-Cherokee Indian, cautiously asked, 'Where's my buddy? What'd you do with him?'

Blue finished my beer. 'He's in the water. I knocked him out.'

The bashed and bloodied redneck was retrieved before he drowned. He was brought back to the party, where he spent the next few minutes spitting blood and what looked like teeth. That night, which finished with us sleeping on the beach, was the only time I recall encountering racism in Vietnam.

BOOTS, BEANS AND BANDAGES

Flinders Ranges, 2000

Today we go for a walk up the creek line—just four of us in shorts and T-shirts, rolling a smoke, looking up and down, scanning the near ground then out to the middle distance. You say that you still do this, even walking down a crowded street: in Sydney recently you exhausted yourself examining every face coming towards you from 100 metres out.

That's what we did in the scrub out from Thua Tich and Xuyen Moc, those small, besieged villages in south-west Phuoc Tuy. In the larger towns, like Dat Do and Long Dien, and even Baria, it was all small houses and ancient buildings with crowds of Vietnamese. Your eyes went over them all, particularly those in the distance. You were always looking, jumping up and down in your skin. We got so good at it, we could almost see through walls.

It's night now, night in the Australian bush, and everything out here has bedded down in peace and quiet. God, how wonderful is real peace and silence. We find ourselves looking for our medication after dinner. Some of us are thinking about a beer . . . need a drink. We start talking again, one-line comments about how we sleep—or more about how we don't sleep, about those months when we could never sleep. And if we did it was like floating on the surface; always one small sound away from full alert and reaching in the dark for your rifle.

At night in Vietnam—out in 'the weeds', as some of us called the jungle—there was some relief, you put your eyeballs back in their sockets. The blackness was absolute, with just the glow of a luminous watch reminding you that you weren't dead and gone to hell.

'It depended where you were—' one man recalls, 'Nui Dat or out in the bush. Some nights there was sounds that were ear-splitting, and at other times sounds so low you maybe imagined them.'

You remember we slept in our tents at Nui Dat not far from the 105s—those howitzers that fired off H and I any hour of the night. They made the ground ripple. On a fire support base they were even closer—bloody gunners sending their shells out into the night with an almighty flash of white. But we slept like babies through that damned noise.

Different story in the jungle at night, though. Out there you would wake up in a sweat when a beetle stopped clicking. You'd sit bolt upright and reach for your weapon when some digger 20 metres away rolled over and you heard his sleeping silk slide quietly over his body. The smallest sound, and you were alert with the noise of blood rushing through your ears. We talked about what a sleep scientist would make of all that.

Tonight it's the sleep of gentle babies, and the one thing that will never change is the snoring and farting.

CONFIDENTIAL INTSUM: July 1966—Binh Ba is a three-hamlet village and the last major population centre in Phuoc Tuy still under Vietcong control. It is estimated that 20 per cent of the population (2300 people), particularly younger men, are actively supporting or sympathetic towards hard core Vietcong cadres within the village . . .

I once heard some smart-arse say, 'A soldier is the most resourceful, independent man on Earth.'

If I recall correctly, this man was an officer—had two lumps or more of bird-shit on his shoulders, anyway—and was trying to impress a bunch of recruits at a training centre in Australia. He also rambled on about the importance of drinking water.

'Drink as much as you can when you can, it's good for you . . . '

I think he was grinning when he said that from his nice little comfort zone. I wish he was here now, packing gear for a four-day bush-bash. Everything we needed was going to be piled on our backs, hung on our belts or shoved in our pockets. After six months or more in Vietnam, I still never ceased to be amazed at the rubbish a man could haul through the war—and every week the experts thought of something new to pile on top. Smaller men, greyhound types, had it hardest. They almost disappeared under the load, and with minimum fat on their bones, the belts, straps and backpack frames dug in and chewed away skin with every click they walked. That was the case with me.

As a Reconnaissance patrol commander, I had worked out what I *needed* to carry, what I was *supposed* to carry, and what stuff to give the flick. I always remembered Dinkum's striped pyjamas when I packed to move out. Clothing-wise, we travelled light: some of us never wore underpants and none of us wore socks.

Recce had been put on a warning order to move: we were stripping cartons, breaking up and distributing rations and drawing ammunition. The scene looked like a supermarket being pulled apart around the six tents, with men haggling and trading off what they'd eat and what they wouldn't. One man who loves egg omelet in a tin trades to get as many as he can, while giving away his US-style pound cake or date roll. There were compressed meats—ham or corned beef—ham mixed with egg, ham and lima beans, sausage pieces in tomato goo, Irish stew, cereal blocks, dry biscuits, cheese blocks, chocolate bars and packets of rice. This was broken down and wrapped into meal parcels with curry powder, Vegemite, jams, salts and soups. Tea and sugar were stashed in side pockets on the main pack, along with brown condensed milk and coffee and chocolate powder. Some men also carried a small bottle of Worcestershire or Tabasco sauce. With those condiments, you could force down anything.

Can-openers doubled as spoons, and we squirrelled away boxes of waterproof matches as backup for our Zippo lighters.

We ratted through what were called 'supplementary packs' for the chewing gum, toilet paper and packets of smokes (Lucky Strike, Winston, M&M, Camel and heavy menthols like Salem and Kool). In heavy demand among the diggers was tinned fruit, from peaches and pears to fruit cocktails. It was tempting to go berserk and load up; you had to remind yourself you were lugging this on your back.

Surprisingly, I had found that I didn't want much food. The other men confirmed what I suspected: our stomachs had shrunk. Just as surprising was how a soldier, even under arduous conditions, could go the distance on very limited food. But he had to have water.

I strapped six water bottles onto my main pack and the pistol belt I wore around my waist, and shoved another two inside the main pack. Water was a mongrel: after ammo, it constituted the greatest weight factor. As a Recon group, we had access to special dehydrated Lurp ration packs—add water and they turned into delicious meals. The Lurps (American Long Range Reconnaissance Patrols) must have accessed water more easily than us—we just could not afford to use our water for meals while on patrol, particularly in the dry season.

Also on my pistol belt were the basic ammunition pouches. Into these I shoved six 30-round magazines for the 'Slaughtermatic', extra boxes of bullets, camouflage cream and a prismatic compass. I carried pencil flares, two hand grenades (with the handles taped down) and two coloured smoke canisters. Somewhere in a pouch I jammed a fig slice or packet of biscuits to chew on while on the move. I wrapped two shell dressings for emergency use in plastic, strapped one to my rifle butt and shoved the other in a shirt pocket.

Next the main pack: a small shaving bag with toothpaste and brush, a plastic mattress cover, poncho liner and thin horse blanket to sleep in, and a hootchie to sleep under in the Wet. Five days' rations went into the main pack, and one day's went into a bumpack attached at the rear of the pistol belt. Also in my backpack I stowed a slab of C4 plastic explosive and a Claymore anti-personnel mine. Slung across the top of the pack was a belt of 7.62 link ammo for the M60 carried by my section gunner, Blue Riley. It didn't take long to figure that a soldier in this new type of warfare was a mobile ammo dump.

'I get hit by a tracer round, I'll light up like a Chrissie tree and then explode,' a digger said to me on his first time in the bush.

Webbing straps went from the bumpack over my shoulders to the front of the belt. This was called 'basic webbing', and it allowed us to drop the main pack and fight, with all our ammo and a day's food and water on the main belt, if it came to a major contact.

Notebook and maps—a topographical and a photo (or 'picto') map—went into the side pockets of my trousers. Every commander also had a Vietnamese photo album that carried printed report formats for situation report (Sitrep), dustoff, and mortar report (Mortrep) slipped between the plastic sheets. The little photo album, with its scenic Vietnam picture, was called a Vui Tui ('photograph') and was already a war icon. Among the last items to prepare were the entrenching tool, which doubled as a pick, and the rifle. The SLR was stripped, cleaned, oiled and daubed with green paint to break up its outline.

Many of us had removed the laces from our boots and replaced them with zipper inserts—easy off, easy on, although now I can't recall a past op where I took the bloody things off—hence my feet were in a semi-advanced stage of Asian tinea. The bush hat, which was similar to what the VC were wearing, had a red band wound through it to identify us as Aussies. A 'Mickey Mouse' Army regulation-style watch was strapped onto my wrist, and all the guys in my section synchronised watches before assembling to be trucked down to Luscombe Field for the chopper lift.

The mission was to take my Recce section up to Binh Ba and report to a senior adviser called Captain George Mansford, who was housed in a French villa—now converted into a fort—on the outskirts of the village. We were going up five days before the remainder of Recon Platoon to train a group of Vietnamese Regional Force sergeants (the Trung Sis) in the art of ambushing.

The pilot of the Huey, we soon worked out, was young and single: he never lifted his machine higher than treetop level on the 6000-metre hop to Binh Ba. He dipped and weaved, and the seven of us saw our lives flashing past at high speed; then a bank and now the thought of going out the doorless machine into the trees. Our compensation for the scare-us-shitless ride was the cool wind gusting into the passenger bay—the last fresh, cool air we'd suck in for a while.

Binh Ba was Charlie country—he was out here in numbers. The village comprised a disused airstrip, a main settlement and a smaller hamlet north across the highway, and the old French villa, now a sizeable military encampment. The population of 2000 or so grew small fruit and vegetable crops. The major source of income was from working the huge Gallia rubber plantation that surrounded the main village and was still owned and run by the French, who must have come to some kind of financial arrangement with the local Vietcong to keep the place working during the war.

The main force of Nogs up here would be from the 274 Regiment and the Mobile D445 Vietcong, according to the INTSUMs.

Mansford, who was consolidating the local Vietnamese force at

Binh Ba, had a reputation as a tough, gutsy and highly effective commander. He was one of those Australian Army Training Team advisers who worked on the edge; he'd had his back to the wall more than a few times. There were two other advisers up here: Warrant Officers 'Sooty' Smith and Jack Copeman. Copeman's nephew Russell had been the first SAS soldier to die of gunshot wounds after action in Vietnam.

It was with all this in mind that I strode up to the Vietnamese senior officer and introduced myself, at the same time glancing across at the scruffy, tall and lanky Caucasian man next to him. He wore baggy Australian-style green trousers, thongs on his feet, and a white singlet. He had snowy hair and was grinning at me; I figured he must be Mansford's driver.

'Hey mate, know where I can find a Captain Mansford?'

The grin stayed and the voice was a raspy Australian growl. 'You're talking to him. G'day.'

Mansford was easy-going but thorough. He ran through the local intelligence reports, introduced us to the Vietnamese Regional Force (RF)—a quite separate group from the ARVN forces—and showed us around the villa. The rubber plantation, the big old French house and even the people were reminiscent of another time in Vietnam: the old Indochina, when life was provincial and changeless.

For a short time the war slipped away, but it came back the minute Mansford started talking about the defences.

'Don't touch the fences or the gates,' he said pointing to both ends of the barbed-wire compound. 'The soldiers have booby trapped them with grenades. They're armed at last light and dis-armed at first light. Don't touch the gates till after 7am, or *boom*!'

I passed word around about the gates and grenades, and while we smeared camouflage cream on our faces I had a final word with my second-in-command, Taffy Cheeseman. He took one group of RF sergeants, I took the other, and we set out to lay ambushes at both ends of the Binh Ba hamlet. We lay in the rubber trees all night and I checked that our charges were laying up correctly. The Claymores had been placed the right way around—'Front Towards Enemy'. We waited.

After two days of ambushing techniques I felt they were getting it right. On the third morning, feeling stiff after a night lying in the plantation, we made our way back to the compound. I always waited until the first sunlight was filtering down through the tall rubber and I could clearly see the ground before I broke up the ambush.

It was during the final hundred metres, with the old villa in sight, that I saw the flash and heard the bang. We started running towards the barbed wire. I gasped when I saw Taffy on the ground, bleeding and twisted in agony.

'For fuck's sake, what happened?' I knelt next to my wounded 2IC, who already had a shell dressing on the side of his face, trying to stem the flow of blood gushing down his neck.

Mansford was nearby, speaking urgently into a radio. He was angry when he saw me. 'I told you blokes not to come in until the booby traps had been bloody disarmed, right?'

The dustoff wasn't long in coming, and Taffy, with his shattered face, was loaded on for the flight back to Vung Tau and the 36th Evacuation Hospital.

I was depressed that night. Cheeseman had taken a big hit: his jaw was smashed from flying shrapnel. I was certain I'd told him the gates were booby-trapped, and wouldn't be safe until first light. Why the hell did he walk in? I hated this job. There was no margin for error, not a single bloody inch. Switch off for one minute and you're dead or mutilated.

Maybe I didn't tell him about Mansford's briefing and the booby-trap warning. Maybe I stuffed up and caused the wounding of a mate.

I looked across at Bob Godfrey, a veteran with experience in Malaya. He knew what I was going to say.

'You certain you want the job, mate?' I asked him miserably. 'I haven't got a good track record: my first 2IC, Tich Tomas, is dead, and Taffy's in a bloody mess and out of the war for sure . . . '

Godfrey just looked at me and grinned. 'Third time lucky, Dogs. I'll survive.'

A TIGER'S TALE

Flinders Ranges, 2000

There are places in Tasmania's south-west wilderness and in Queensland's Daintree rainforests where you can walk 100 paces off the road and be totally lost. Turn left, turn right, look ahead, look back. Everything looks the same.

We know places just as bad where a set of circumstances comes about and it's 'Where the Fuck Are We?' time. Then comes the unease, the anxiety, the desperation . . . the panic.

Out in open country, like here today, there are creek lines, rocky outcrops and a fence line to follow.

You stop us, turn around and ask, 'Hands up anyone who ever got lost in Vietnam?'

Silence, then a laugh. 'Never lost, mate, always geographically embarrassed.'

Okay, let's talk about navigation and map-reading. Let's see if we can get those old skills back. There were a number of occasions in Phuoc Tuy Province under thick canopy on a dull day when all the features were shrouded in shadow and, for as far as the eye could see, the ground was covered in green mats.

Thirty years after the war, and time for a bit of map-reading. We sit down in the low grass and each man takes a turn studying the map of the Eregunda Creek line. Turn it left, turn it right, make that east and that west. Remember how to shoot a compass bearing? Remember 130 paces equalled 100 metres on the map . . . or was it 140?

A man crouches over the map. 'Over the years I lost my ability to map-read, and I regret it. It was a skill I had, and I always sort of admired myself for having it.'

Okay, you know where we are, Mr Map-reader, but we admit it: we're lost . . .

CONFIDENTIAL INTSUM: 1 July 1966—Patrol Reports: All patrols should bring back at least topographical information which is not shown on maps. Information from troops on the ground is probably the most reliable of all sources available to the battalion.

We had a two-day patrol, and Deak called us together at the Binh Ba villa.

Deak loved maps. Blue Mulby and Bernie Smith loved maps. Dogs Kearney did not love maps. I was never good at figures, distances, bearings, playing around with compasses. It was my belief that those who loved maps were born with some sort of special gift, like grid lines in their brains. They could grasp concepts of distance, shoot bearings and in a flash translate them to a map, even in the blackness of jungle. They gazed at horizons and could calculate distances. Me, I was a school drop-out. I was never taught advanced map-reading, which was a prerequisite for command in Vietnam. They looked at me back at Holsworthy, saw the red beret of Airborne, and said, 'You're needed as an NCO, you're a leader. Now you're a section commander.'

I didn't get in a lather over my map-reading, but my lack of confidence when it came to navigation sometimes turned to an anxious sweat. I was sweating a little now as Deak spoke.

'We're doing a recce and clearance across 10 grid squares because the battalion is moving out on a major op east of Nui Dat. We'll break into four patrols—Blue, Bernie, Dogs, and I'll take the fourth.'

Mick swung the map around and moved his finger over what looked to me like a huge swathe of unbroken green with a few brown contour lines running through it. This was jungle, and those spaced-out contours meant the country was relatively flat.

'It'll take two days, three at most, following the high ground, and we keep about two clicks from each other. We will rendezvous with Bruce McQualter's Bravo Company. The plan is avoid contact; we're looking for any signs—VC movement, camps, bunkers—but detour around them. We don't want a shit-fight with six-man patrols.'

We ran a last check of our gear, smeared on camouflage cream, and packed on four days' rations. The load was crippling but we needed it all.

I swung the compass and took a bearing through the thick bush ahead. My scout was Pagey, who already had his secateurs out: he would carefully cut away thick growth as he scouted forward of me. When he looked around I would swing the compass again and wave him left or right to keep him on the bearing. In the thicker stuff the idea was to sight the compass on the bearing and pick out a significant tree 30 metres or more ahead. With a waving motion I would point Pagey in that direction. My other scout, 'Little Mac' McLaren, or my 2IC, Bob Godfrey, strapped sheep counters to their rifles. They counted off the paces: 140 paces was the equivalent of 100 metres on the map. Bob walked behind my M60 gunner, Blue Riley, and behind Blue were Max Campbell and Barney Gambold. We were a tight group: we knew each other's habits and peculiari-ties, and our collective understanding and skill in bushcraft was such that we could move on a whole day's patrol without saying a word.

I had absolute confidence in the Recce group, and they had confidence in me—and my map-reading. They thought I knew where I was going. Most of the time I did, but not always. I had never been put through an NCO course with intensive map-reading. For me the whole war was on-the-job training.

Blue Mulby and Bernie moved out to the east while Mick

Deak and his platoon headquarters group took the centre. My patrol worked west.

The day wore on soundlessly in the jungle. The foliage was thick on the ground and above us. Jungle is classified as single, double or triple canopy; three tiers. The triple is the highest, with little light pooling down to the jungle floor. Double canopy allows in considerable light, so there is significant growth at ankle and shin level. The worst of these three types to travel through is single canopy, with maximum growth below. Yet even more frustrating than that to negotiate is scrub with bamboo and wait-a-while vines.

The Recce team knew how to 'work' the jungle: slow travel, gently moving branches and shrubs aside. In the thick stuff, cut vines and entanglements carefully with the secateurs. Never use a noisy machete. If you fight the jungle, the jungle will take you down in an hour—reduce you to a sweating, gibbering heap, physically and psychologically wasted. Patrolling was slow and silent because I needed to accurately navigate. I would turn back to Bob Godfrey every so often, he would look at his sheep counter and hold his fingers up, showing the number of 100 metres we'd covered. I would call a break every 20 to 30 minutes and pull out the two maps: the topo, with each grid square indicating 1000 metres; and the picto, a representation of the country made from aerial photos.

I struggled to identify a landmark, but all we had were the deepest creek lines marked on the map. There was no steep rising ground, and no man-made tracks or constructions like huts or buildings. This was, as any digger would tell you, shit country.

After a few hours I began to feel uncomfortable. We had done maybe two clicks and I still had no confirmation that I was holding the correct bearing. The bearing I shot from the prismatic compass corresponded to a thin, straight, red line I had marked with a chinograph pencil on the map. I should have hit a sizeable creek line, but I hadn't. All I had were countless minor dry stream beds around me.

I consulted with Bob.

'Seems okay, Dogs,' he said. 'Stop worryin'.'

But I *was* worrying, and 100 metres later I spread the map again.

'Look, this bloody creek should have been here 100 metres back. What do you reckon?'

Bob looked at the map, blew his cheeks out and said, 'You're wrong. In fact I think you might be about 500 metres off your bearing.'

Stuff it, I didn't needed this.

I decided to call up Deak on the radio and send what I thought was our Locstat (Location status). Then I felt the first twinge of panic.

Where exactly are we?

The others were looking at me. I didn't need this at all.

'Can't get the skipper, Dogs. No communications.' Little Mac shook the handset at me and shrugged. Now I was really worried.

Should I call for a Mark Mission?

A Mark Mission was a last resort. It involved calling up artillery and getting them to fire a shell some distance from you, then another a distance away from the first. You determined the direction of the explosions and shot back bearings with your compass. Where the back bearings intersected gave your rough location The problem—the huge problem—with this was that you'd better be bloody sure you weren't standing where that shell came in. If I picked two creek lines a click away I'd be safe. But then some cranky bastard back at the fire base would be blabbing on: 'Recce's lost. Dogs Kearney's lost.'

I decided to push on; stumble and fumble and hope. I gave the order to get up and waved Pagey forward to the next big tree. What the hell was I going to do?

Fuck the compass, fuck these stupid maps, fuck this jungle.

We had gone just a few paces when I heard a commotion behind me. There was crash in the bush to one side, a cough like a man loudly clearing his throat, then a crash on the other side of the patrol. Momentarily panicked, I wheeled and shot an anxious look at Barney, the tail-end Charlie. The expression on his face was one of shock: his eyes were as big as dinner plates, and his mouth gaped.

'What the fuck was that?' I hissed at him, at the same time taking a kneeling position, rifle close to my shoulder.

Barney swallowed and whispered, 'A tiger just ran out behind us.'

I thought I'd misheard him. 'A what?'

'Tiger . . . stripes, big tail . . . you know, a fuckin' tiger!'

Bob was next to me now, and as each man in the patrol heard about it, he hit the ground and clicked his safety catch to AUTO.

Bob gaped at me. 'He said "tiger". He did say "tiger", didn't he?'

Barney was squatting and moving back to us now, his eyes and head swivelling like a sideshow clown with its mouth open.

'I read that one of those fuckers came in a hut one night and dragged the poor bloody Indian headman off by the leg, and then ate him.'

I spun around. 'Shut up, Barney, and cover our arse.'

I turned back to Bob, whispering, 'What do you think—are there tigers in Vietnam?'

''Course there is, Dogs—elephants, pythons, tigers . . .'

'Yeah, yeah, but the type of tiger that eats people?'

Barney butted in. 'It ate that bloody Indian, they didn't even find his head.'

I'd had enough. 'Barney, shut up or I'll feed you to the fuckin' tiger!'

The other men were now shooting anxious looks at me between peering into the bush.

Jesus, they don't look this worried even when Charlie's prowling around.

I fought to regain some sort of self-control.

Let's see: I'm lost, I've got no radio contact with my platoon commander—and a fucking huge cat is stalking us. Do we shoot it?

Problem: the 5th Battalion's mascot was, of all things, a tiger. The Tiger Battalion, that was us. Before coming to the war we had adopted and sponsored a tiger at Taronga Park Zoo in Sydney. His name was Quintus, and although far from full-grown when we got him, he still ripped open the handler's arm first time on parade.

This had all the makings of a huge stuff-up. Arrive back at the 'Dat and Commanding Officer Warr rolls up in his Land Rover—his usual form when Recce got back—to drop us at the Intelligence Officer's tent.

'How did things go, Corporal? Much of interest for the IO?'

'Fine sir, we shot the battalion mascot.'

I motioned to Bob Godfrey. 'We'll take a breather and watch for a while. Pass it on: if anyone sees this tiger, don't shoot it. But if it comes on and has a go, brass the fucker.'

I needed to sort things out and give myself time to check my map-reading. I tried to boost my confidence.

I am a good section commander. I've got a top team and a top leader. I can work through this with a cool head.

Darkness was falling, and I decided to go into a hide for the night.

I'd seen elephant dung on patrol, and seen the marks they left when they rubbed against trees. I'd seen big snakes and small snakes. I'd seen cranky water buffaloes trying to kill Dinkum. But a tiger? Christ, no. Vietnam was a circus. We had elephants, we had tigers and pythons, even bloody monkeys. We even had tents. I was starting to feel like the clown.

We slept recce-style, feet to feet. Most men had one hand on their rifle. I didn't sleep, didn't even doze. All night I saw two shining eyes looking down at me, and I heard that deep cough down in the throat. Tiger! No—the eyes receded and there was no sound out in the thickets.

I figured if the animal came in, we'd blast it and run.

Morning light, we were up and moving south. I kept the compass on the southern bearing and pushed Pagey forward as fast as I could while still keeping security. I was having an anxiety attack. Where were Bernie and Blue? Suddenly Little Mac dropped to his knee and grabbed the radio handset. 'Dogs, it's the skipper. Deakey!'

I repeated our call sign. No reply. I did it again. Nothing. *Hopeless.*

Then Mick Deak's voice came through, calm, controlled, all authority. He had received my earlier message calling for a Locstat. He knew I was having trouble.

'I am picking up your carrier wave. If you can hear me, press your pressle switch twice.'

I depressed the voice switch on the handset twice.

Deak: 'You pressed twice. Just to be certain you hear me, press four times.'

I carefully counted out four presses on the pressle switch, scarcely able to breathe.

Deak: 'If you think you are to the east of our position, press once. Twice for south, three times for west—God forbid—and four times for north.'

Deak was right: if I was west, we'd have run into him and probably had a firefight by now.

I pressed the switch five times.

Deak: 'That was five times. Do you mean north? Press once for yes and twice for no.'

I pressed the switch twice.

Deak: 'So, you are not north, and you pressed it five times. Do you mean you're north-east of our position?'

I pressed once.

Deak: 'Good, so you are to our north-east. How far away from us do you guesstimate you are?'

I pressed down 15 times for 1500 metres.

Deak: 'If you think you are a click and a half to the north-east you should be able to see a pretty deep creek to your front with a small knoll to the west. Can you see that?'

I hastily scrambled around and found the spot that matched Mick's description. Relief poured through me. I depressed the pressle switch on the handset once.

Deak: 'Good, you are at grid reference 834-987. I'll see you in one hour.'

Later that day we RV'd with Deak, Bernie and Blue Mulby and walked the short distance to Bravo Company. Mick Deak spoke to me during a smoke break. He could see I'd had problems, and he knew I'd tried to work them through. He stood up with a parting remark.

'Give me a cautious, nervous, thinking professional every time, Dogs. I'll follow him anywhere.'

I wondered when to tell him about the tiger.

Above: Ready to roll. Reconnaissance Platoon aboard armoured personnel carriers at Nui Dat prepare to move out on operations. Platoon commander Mick Deak is standing, holding onto radio antennae. (M. Deak)

Top: The French Connection. Australian military advisors and Recce Platoon occupied an old French villa in the town of Binh Ba. The platoon had an unfortunate accident which saw a serious wounding at these gates during one operation. (R. Kearney)
Above: Contact! Platoon machine-gunner Anthony 'Bluey' Twaits (R) pulls his M60 onto his shoulder during a firefight with the enemy in the Long Hai Hills. (Daryl Henry)

Top: Hard landing. A resupply 'huey' approaches the rim of the Horseshoe Fire base. The Horseshoe became a base of strategic significance during operations to Phuoc Tuy Province.

Above: The enemy. The faces of the North Vietnamese Army soldiers. Tough, well-trained and resilient, the NVA were a formidable foe during actions against Australians during the Vietnam War. (5RAR Association)

Above: End of the line. A female Vietcong soldier lies dead on a bush track while members of the Recce Platoon hastily dig a grave. Blue Mulby is the soldier closest to camera. (Daryl Henry)

Above: Fronting up. Reconnaissance Platoon lines up for patrol briefing from platoon commander Mick Deak at Nui Dat. Bands were worn on the bush hats to prevent confusion with the enemy who wore similar hats in the jungle. (Daryl Henry)

Top: Hannigan Gap in the Flinders Ranges. This is part of the spectacular backdrop to Trojans' Trek where veterans seek solitude and rehabilitation. (R. Kearney)
Above: Memories of war. Bob Kearney discusses life issues with a fellow veteran during Trojans' Trek. (C. Henschke)

Above: Road to freedom.
The Blinman Road into the
Flinders Ranges, the first
view members of Trojans'
Trek see on the approach
to their camp. (R. Kearney)

Left: Over the edge.
Vietnam Veterans go
through another adrenaline
rush during abseiling at
Eregunda Creek on
Angorichina Station in
the Flinders Ranges.
(R. Kearney)

Top: Firing away. Campfire discussions on the war with Trojans' Trek members and Bob Kearney (second from left). (R. Kearney)

Above: Reunited again. Several members of the 5RAR Reconnaissance Platoon at a 2000 reunion. From left: John 'Blue' Mulby, Ken Skaysbrook, Mick Deak Von Berg M.C., Daryl 'Butch' Moroney, William 'Suave Harve' Harvey, (front) Robert 'Dogs' Kearney, Peter 'Doc' Fraser M.M. (R. Kearney)

THE BABY AND THE BOMB RUN

Flinders Ranges, 2000

We are sitting around a table in an old house you've brought us to. Outside the wind is blowing over the plain and up over the building, thumping and banging on the windows and the old galvanised roof.

One man comments, 'I remember that Yank who said that the wind didn't blow in Vietnam—it sucked.'

What comes to mind is leadership, as we had some leaders in Vietnam who really sucked. We also had some fine leaders in Vietnam, from the Battalion Commander down to the corporals, who really looked after their men in the field. Some of the officers were National Servicemen who had made the grade at Officer Training School and went on to show they were the right stuff in the bush. In fact, we grunts probably never really appreciated the weight and pressure of command. When you think about handling and taking responsibility for a bunch like us, it was a big ask. They took it on and did it well. There were a few exceptions; rare, but they were out there.

One man sits down with a coffee and tells a story of one such exception.

'There was one platoon commander we had in the war, he was a regular soldier. In Australia he comes on with the professional hard-case act: how he is a born leader and is destined for greatness—to lead men into combat like his old man did in the Big One. Hell, the shit was so deep around this guy you needed shovels to get above it.

'Back in Australia you'd only follow this bloke out of curiosity. Every sign was there: he strutted around the parade ground with a baton under his arm that had a polished bullet jammed in the end, for God's sake. Soldiers who had already done a year in Vietnam were watching this bloke and getting seriously pissed off.

'So we arrive in Vietnam, go straight out bush, laying ambushes and doing patrols, all that crap, with this looey stirring us up to get him some action. You know what he does in our first ambush? Bastard goes to sleep—holding all the firing devices for the Claymores we've put out front, if you don't mind.

'Unbloodybelievable, but it gets worse. While this goose is asleep, a platoon of Nogs comes trotting through, whistling and carrying lanterns. Did we open up? No bloody way while all the Claymore clackers are held by Sleepy. That night, you could say, every bloke in our platoon was blind in one eye and couldn't see out of the other.

'Next ambush, he does it again—he's fast asleep while we're shaking like a dog shitting razor blades.

'Well, you can imagine the boys got a bit irritated by all this, and there were a few suggestions made about "taking him out". But no, we do it properly—we rubbish the shit out of him next time he comes up the boozer to have a beer with the boys, tell him how we can't stand him any more. Poor bugger has the breaking point of a Mars bar: he cracks up and goes bleating to the Commanding Officer about how he's lost the confidence of his men.

'Next morning he's gone, and we give a big hooray. Not for long, though: the CO fronts us section commanders up and bawls us out. Didn't we know how we'd ruined a promising officer's career? How-bloody-dare-we? For the rest of the tour we get every shit job you can imagine. Nearly killed us I don't know how many times. As for the poor luckless looey, he got sent over to PsyOps and threw leaflets out of planes for the rest of his trip in 'Vietnam.

'Thirty years on, and a lot of us are still dark on that bastard with the baton. We saw him one Anzac Day and wanted to kill him. No justice. Just no bloody justice.'

The wind didn't blow in Vietnam—it sucked, like everything else.

CONFIDENTIAL INTSUM: December 1966—Recce Platoon on orders from Battalion HQ move to and occupy ambush positions in the vicinity of NW, NE, SE and SW corners of Binh Ba village.

I'd had my confidence shaken up again. Six-man patrol, Binh Ba, and we had just walked straight past an enemy bunker. In fact, scout Pagey and I had just walked past, but Gunner Blue Riley and Bob Godfey saw something. The sound of an M60 machine-gun going off just a few metres behind you is one of the most terrifying in the war—like an electric shock shooting up your back, and at the same time you are momentarily deaf. If the rounds are going out, great. If they're incoming you wouldn't hear anything anyway. You'd be stone cold dead. Blue Riley put three 10-round bursts through the M60 and I almost had a heart attack. Every man hit the deck. I took up a fire position while I crawled back to Bob.

'What the hell is it? What are your firing at?'

'In there,' Bob jabbed a finger to my right. 'Group of Nogs.'

Blue let off another half-belt, and I felt my head was going to explode. The gun jerked violently backwards and forwards, shaking the gunner's shoulders. A stream of cartridge cases spewed out on the ground in front of me. The best way to mobilise the mind and the body and deal with the din, I had found, was to cut loose yourself, so I switched my SLR to AUTO and put a full magazine into the bush. Bullets and tracers shredded the undergrowth and sent small sticks and dirt up in a thousand small explosions.

Silence. The smell of gunfire. We waited.

'Up and go, go now,' I passed the word down the section and the men spread in an extended line, moving forward in that curious half-crouch they adopt when expecting return fire; as if making yourself about six inches shorter will somehow save your life.

Enemy gun pits, empty. A washing line with clothes and sweat-rags blowing in the wind. That's what my gun group had seen initially, I figured. Bob was next to me.

'Dogs, there were four of them sitting just in here,' he whispered breathlessly. 'They've shot through. Jesus, they must have moved. Riley was right on 'em.'

I called Little Mac over with the radio and grabbed the handset. Mick Deak was back at Binh Ba: I told him we had a group of VC moving off at high speed, so get the artillery in.

Bad dreams and nightmares revisited me all the time in Vietnam, and now I was back on Nui Nghe and Tich Tomas was talking to me . . . Nannup and a holiday on his farm . . . then the round came in, overshot, and a single piece of shrapnel killed my friend. I now had seven friends relying on my ability to get this right.

Stuff anything, Dogs, but don't stuff a fire mission.

I called the fire mission in front of our position. My mouth was dry. The first rounds fell too close; I panicked, grabbed the radio and called Deak back.

'Check fire, check fire!'

I cancelled the mission without adjusting fire. I just couldn't do it. We followed the enemy trail for another 300 metres. Nothing.

Several days later Recce Platoon patrolled through Xa Ngai Giao, a small hamlet at the end of Binh Ba airstrip. Route 2 divided this ramshackle collection of houses and huts straight down the centre. I suddenly had another flashback: it was on this very airstrip not so long ago that I'd stood with Charlie Company, smoking and watching a group of Phantom jets pulverise the cliffs of the Nui Thi Vai. It was 12 clicks from the end of the strip to the mountains, and the day had been clear—perfect for an air show.

We placed bets on the pilots. Two of them went in and dumped their load, then pulled up into a safe climb, easily clearing the top of the mountain. It was the third guy who caught our interest: a maverick, reckless, getting off on super-low runs at his target. We watched him wait until the last heartbeat before he pulled back the stick and heaved his machine just over the ridge.

'Bet ya he's young and unmarried,' said Bernie Smith, himself married with children.

Gunner Bones, with his Coke-bottle-bottom glasses, looked at Bernie and then gaped for another minute at the bombing run. Bones was struggling to understand what Bernie meant.

'What do you mean, he ain't married?'

Bernie looked at the tall, lanky gunner like a man trying to teach an ant algebra. 'Bones, it's all about risk-taking and being a dumbshit, a bit like you. He's leaving himself no safety margins. You watch him hit the mountain on his next pass.'

Bones and the rest of us shielded our eyes as the three Phantoms dived in again. There were two fireballs of napalm. Pilot three hung on that second or two longer. There was the flash of shiny fuel canisters full of the explosive petroleum-jelly, a flash of orange and, before the sickly, black smoke could rise, a second detonation as the Phantom jet slammed into the cliff. Bernie slowly turned around and walked away, not even bothering to look at Bones, who stood motionless, transfixed by the needless death of a gung-ho American pilot.

Mick Deak was trying to be patient with me. I was in one of my 'obstructive' moods, where I considered the world owed me a few favours and Deak wasn't giving me any. We were back at

Binh Ba and it was taxation time. This generally meant the Nogs were coming into the area and squeezing money out of the locals. Charlie came at night, so a night ambush was on the cards. Deak spread his precious map and turned it towards me.

Pointing to some jungle outside Xa Ngai Giao, he said, 'Lay your ambush in here on this track. When you're in position send me your Locstat.' Deak glanced up at me, knowing full well that Locstats weren't my strong point.

'When you're in position I'll lay a couple of DFs in, so if you get bounced I'll call arty in straight away.'

This was standard procedure. The pre-planned coordinates where the shells would fall would be relayed back to the fire base, and all the gunners had to do if we called fire for effect was to shove shells into the gun and let it go. The laying of these coordinates was called Defensive Fire or DF.

Deak looked up from his map. 'Lay up ambush for one hour, then go and see what's going on in Ngai Giao.'

I struggled with the concept for a minute. 'Well, that sounds brilliant—like a Cordon and Search at midnight with a section of seven men instead of a battalion? What do we do if we find tax collectors in the main street . . . ?'

'Stop being negative, Dogs. You follow them—they'll have lamps. When they get out of town, tell 'em to surrender.' Deak leaned back. 'It's not like I'm asking you to wander around Pitt Street; it'll be black as a dog's guts in there and it'll just be bad guys on the streets.'

I pressed on, being an irritant. 'And if they choose to run instead of throw their skirts up and surrender?'

Deak shot me a serious look. 'We came here to kill Vietcong, Dogs. And that's exactly what you'll do. This isn't a "Find and Follow" mission.'

'Deak was right about the blackness,' I whispered to Bob

Godfrey, who was crouching, along with the other six Recce men, near the closest shack in Xa Ngai Giao.

Moving in the dark was, for the combatant, full of hazards and horrors. I remembered being tied with toggle ropes, falling over pigs and into shit-pits during that night cordon in the early part of the tour, and now I was glad to be with a small group who knew what they were doing. Still, there was the problem of kicking a bucket, falling over those huge vats the Vietnamese stored their drinking water in, or tripping over a dog. Dogs? I hadn't really thought about barking dogs, or about being impaled on a water buffalo's horns.

We worked our way further into the hamlet using a technique of dry fire and movement, where we covered each other as we moved. We stopped at cracks in walls where light from an oil lamp shone through; we peered inside like Peeping Toms. I ran across a laneway between two houses and stopped, waving the next man up while I covered the blackness ahead. I could feel the adrenaline rising: my breathing and that of the others was short and sharp.

We'd already made our minds up: anybody skulking about in a black uniform would have about one second to drop his weapon, or he'd be brassed up. No self-respecting Vietnamese peasant or rubber-tapper was going to be out here tonight with the VC taxmen in town. The village headman surely would have already cautioned his people about that. Rifle at the ready, I peered around the side of the hut—and found myself looking straight into the eyes of a baby being bathed by her mother. The infant peered at me—sweat band around my head, camouflage cream all over my face—pointed at me with a stubby finger, and let out a scream to wake the hounds of hell. The mamasan spun around and her mouth dropped open before she joined in with a scream of her own.

The seven-man Recce patrol turned and ran.

'Well, that was great, just fucking great. A stealth attack on Charlie, and we're sprung by mamasan and babysan. What's next, Dogs?'

Little Mac was speaking for the whole section while I was trying to explain to Mick Deak on the radio that things hadn't gone quite to plan.

'It gets worse,' said Deak when I met him for a debrief at Binh Ba. 'Seems the headman called the Task Force Commander and bleated about the whole village being awake all night expecting a firefight between VC at one end of his peace-loving village and some Australians covered in war paint at the other.'

The patrolling in and around the Binh Ba rubber and the military outpost went on relentlessly. Since arriving in Vietnam, the twin demands of establishing the ATF base and conducting major operations had meant that each man in Recce had been able to take only one day's break a month from patrol work. This came at enormous physical and psychological cost: several of us had already been sick. I had a good look at the platoon during one of the rare days we were together. There were doses of diarrhoea, skin diseases you couldn't find in a medical dictionary had spread through the platoon, and our feet were in terrible shape from a combination of saturation in the Wet and blistering and chafing in the Dry. Blue Mulby had suffered a bout of leptospirosis—a rat-borne disease—and experienced an alarming drop in weight. We all had that Death Camp look, as did most men in the 5th Battalion. The war was like water on a stone, dripping and wearing us away, layer by layer.

But it was now Christmas, Binh Ba-style. First came a stirring message from Task Force Commander Brigadier Jackson. He sent us his best wishes for Christmas and the New Year, 1967.

'In our seven months of action we have come a long way together. Much has been achieved, but we all know there is much to be done. I know well

that on many occasions a great deal has been asked of you, and always without fail you have responded in the true tradition of the Australian soldier. I am deeply proud of your achievements and you have every cause to share in that pride.

During this time of celebration and thanksgiving we will all be pausing in our rare quieter moments to think of our families and friends at home, the events of the past few months, our fellow soldiers who are no longer here, and the future. Many thoughts and prayers will be with each of you, and from them we can all draw strength and determination for re-dedication to our tasks here in Vietnam.

We need to have no fears for the future. It is now clear that Communist aggression against the people of South Vietnam will fail.

Good luck.'

We cut down a lemon tree in the backyard of the Binh Ba villa and decorated it with toilet paper, string, barbed wire and bits of silver paper from cigarette packets. Blue and Bernie organised their sections to hang ration cans on the tree as ornaments, and I took my men out to scrounge for fruit and for spare hootchies to use as tablecloths—anything that would take our minds off war.

As one of those more touching gestures, most men found something to give their mates: a pocket knife, a torch, playing cards—anything that didn't resemble Army issue. John Lea-Smith and Mick Deak drove into Ngai Giao and procured cartons of American beer. Each small thought and action had a huge impact on all of us: Christmas was a small piece of normality in a place that was everything but normal. Deak later spoke quietly to us about Reconnaissance Platoon being a family. Those words, from someone as tough as a grunt's boot, had a further soothing and cheering effect on men who were close to running on empty.

RUNNING FOR COVER

Flinders Ranges, 2000

By late afternoon we have walked some distance. We are strung out in single file. Some of us speak briefly to each other, beginning to break down the initial shyness. Others, we notice, hang back; they seem a bit withdrawn and aloof. We are about to inquire of one of the men how he feels when he says, 'Got to have my own space. Sorry, it's nothing personal . . . '

As we trek on, we notice the odd grumble here and there about not being fit any more. That night we reach Moolooloo sheep station and have a top meal. Some of us are good cooks, and nothing breaks down barriers like a hearty feed.

Before we struggle into our swags, the subject of certain 'medical' problems comes up. You tell us about yours—how veterans suffer hyper-vigilance. Even at night, even when dead tired, the brain still spins about like a tree full of fruit bats. Then there is myoclonus, an affliction that causes involuntary muscle spasms. You tell us of vets so deprived of sleep and twitching so badly that they drag their sleeping bag into the lounge because the wife can no longer stand sleeping next to this wired weirdo.

We get back to the problem of stand-offishness, that feeling you have where you have to move away from a group at a party like you've just farted. It's real panic stuff sometimes—the sweating without heat, the need for air, space, isolation. You feel you have to create your own perimeter.

It's not so much that we feel stupid doing this; it's more that none of us ever used to be like this . . .

CONFIDENTIAL INTSUM: September 1966—The North Vietnamese Communist leadership has 'professed its determination' (in the words of Ho Chi Minh) to prolong the war for five, ten or twenty

years and more if necessary to achieve its
ambitions for the domination of the entire
country. The prospect of an interminable war
must weigh heavily on the North Vietnamese Army
regulars and the Vietcong.

The two Hueys droned south from Binh Ba. From 2000 metres
out we could see the massive Australian base taking shape in and
around the Nui Dat rubber. In just a few months, engineers had
cut dirt roads through the plantation, members of 5RAR and
6RAR had thrown up huge triple-tier concertina barbed-wire
fences across their perimeters, and machine-gun emplacements
had been constructed, sandbagged and sighted to give comple-
mentary crossfire. In the shade of the rubber there was a sea of
tents—called 'lines'—where beat and buggered diggers could
snatch some time off in relative security before they walked back
out through the wire looking for Charlie. Corrugated iron buildings had mushroomed across the base—mess halls, administration
offices, workshops, sheds where armoured personnel carriers
were stripped and repaired. There were big gun pits where a
battery of 105 howitzers waited on the call for fire support. All
around the inside of the gun pits were men stripped to the waist,
stacking shells. It was a similar picture over at the 5RAR and
6RAR mortar pits—mortar men ready to send out a lethal
bombardment as soon as their mates got into trouble.

The ATF bristled with ordnance and armament, and it was
getting bigger by the week. Through vigorous and aggressive
patrolling, the men from the two infantry battalions had secured
safety zones out from 1ATF. These were called Tactical Areas
of Responsibility (TAORs), and platoons patrolled them and
ambushed day and night. Any VC force trying to get close to the
main base—as they had nearly done at the Battle of Long Tan—

would bump an Australian unit, which would promptly call in artillery or mortar support.

The ATF senior commanders figured the base was big enough to stand on its own feet, and the battalions could now spend more time on Search and Destroy missions much further afield. But take your eye off Charlie and he would shit on you from a great height: he had proved he had the ability and guts to take on any force of any size. Uncle Ho had already revved his men up with the promise that they were going to win this war. We were being told that we would.

Fifth Battalion Commanding Officer 'Wingy' Warr always came down to meet us when we disembarked at Luscombe Field: he wanted to know first-hand what Recce had found on its latest patrol. Warr's voice was clipped and proper, cultured.

'Good trip, Corporal?' he would say to me if I was first in his Land Rover. 'Got much for the IO?'

The Intelligence Officer (IO) was Captain Robert O'Neill. To many of us he didn't fit the usual mould of other intelligence officers, who stuck pins in maps and sent the grunts out chasing invisible VC battalions or platoons of monkeys. O'Neill was at first sight an awkward, uncoordinated man, but he was a Rhodes Scholar and an author, and he held a PhD. His laser-sharp mind could make sense out of a Chinese jigsaw, discard the rubbish and the inconsequentials, and he could almost second-guess Charlie's next move. We had coffee and flipped through our notes: enemy movement here, deserted bunkers there, cooking fires that were hot or cold, trails that indicated many feet moving in a specific direction—all these signs built up patterns for O'Neill, who sifted and sorted through other intelligence gathered from battalion enemy contact and SAS patrol reports. Somehow this helped frame the Big Picture of main force enemy intentions in Phuoc

Tuy Province, and formed much of the basis for the INTSUMs that were then passed back to infantry commanders. Reports also went to Task Force Intelligence, which in turn formulated a battle plan and the next major operation. Intelligence in the Vietnam War was everything: good Intel meant that the Australians hooked in first and bloodied the Nogs' noses. Poor intelligence could lead us into hell on Earth.

We struggled back to our tents. Recce lines again looked like a pigsty, but we ignored the mess, grabbed the mail, which some clerk had dropped on our mosquito nets, and devoured news from home.

Blue Mulby was talking about his son, Vince. I sat on the tent floor watching him smile and comment on his news from home.

'Why did you call your son "Vincent", Blue? Why *Vincent*? Isn't that a headache pill?'

Blue thought for a minute, then tightened his lips as if he was going to drag some errant Yank out for a punch-up.

'Not sure, Dogs. "Vince Mulby" . . . Don't you reckon it sort of sounds special?'

I started to brew up using my canteen over a small Hexamine stove. Mulby was tough, humorous, dependable and had a great rapport with his section. He wouldn't suffer fools—unless they were his own men, in which case he'd quietly put them right, then offer paternal comfort and advice. Like he did with the man who had ratted through the supplementary pack and came up with American chewing tobacco.

'What's this stuff, Blue?' he'd asked.

Mulby was packing his gear for a patrol. 'Chewing tobacco. Yanks use it instead of smoking fags.'

I watched with growing amusement as Blue slyly observed the man unwrap the packet, bite off a sizeable chunk and begin to masticate.

Was he, or wasn't he?

Blue obviously considered that mistakes made in life by young diggers were character-building. Sure enough, the soldier swallowed the evil black lump of guk. There was a moment's silence, then the poor tobacco victim began to heave. His eyes spilled a shower of tears.

'Fuck's *sake!*'

More spluttering, then a gargle, and the soldier shoved his head into the closest water bucket.

Blue watched, shaking his head, and called over, 'It's called "chewing" tobacco, not "swallowing" tobacco. I think you're s'posed to spit it out, like in those Western movies where John Wayne gobs on the bad guy's boots.'

Two days at the 'Dat, hot food at the mess hall, cold American beer in the Wet Canteen, and then we were out on the Song Ca River about 6000 metres from Nui Dat. Here trails wound through a mixture of thick bush and moderate jungle. To the west the Nui Thi Vai reared up; most of the trails led towards the mountain range. That range and the nearby Nui Toc Tien created a natural funnel for enemy approaching or leaving the west of the province. This was ambush territory: a lay-up here and a patient wait would certainly pay off with a kill.

Late morning, and we had been moving quietly along the Song Ca. It was nerve-jangling territory: dry and almost impossible to walk through without the crackle of dry bush underfoot. We moved as a platoon—Mick Deak had decided the enemy threat was too great for us to split into smaller patrols—and progress was agonisingly slow, each man straining to see or hear each time the scout stopped for a breather. Recce Platoon adopted the same practice as SAS, laying-up for up to an hour to watch and listen. Once again our task was to avoid contact; if we did unexpectedly hit a large enemy force we were to shoot, break contact and put some distance down so we could call for fire support.

Deak called a lunch break and we formed a circle, with each man sitting or lying within sight or reach of another. I was putting my section next to Mulby's when he suddenly kicked what looked like a mud-covered soccer ball over to me.

'Dogs, check this out,' he whispered.

I watched the ball roll over to me and gave a fancy back-kick return to Blue. It wasn't as soft as I'd expected. 'Hey, that's hard. What is it, a bloody rock?'

'Naw,' Mulby said quietly. 'It's a head.'

I froze for a moment, looking at the object covered in straw, mud and twigs.

'You're pissing in my pocket, right? Give me a look at that thing.'

I began to scrape away the debris with a stick while Blue stood and lifted his rifle into a ready position. Still scraping at the mud I watched the big man begin to quietly search the surrounding bush. Mulby prowled like an emu on alert; one foot lifted from the ground, wiggled a bit, then placed down while the other came up. He bent slightly at the waist and his neck and head—which switched left and right like a chicken checking for seed—extended far beyond the rest of his body.

Suddenly I saw two empty eye sockets. It *was* a head, and it had to be enemy—I hadn't heard intelligence reports about any diggers losing their heads.

Blue found a boot in the ground, pulled it out and whispered, 'One boot and a sock inside it.'

Other men had now joined in the gruesome hunt, and we examined the boot with its laces still done up.

'How the hell did he do that?' I asked.

Blue took the boot back. 'Do what, dickhead?'

'How did he take the boot and sock off without undoing his laces?'

Blue pushed his face up to mine. 'He didn't take it off, Dogs. Sometimes you're as bright as a one-watt bulb. H and I blew it off him. This place has had a full-on arty strike. The Nogs were probably having a brew and rice when *boom,* this fucker gets a round straight on top of him.'

Mick Deak ordered the bits buried, but not until we'd had another debate.

I made a suggestion. 'Leave them on the ground so the relatives can come and collect them after we've won the war, skipper. What do you reckon?'

Deak ignored that idea. We finished our lunch, then the burial.

Less than an hour later we saw the first enemy gun pits, the first of a bunker complex. We froze. Mick Deak broke us into three sections and we sat quietly, listening. It was the biggest bunker complex we'd ever seen, and it was unoccupied. The system of tunnels and hides and machine-gun emplacements actually traversed the nearby Song Xoai River. It was capable of housing what we first thought was a battalion-size VC group. Then we revised our estimate to regiment-size.

Shit, I thought, *it's just four clicks from Binh Ba rubber.*

Elaborate kitchens were constructed with cooking systems that filtered the smoke through herring-boned ditch funnels. Tunnels veered off at sharp angles to avoid incoming shrapnel or gunfire. We wandered through like ghosts, each man thinking the same thing.

This is the enemy's home, where he sits, talks, jokes, lives and trains. Here he is treated for wounds, here he undergoes indoctrination, straps on his pack and rice bag and goes out to take on the Australians.

Question: Where was he right now while intruders walked through and made notes and sketches of his small city under the trees?

At 1100 hours next morning, Mick Deak gave the word that we were heading back to Nui Dat.

'Break up into four patrols, 1500 metres apart,' he said.

Little Mac scouted for my group. Gunner Blue Riley and Bob Godfrey took the middle ground, and Max Campbell and Barney took the next positions. Pagey was tail-end Charlie. In Vietnam the terrain and topography are constantly changing: you can work your way through jungle, low thickets and bamboo during any given day on patrol. Infantry prefer cover, trees and shrubs. The soldier is dressed to blend in; in the bush you can hide, sleep, observe. The soldier on patrol hates clear ground, where he is exposed and vulnerable. This particularly applied to Reconnaissance Platoon, where stealth and camouflage were always desirable ingredients.

At 1400 hours we struck one of the biggest clearings I had ever seen. It was the size of five football fields. Tactics dictated that we move around the grassy clearing, but that was going to take ages: we'd still be walking by nightfall.

I called each man forward to take a look. 'This is the way I see it,' I said. 'If we go around we'll still be moving in the dark. We go through the guts, we'll save time. We get sprung, hit the deck and snake over to the buckled tree on the far side—that'll be our RV. It's not a good move, but I say let's give it a go.'

I got nods of agreement all round, and Little Mac moved out. He'd covered 50 yards when I moved forward, running and weaving.

We're in the open now, Nogs can get a clear shot any minute. Move, you buggers, keep going . . . weave and keep down. God, I know I've been a bastard, get me through this and I'll change, I promise. I'll go to church, I'll give up the piss . . . keep moving. Zig and zag . . .

The minutes dragged like hours before we all crashed into the bush, collapsing in a heaving, wheezing pile of bodies. We worked further into the thicker growth and I sat up ready to congratulate each man when suddenly Pagey froze, then jerked his Armalite up into a fire position. At that same moment an Australian soldier stepped from the thick scrub, lifted his rifle and shoved it into Pagey's face. It was split-second decision time for both men—neither squeezed the trigger.

Delta Company's Lieutenant Dennis Rainer approached me and squatted down. I stiffened. Of all the blokes in the battalion to run into it *had* to be Rainer. The platoon commander was one of the most respected in 5RAR—courageous and aggressive, Rainer had led his men into several successful contacts with the Vietcong, and Charlie had lost every time at extreme cost. In his last contact Rainer had recorded 10 dead confirmed by body count.

'We've been watching you for some time, Corporal,' he said quietly. 'Thought you were VC. The rest of D Company are going into a blocking position to cut you off.' He pulled out his map. 'Show me where you think you are.'

I did so. Rainer pointed down to my map, a picto.

'You shouldn't rely entirely on the pictos, they are a bit inaccurate. You're 500 metres out and in Delta's zone.' He folded his map. 'We were going to ambush you, you know. Just a few minutes more and . . . '

I quickly apologised. He smiled, studying me quietly like a Cobra watching a rat, then melted into the jungle.

THE SECRET OF NUI NGHE

Flinders Ranges, 2000

Pills and tablets. If you can't shut us up, dose us with pills and tablets. Medicate the Vet and he'll go away.

You recall that, back in the early days when vets were going out helping other vets, you had an appeal from the wife of a veteran. She was very worried and asked if you could come around and talk to her sick husband.

That was the late 1970s and quite a few veterans were starting to melt down. The 'Post Traumatic Stress Disorder' tag hadn't been dreamt up then, and any vet who was 'going off' was displaying normal post-Vietnam War behaviour. To the public it was a legacy of the baby-killing syndrome a lot of us had been branded with—'he's a vet, he's bloody mad'.

Anyway, you walk into this guy's house and there's a bad feeling coming out of every room. The wife is standing near the fireplace, swivelling her eyes to indicate he's in the kitchen. You notice a picture of the bloke in a frame sitting on the mantelpiece. He's wearing a slouch hat in one of those photos we all had taken when we were about 19 and had just finished recruit training—fresh-faced with that shy grin. If you could see innocence in a picture, it was in those early Army photos. And it was strange how those pictures all look the same: even the men from World War II had that same Aussie-boy-hasn't-seen-bad-things-yet look. They didn't have the stare of the haunted.

You walk into the kitchen and he's sitting at the table. There's a beer in his hand and a few crumpled, empty cans next to an overflowing ashtray. The guy looks about 50 years older than he does in the photo. The eyes are slightly watery and glazed over: it's obvious straight away this bloke's a drinker, and he's melting down.

Not a word.

How many times have you seen this . . . poor me, poor me, pour me a drink. You pull out a chair and start to talk. Your gaze moves around the kitchen and stops when you look at the refrigerator. On top of the fridge is a mountain of medication, dozens of pills—green, yellow, red, white. They all come from shrinks and psychs, and this man is a walking pharmacy. He's a doped-out digger who's had pills shoved down his throat to shut him up, keep him quiet, rest him in peace until he's dead.

You felt depressed for days after seeing that . . .

CONFIDENTIAL INTSUM: 8–14 August 1966—To uncover the enemy's favourite hiding places under the thick canopy of jungle leaves, cargo planes equipped like crop-dusters fly low over the treetops to spray defoliant agent that will kill the growth and force the enemy to move on . . . To soften up the enemy in other ways, the Air Force also engages in various kinds of psychological warfare. Millions of leaflets are dropped over hostile areas each month, describing various Vietcong atrocities . . .

There wasn't a soldier at Nui Dat who didn't hate Hoa Long, the displaced persons' village just a click outside the Task Force. Unlike the residents of other small towns and villages around the province, those in this scungy hamlet were a sullen, moody lot. The place was full of VC and their sympathisers, as well as those moved from other villages that had been bulldozed to make way for the ATF base. I suppose a few in Hoa Long had reason to be permanently angry at the *Uc Da Loi*.

I thought back to a month before when we were tasked to ambush just outside Hoa Long. Deak said the VC were getting a bit cocky about moving in and out of the place to resup and see the relatives. We'd sat in an ambush for a few hours when someone hissed that there was a light in the distance winking on and off.

'Dogs, take four blokes and check it out,' Deak whispered. 'Watch it. Any Nog makes a break, brass 'em.'

We set off at a trot towards what had now become a glow from a hut, and in a minute we were up against the timber wall, peering through the cracks. The image was one I'll never forget: men shuffled around inside with rags wrapped around their bodies.

Oh, sweet Jesus, they're lepers.

Nothing had prepared me for that. I felt surges of pity, sadness, revulsion, regret, guilt. The slow movement of the men, the shuffling and murmuring . . . these weren't Hoa Long enemy, they weren't bad and evil men. They were outcasts—outcasts in a war zone. How bad can things get in life? Hoa Long was truly a place of nightmares.

Lying flat on my stomach with a .50 calibre machine-gun firing over my head in the dead of night didn't improve my impression of the place. The reason for my predicament was another Cordon and Search operation. We had been tasked to lead a rifle company into the village, which we had recce'd on several occasions, when an enthusiastic, 'friendly' Vietnamese Regional Force soldier heard us and opened up. The platoon went to ground and the bullets cracked away just over our heads. The worst thing was, I was straddling a small barbed-wire fence when the action started, so I dropped down on top of the wire. I now lay like a huge turtle, arms out, massive pack on my back forcing my head down and a determined soldier pumping sustained bursts from the big gun.

Deak was frantically radioing through on the Battalion Head-quarters channels trying to get them to contact the village liaison officer to call off the zealous fool. I was now seriously regretting a heavy night on the grog at Bravo Company's boozer, *The Vile Inn*. I was enduring a wave of nausea and fatigue. All the other Recce men were head down and arse-up; unable to move, I just closed my eyes, opening them only at the odd burst the Viet-namese soldier was sending out.

Thump! Something hit my shoulder.

'Fuck, I'm hit. *I'm hit*,' I yelled.

Then I heard a voice from the blackness nearby. 'Wake up, Dogs, and stay awake.' Bernie had thrown a full water bottle at me, striking my arm. 'The skipper and half the bloody platoon have been trying to wake you up.'

I peered around, indignantly. 'I wasn't asleep, I just had my eyes closed. I can't see a bloody thing with this load forcing my head down—and you reckon *you* can zonk lying on barbed wire?'

It wasn't easy to anger Bernie, but he was plenty cranky at trying to wake me. 'Yeah, well you were snoring like a bloody hovering Chinook!'

I wondered after we got up to move off if I had that effect on a lot of people. I thought I was a good section commander, but maybe I was also an irritating bastard.

Two days later, new orders and a return to Nui Nghe, that peg of granite which protruded from the jungle north of Nui Dat. More bad flashbacks . . . the death of Tich Tomas, the knowledge that VC were still thick around the small mountain, and the prospect of bush-bashing around boulders and swamps were foremost in my mind as we trekked out towards the menacing landform. Reconnaissance was moving two hours ahead of Alpha Company. If we detected Vietcong it was a matter of breaking contact or dropping and bringing the main Australian force up.

That night we stopped short of the hill and RV'd with A Company before having a quick bite and getting some sleep. I thought about 8 July 1966, the day of my friend's death on Nui Nghe.

Why didn't I tell the section to go to ground before the arty came? Why did Tich die and not me? Why have I still not written to his family explaining—telling them what really happened? Not what the Army most likely told them: 'we regret to inform . . . your son has been killed in action . . . ' I'll write myself when I get home.

It was almost black now. I lay on my back and looked up through a break in the tall trees: stars above and a moon rising, which suddenly threw a glow around where I rested. It was moist in here, dank—that curious smell of rotting where billions of leaves broke then crumbled and decomposed to mould on the jungle floor. Leaning to my side I could feel the coldness of the SLR and the roughness of the webbing we always laid out alongside our body, ready to throw on if firing started. Above me, so close I could reach up and touch it, a firefly passed over, winking the light in his abdomen to attract a partner for the night.

I ran my fingers down through the humus and felt the wetness beneath the leaves. I looked up and froze: a venomous green tree viper was extending almost two-thirds of its body length out towards another tree. For a moment my mind went back to Willy, the soldier in my section when I was still in Charlie Company.

Willy was an inveterate rat-catcher. He caught Vietnam's biggest rodents between the fly sheets on the tents, and when he had a box full of rats, he grabbed several containers of lighter fluid and showed us how to jet-squirt the fluid by squeezing the sides of the cans. Willy tipped his rats into the bottom of a gun pit and we all shot jets of lighter fluid at them. Then he gave the signal to light up and we all flicked our Zippos. The man's face took on a certain look of rapture when the flames raced up and engulfed the rats—it was just short of an orgasm. But Willy's games didn't stop at rat-burning: he caught scorpions and massive Golden Orb spiders, put them in a steel baking tin and heated it over a Hexamine block. Heat and hate propelled the two protagonists into mortal combat. Willy took bets on the outcome; the spider always won.

One day, after losing my money, I asked, 'Why do you like killing things, Willy?'

'I don't,' he replied. 'I just like killing rats and those fucking spiders that put their wet webs up that I walk into every night. They're gangly bastards that make my blood run cold. I'm more scared of them than I am of getting shot.'

An hour later and I was still awake. There was almost total silence, but if you put your ear to the ground you could actually hear a million small feet scuttling along in their tiny world. The jungle was pristine, clean, pure.

Next morning Deak briefed me: I was to take the lead up the thick slopes of Nui Nghe. I shook out the section and Pagey stepped up, unhooking his secateurs. Ray Ferrier, Blue Mulby's scout—and one of the most experienced in the battalion—came up close to Pagey and whispered, 'Careful, mate. Really careful now, plenty of time . . . '

We worked our way gradually up alongside a re-entrant. The bush was so thick we were sweating from exhaustion after only a few minutes. The main danger here—apart from being dropped by a sniper—was stumbling, falling and simply twisting or breaking an ankle. No-one would be happy bringing a Medivac chopper in here. I knew that for a fact: it had taken an agonisingly long time to get a wounded Tich Tomas out during the Casevac.

Field signals came back from Pagey—'Stop, wait five.' His fingers formed a circle around the eye: 'Wait and have a good look.' I studied my map, although I didn't need any bearings moving up a small mountain: the top from the bottom was obvious to even a dill like me.

Suddenly Pagey passed word back instead of a field signal: 'Rocket.'

I was flummoxed. 'Rocket?'

I pushed forward to the scout, and sure enough, there was a rocket lying in the bush—the sort that was carried by a chopper or a small plane. I motioned my scout to go on, and within a minute he whispered back, 'Wheel.'

I looked at the wheel of a small plane. 'There's a wreck around here . . . some bastard's gone down, mate.'

Pagey nodded and moved a few more metres into the bush, then, 'Dogs, wing.'

I put my section down in an arc covering the immediate front and signalled back two fingers on my shoulder for Mick Deak to come forward.

Deak looked at the wheel, bent down and pushed it around.

'It's been here for a while. Dogs, get Pagey and let's check further up.'

Forty to 50 metres on, we found the smashed aircraft, a crumpled wreck that had brought trees down with it. Typically, the jungle was already devouring the scene: vines had begun to encircle the main fuselage, half-obscuring the American star and stripes. A Company moved up behind us, and Company Commander Max Carroll threw a secure cordon around the crash site. We then began a detailed examination of the wreckage.

The Forward Air Controller (FAC) was a small, lightweight aircraft for carrying two people. The plane was a Vietnam enigma: it flew slowly over suspected enemy positions, attracting fire so it could then mark the site with a smoke rocket. Helicopter gunships would be called up to strafe the killing zone, or Phantom jets would pound and napalm the area. FACs had one of the most potentially dangerous tasks in the war: they went out as virtual bait, luring the enemy into exposing himself. Small-arms fire could bring the FAC down, and the pilot and his observer had little more than an Armalite or pistol to defend themselves with—if they survived the crash.

In the front seat of the wrecked aircraft were the skeletal remains of the pilot, killed on impact. As for the passenger, or observer, a tale of true heroism was revealed as we scrambled over the wreckage, trying to unravel the last hours of the FAC flight and these two men who were obviously Missing In Action.

(Years later, we discovered that the pilot was Major John Charles Jacobs, a 10-year US Air Force veteran and a 30-year-old married man from Indiana, sent out over central Phuoc Tuy Province in support of Australian operations. His co-pilot was Charles Franco, 25, a New Yorker. They were headed towards the slopes of Nui Nghe when their small aircraft was suddenly hit by ground fire. The FAC plane plunged down through the curtain of tall trees onto Nui Nghe.)

It was the NVA 274 Regiment commander who sent his troops in to check the wreck and kill the airmen if they had survived. Jacobs was killed on impact, but a badly injured Franco had crawled from the wreck and slumped against the fuselage, preparing himself for what he knew was coming. Franco had smashed his femur, and as the enemy crept up on him, he began firing with his Armalite rifle. The enemy was closing in. Obviously in agonising pain, Franco changed magazines and sent a wall of automatic fire into the advancing NVA. He ran out of ammunition and pulled out his service pistol, shoving it down behind his back. He was determined in those last moments to take one or more enemy out before he died. But an NVA soldier worked his way in behind him and killed him with a single shot to the head. Franco remained slumped against the plane while the NVA laid an ambush for Australian troops, who they thought would come looking for the lost FAC. We never came that day.

We prised the dead Charles Franco—his hand still clutching the pistol—from the mud with as much dignity as we could muster while a chopper was summoned from Nui Dat to remove the remains of the two men.

We sat and watched while SAS Warrant Officer Mick Wright was winched down with body bags. He carefully placed the men's remains and dog tags into the bags, then the Huey turned and clattered away. Two men, missing for months, were now on their way home. At last their relatives and friends would know the real story of their death.

I looked again at the scattered M16 shells. Franco had put up a fierce last fight for his life. Both men should have been awarded medals, and Franco was a contender for the Medal of Honor.

Think about it—the terrible loneliness, the inevitability of the predicament, the decision to fight and die, and not surrender. And all the time aware of your dead mate just metres away, a silent companion in your final minutes on Earth.

MINES AND MOATS

Flinders Ranges, 2000

Rabbits. Millions of them used to run around out here in the lower Flinders a few years ago. There were more bunnies here than there were men in the North Vietnamese Army, then the calcivirus came and wiped most of them out. Most, but not all.

See that burrow? We'll put a snare in there—when the rabbit comes out it'll be caught. We'll use trip wire, like the wire we used on the Army trip flare. Remember the type we strung out across a track before an ambush? Charlie would come along and snag the wire and the flare would explode with a sort of *phoot*! A brilliant, spluttering light would silhouette him and his mates while we shot them.

Two ex-soldiers question the use of rabbit traps: they don't want the rabbit to be caught by the snap-clang, steel-jawed, mongrel thing that springs from the ground and cuts off its legs. Not too hard to work out why those guys have an objection to the rabbit traps: real bad vibes, man. There is possibly nothing, you once said, that flooded a soldier with fear more than the knowledge he was in an area where the enemy had placed anti-personnel mines.

Isn't that the most horrible of descriptions—'anti-personnel'.

Mine warfare is both psychological and physical. Anyone who ever had an experience with landmines is likely still stuffed in the head. Mines terrorised you, maimed you. If you were fortunate, soldiers said, the mine killed you. If you were unlucky, you were mutilated: an arm, a leg, or, God forbid, your eyes were taken from you. Amputations and crippling wounds in Vietnam were 300 per cent higher than in World War II. But it was okay—we could be taken to hospital in one hour, tops.

You couldn't see mines, there was no warning. The M16 American-designed 'jumping jack' was fitted with three prongs that protruded just above the soil. You trod on it and heard a click—the most horrifying sound in the world. You lifted your foot and the main charge sprang from the ground and exploded at waist height. What wonderful mind sat in some military laboratory and dreamt up that obscenity?

Then there was the Claymore, the one we carried. Unfold the twin legs on the book-sized device and aim it towards the enemy, screw in the detonator and roll the cord back to where you lie and wait. Charlie comes by, we squeeze the 'clacker' and send 700 steel ball bearings at him. Another fine example of creative killing.

These are things the best-trained soldier in the world had to deal with. We never dealt with it, never forgot the scream many of us heard a long time ago—'MINES, FREEZE!'

CONFIDENTIAL INTSUM: January 1967—The purpose of the Claymore is to kill as many attacking enemy as possible without wasting small arms ammunition, and to discourage the enemy from vigorously maintaining the momentum of his attack. Correctly sited, the Claymore is capable of achieving the result for which it was designed.

Armoured carriers are people carriers. A section of men can sit cramped inside the machine or can ride topside, but whether you sat in it or on it, an APC was bad news. The people carrier was not people-friendly. If you sat inside with your back against the wall, you faced each other, had to shout above the din of a racing V6 motor, and the squeak, clank and thud of the twin tracks that drove the 11-ton machine. You tried to get your mind off a Bad Thing happening. Bad Things often happened to APCs: they were natural targets for rocket-propelled grenades—the dreaded RPGs—or, worse, an anti-tank mine.

The turret heads, as we called anyone associated with tanks or APCs, sandbagged the floor of the machine against possible mine blast, but could do nothing about an incoming rocket. The open hatch above your head—through which you could look if you were game enough to stand up in the rocking, bucking carrier—was also an open invitation to a satchel charge thrown from the roadside, which would explode inside the machine.

Those were some of the elements of paranoia diggers got riding *inside*. Up above, clinging to anything that would prevent you being thrown off, you could see and hear what was happening around you. Problem was, anyone out in the jungle or along the road could also see you, and obviously shoot you. Then there was the possibility of falling off a carrier travelling at high speed and being run down like a pedestrian by the machine hammering up behind you.

I was inside an APC now. The hatch was down and I was shoved up against Barney and Little Mac on a night trip. This was another one of our 'deception' plans: close the hatches with all the men inside, and the enemy will think the APC isn't carrying troops. We clenched our teeth and hung on in the dark like kids waiting for something spooky to happen as we rattled along at full gallop towards the town of Dat Do. The town was an RV point, but this operation was in fact another Cordon and Search in a hamlet called Ahn Nhut on the road into Dat Do. Ahn Nhut was truly a 'Nowheresville': a flyspeck on the map, a collection of houses and shacks and a military camp, all surrounded by a moat. We were told it was a moat, though I'd always thought that moats involved drawbridges and the whole Medieval thing.

One man in each Recce section carried a starlight scope, a recent hi-tech addition to the Vietnam War. The tube-shaped device drew in all available ambient light at night—from the stars and the moon—and magnified the illumination, so when you peered through the scope you saw green-tinged, floating images, and maybe enemy moving towards you. A flash from a match or a drawback on a cigarette returned a brilliant glow. Like most new, hi-tech war accessories, the starlight scope worked when it felt like it. It was really just more crap for the grunt to lug.

We pulled alongside Dat Do airstrip, struggled out and trotted over to Mick Deak. Before the battalion cordon could be thrown around Ahn Nhut—and we once again set out to 'win the hearts and minds' of the locals—a recce had to be done. Deak crouched down and gave his brief. He spoke to platoon sergeant John Lea-Smith.

'Take Dogs and a few of his blokes and Recce the outer fence around that moat. See if there are any gaps in the wire or places to cross the moat. The Nogs will use any gaps if they try a breakout during the cordon. On the way over, stay alert and spread out—it's all open paddy country and you'll stick out like spare pricks at a wedding.'

The five-man Recce group trotted towards the village. We all winced inwardly at being silhouetted against the paddy fields glowing in the blackness. Every so often John waved for us to space out. There was no comment as to why were spreading out in the open—jumping jacks.

Mines, bloody anti-personnel mines. The M16 mine, the jumping jack . . . Close off that part of your brain, hose down the mine paranoia. Don't think about them . . .

We could now clearly see the profile of the village, and John pulled us up at a low barbed-wire fence.

'Dogs, leave the other three here to cover our arse, and you and me'll go and check this moat out.'

I thought for a moment about the absurdity of a moat in a modern war zone. 'What are we having a closer look at a bloody moat for? I thought a moat was a moat that circled a castle, with the only way in over a drawbridge . . . '

'This isn't a "moat" moat, you drongo. It's a ditch to catch water and stop the bloody village flooding in the monsoon. Look around you—it's as flat as a billiard table, all paddys.'

I argued on. 'It won't be a ditch, it'll be a bloody sewer. It won't be a cutesy little paddling moat, John, for Christ's sake.'

'Who gives a shit? Dogs, stop whingeing and let's go.'

Thirty metres from the moat and still in a semi-crouch, I heard a Vietnamese call out. *'Bai min, dung loi, dung loi. Bai min, bai min!'*

The platoon sergeant spun around to me. 'We've been sprung. What's he going on about?'

John noticed I had frozen and couldn't speak. 'What's he gibbering about?'

For a moment I was paralysed. I knew what the words meant— or at least one of the words.

'Don't move! He's telling us we're in a minefield!' My voice was dry and croaky. I couldn't swallow. Every inch around me was now explosive. I felt my skin begin to prickle.

John squatted and looked at me. I could see his eyes wide and white in his sweating face. He was whispering, 'Bullshit, there used to be mines around here but the ARVN pulled 'em all out. Didn't they?'

I was beginning to feel sick. 'If they didn't, we're in more shit than Ned Kelly. Can you remember our route in?'

At that moment an Australian voice called out in the dark from the village perimeter. 'I'm the LO here, and you blokes are in a bit of a shitty spot right now. You're in an old minefield. I understood you were only supposed to come up as far as the first fence. That right . . . ?'

John gave me a desperate look. 'How many fences we come through you reckon?'

'Well, that bit of barbed-wire behind us where the other guys are—you couldn't call that a fence.'

'No, not by Aussie standards, but maybe by Nog standards. We must be between two fences now and this area is fucking mined. Jesus!'

'John, what's the date today?'

He shot an odd look at me. 'What? What do you want to know the bloody date for—you keeping a friggin' diary? Shit, fill your diary in when we get the fuck outta here!'

By the time we'd made the fence, picked up the men and reached the road back to Dat Do, we were drenched in sweat. The night was cool, but fear had caused torrents of perspiration to pour out of us. I guzzled down a full water bottle.

John caught up with me while we took a breather. 'What was all that crap about a date? Are you losin' it, mate?'

'I lost it a long time ago. I wanted to know the date because it's my birthday on the 27th, and I don't want to die before my birthday.'

'It's the 13th, today. What's so important about your bloody birthday?'

'I'll be twenty-one. I'll be a man.'

Next morning the village Cordon and Search started. At 0915 hours we heard the explosion and saw the black cloud of smoke near Ahn Nhut.

It was a mine or a booby-trap—probably an unexploded bomb—rigged to go up after some unsuspecting Australian stepped on it. The detonation was huge: red-hot steel fragments ripped through the command group of my former company. C Company commander, Major Bourne, was killed, along with his second-in-command, Captain Milligan, and Captain Williams, the artillery forward observer. Five other men were badly wounded. One mine effectively wiped out an Australian rifle company's entire command unit.

On 27 February Mick Deak called me down to his tent in the Reconnaissance lines. The tent flap was closed with a flysheet and I couldn't see inside. Mick pushed me into his tent and all the men from Recce were crammed inside. Bernie leant over and lit the 21 candles, and Mick slapped me on the shoulder.

'Well done, Dogs,' he said. 'You made 21.'

BAD DAYS ON THE LONG HAIS

Flinders Ranges, 2000

We have been walking for about an hour when we stop near a rockpool. It is one of those beautiful springs caught between huge rocks where small yabbies scoot about and a yellow-footed rock wallaby, ears twitching, looks down from the small hill above. Here is a place you can take a breather and talk about a subject we have been avoiding for the past few days: mates killed in action.

When veterans speak of friends lost in war it is always in the context of an event. We can't help but notice when you speak about Sammy, who died, it is 'while we were up in the Warbies on a shitty operation'. If someone asks when Snow got killed, it is 'during that bloody patrol on the Song Ca River when we hit a platoon of Nogs'. No one ever speaks in isolation of the death of a soldier, or goes into detail about how the man took his last breath or bled to death. That is too personal for an Australian soldier.

The Vietnam War was all about mateship and loss. Today we weep inwardly: eyes moisten, but there are usually no words spoken, just haunted looks.

Someone once said it hurt so much when a soldier died because it was the loss of youth. The death of a young man—or woman—seems to scar so much more deeply than if dear old dad died yesterday.

You recall the day you staggered back to your tent after an operation and collapsed on your cot. You looked across at the bed opposite. Your eyes went down to the foot of the bed where there was a steel trunk. Next to that trunk was a set of boots. In the centre of the tent was a table, on the table someone had left an almost empty coffee mug—the last brew he had before we went out on ops. But worst of all you noticed someone had left some letters from home on the empty cot opposite, expecting the digger to read them when he came back in from the bush. You rolled over and stared at the sandbagged blast wall around the tent. You knew the man who slept in the bed wouldn't be back to scrape the muck off his boots or read the letters because the day before yesterday you loaded his body onto a Huey.

Jesus, sometimes in the war we did it hard, really hard. And nothing was harder than the death of a digger.

CONFIDENTIAL INTSUM: February 1966—The Long Hais have been used as a base and refuge by the VC for many years. From the security of their bases in these hills the enemy have spread their influence throughout Phuoc Tuy Province and have, since 1965, controlled areas of Dat Do and Long Lee.

Mick Deak studied the INTSUM for Operation Renmark, then spoke to Blue, Bernie and me. 'The op begins on 18 February. We'll hold an O Group in my tent tonight.'

Mulby, Harve and Bernie came into my tent after the O Group and were putting on a brave face after learning precisely where Operation Renmark was taking us—into the Long Hai hills. Recce Platoon was to have the 'honour' of being the first Australian platoon to operate in the Long Hais, we were told.

Honour? Maybe some other pricks would like the honour.

Bernie Smith pulled himself up onto my cot and curled his legs up under him. Bernie always wore thongs around the Recce lines. He had a peculiar manner when he would sit in a chair, on a bed, or even on the ground, where he would cross his legs, then wrap one of his feet back under his leg. This caused Bernie to have a hunched, part-foetal look. He rolled a cigarette and held it claw-like between three fingers when he shoved it into his mouth.

We were contemplating pack-muling up another mountain, a mess of rock, jungle, bamboo and re-entrants with another full load on our backs. We'd been in awe of the low mountain range since the day we arrived in Phuoc Tuy. The Long Hais rose steeply out of the flat, paddy-covered plains to the north, and on the southern side seemed to curve almost gracefully upwards from the beaches that rimmed the South China Sea. Even relaxing on 'R and C' in Vung Tau, you just had to look at the Long Hais. The jungle-covered feature was splotched with ugly splashes of brown and white, and to call the range a hungry, menacing animal wouldn't have been putting too fine a point on it. The enemy had been tunnelling and digging into the Long Hai hills ever since the French were kicked out of Vietnam in 1954: it was a fortress of bunkers, protected by machine-guns, booby-traps and mines. The Long Hais were not unlike the Nui Thi Vai in many respects: both had been pounded by B52 strikes with massive 1000-lb bombs, shelled by artillery and naval guns from ships in the South China Sea, mortared, and rocked with air strikes. Anything that burnt or exploded had been hurled at those huge lumps of stone, but still Charlie came out and thumbed his nose, almost goading us to have another go.

The conversation swung around to the enemy. The VC were spoken of in dismissive terms: their skills, cunning and ability to fight were never discussed. To most soldiers the VC were merely targets on a shooting range: there was nothing personal about shooting them. And they probably thought the same way about us, the invaders.

Bernie was philosophical. 'They never got us on the Warbies, they won't get us on the Long Hais.'

I wasn't so optimistic. 'I think we're getting a bit close to the end of the trip over here to be buggerisin' around on another mountain.'

Suave Harve nodded. 'I'm with you, Dogs. I say leave the bloody Long Hais to the next lot that get over here.'

Mulby gave me one of the most serious looks I'd got from him since he threatened to flatten me back in Holsworthy.

'I think these bloody hills are going to be the worst place we've been to yet, no worries.'

Outside the tent a few minutes later Mick approached me.

'You're not going out on this one, Dogs,' he told me. 'You've got R and R due in Taipei, and you're taking it.'

I felt I wanted to be part of this op, and began to argue that my section needed me. But Mick cut me off.

'Bullshit. You're not so special that we can't do one operation without you. You're going, so get some clean clobber and wear it.'

I went.

By 21 February Operation Renmark was up and running. A B52 air strike had been called in to bomb suspected bunker positions, and like us, the enemy never saw the huge bombers at the height they flew—there was just a sudden, massive ground-shaking rumble when the bombs struck in a series of orange flashes. At night a B52 strike was mesmerising—a series of dazzling flashes like a string of beads bursting across a ridge line. For those beneath a pattern-bombing attack, it must have seemed like the gates of hell had been swung wide open.

Mid-afternoon, and Bravo Company was moving into position to search the southern half of the Long Hai hills. In the heat and dry of the February day, the company had been working its way through jungle alongside a track and the leading APC turned to cross the track towards the Long Hais. At that moment—

1407 hours—there was an enormous explosion. The detonation had the power of a 500-lb bomb: it blew a two-foot-wide hole in the bottom of the machine, and lifted the 11-ton vehicle 10 feet into the air. A digger riding on another APC later said that the force of the explosion threw one of the carrier's steel wheels 50 feet into the air. At the same time its back ramp was ripped off and hurtled into a soldier walking behind it, killing him instantly.

The blast immediately killed some of the men sitting inside the APC, while the shock wave blew others out onto the ground. One digger sitting atop the vehicle was crushed when it landed on top of him. Some of the survivors wandered around in shock, others were blast-burnt after the explosion. The following APCs immediately swung into ambush drill, with their .50 calibre machine-guns sweeping the surrounding jungle.

Bravo Company commander Major Bruce McQualter alighted from his carrier, rallied his men, then moved forward to the wrecked APC with stretcher-bearers to offer assistance. Near another undamaged carrier, platoon commander Jack Carruthers and his sergeant, 'Tassie' Wass, had also jumped from their machine and were desperately trying to assess the horror in front of them. Suddenly someone in McQualter's group trod on a jumping jack. The effect of the main charge as it bounced into the air and exploded was devastating: McQualter was struck in the head and collapsed instantly. His medic party was also flattened, and Carruthers and Wass were felled by flying shrapnel. It was a slaughterhouse.

For the next hour men performed acts of great bravery, struggling to recover and save the lives of their wounded mates, constantly aware that every square metre of ground around them was seeded with jumping jacks.

The massive blast left a crater six feet wide and four feet deep. The number of dead and wounded was at first overwhelming,

and the Battalion Regimental Medical Officer, Tony White—
flown in by Sioux helicopter—was stunned. What he first
thought were blackened and discarded uniforms were in fact his
soldiers, burnt in the horrific blast. The body of the carrier driver,
cut in half, was just visible from beneath his shattered vehicle; on
the other side of the APC the arm of a dead B Company digger
protruded from beneath the hull. McQualter lay on his back,
reaching his arms upwards, wanting to be helped to his feet. But
he could neither hear nor speak as a result of the wound to his
head, and he lapsed into a coma. Carruthers was on the ground,
his big, bushy red moustache streaked with blood.

The air around the blast site was thick with shock and silence,
and the stink from the explosions hung in the air. Training proce-
dures now took over, and men scrambled to create a defensive
perimeter around the mine ambush. Australian sappers were
choppered in, but even clearing a landing site for the engineers
and their mine detectors—and the dustoff helicopters—was an
ordeal, with the ever-present risk of another mine explosion.

Nine men died and 31 were wounded in this, Australian's worst
mine incident of the Vietnam War to date. It was an afternoon of
despair, frustration, anger—not a single enemy was sighted during
the incident, and the men had not yet even started climbing the
Long Hais. Adding to the devastation of this huge loss of life was
the fact that it had come just a short while after C Company lost
its command unit in the Ahn Nhut mine incident. Groups of
men died or were wounded during operations: at Long Tan, for
instance, there was a sudden, huge loss of life in just a few hours.
But what happened at Ahn Nhut, and now on an even larger
scale near the Long Hais, involved the loss of men and senior
commanders in two sudden hits. Bravo Company had lost all its
commanders in two explosions in just over four minutes.

At times like this your mind went back and replayed events associated with sudden death or maiming. They were the constants of war—any day one of us could cop it. This relentless pressure triggered some very black humour, intended as a defiance of death. And no-one was better at sick humour than Recce Platoon. Most of the bad jokes were aired back at the platoon lines.

Bernie Smith was soon going home: the section commander's tour was almost over. Said he: 'I can't wait to get home so I can go dancing.'

Blue Mulby and I: 'You'll step on a booby-trap tomorrow, blow your legs off. Some dancin' you'll do then, Bernie.'

Bernie grinned at us and gave us the finger. He wasn't big on dancing, so I dropped to my knees and jerked and wriggled in the dirt outside his tent. It wasn't meant to be funny, it wasn't meant to be serious. It was just typical of the sort of loony talk on any given day on the Funny Farm that was Vietnam.

Already working along the ridge line on the Long Hais, Mick Deak and some of his men saw the huge plume of black smoke when Bravo Company hit the mine ambush. Soon the radio transmissions cranked up with the bad news—the number of KIA and WIA, and the urgency and breathlessness in the voice calling for dustoffs.

'Jesus, this is dreadful,' said Deak. 'The poor bastards . . . '

He called the section commanders in and gave an O Group update.

'There's every chance the Nogs are going to use this—they've probably been waiting for it. They may well mortar the blokes down below, so we've gotta stay absolutely switched on.'

BREAK CONTACT

Flinders Ranges, 2000

At last light the sun gleams off the rocks high up on the cliff. The colours are raw red and brown, but further down they wash out and there is a loss of perspective. Things seem to move slowly; only a corella, silent for a change, hops about near the top of a river red gum.

As veterans we remember the approaching night. In Vietnam the time of last light was when we 'Stood To' in the jungle: we slid quietly down onto our stomachs, or wedged ourselves in a sitting position against a tree, and waited for the blackness. This was supposed to be the time the enemy was most likely to attack. That really was bullshit, wasn't it? What silly bastard was going to have a go when he was suffering night blindness as much as we were? And the VC were going to mount a massive human wave assault in the jungle in near-darkness? Get real . . .

There's another sort of blackness—you call it the Fog of War. It's not the fog described by that 19th-century military theorist Karl von Clausewitz, who used the expression to describe confusion among commanders caused by the intangibles of battle and the Big Picture. No, it was more like that scene in *Saving Private Ryan* when Tom Hanks is on the beach getting the shit shot out of him and he can't hear anything. You remind us of your Fog of War.

'I can tell you what it felt like—scuba diving. That's right, you're wearing a diving mask and all you can see is what's straight ahead, all you hear is your own breathing and a rushing sound in your ears. Outside that mask is just silence, like someone turned a radio off but it keeps coming back in bursts of horrible loudness. There is a crack above your head then a real loud bang and your ears shut down to all noise: they're overloaded. Then there's silence again, a silence you want to stop.

'What you see now is either super-slow or super-fast. You look at trees from a sideways-lying down angle, or at the sky from on your back. Then you are up on your feet and running with that scuba mask on again. You feel tight in the chest, your mouth screams for a drink and you shout, but you can't hear anything, or you're shouting and nothing is coming out. The Fog of War drains every ounce of energy out of your body in a rush. But that's when the reflexes of training kick in to keep you alive. You have never been so terrified in your life—but never been so capable and determined. It's totally weird being under attack.'

CONFIDENTIAL INTSUM: February 1967—Likely enemy reaction in the Long Hai Hills. Any sizeable VC unit will go into a counter sweep operation, taking evasive action except where it is possible to lead our troops into an ambush or onto booby traps.

It was a week later and I sat in my tent on my cot, legs drawn up and resting back against the sandbags. Blue Mulby was sitting in a chair, legs crossed up on the table. He was telling me about the drama of the past days on the Long Hais.

'You're shagging yourself stupid in Taipei, and we're eating dirt up on the mountain. Nice move, Dogs. We had some quite wonderful bloody times up there.'

Blue then relived those dirty days in the Long Hais—that first firefight, with scout Ray Ferrier making first contact with the enemy . . .

Bravo Company had taken a savage mauling and the Tiger Battalion had suffered a serious body blow in the mine incident, but the operation to clear the Long Hais had to go on. Mick Deak kept his Reconnaissance Platoon, now numbering 21 men, in one tight group as they negotiated a dried-out creek line ahead of the advancing rifle company, Delta, which was about two hours behind.

Scouting ahead, Ray Ferrier—'the Ferret'—may have been the first to see movement, the first to notice the freshly cut green leaves that were appearing around him. With the in-built antennae that forward scouts automatically grew after a month or so in the war, the Ferret sensed something was coming: there was a presence ahead. To the Ferret, scouting was like hunting: stop, listen, turn the head one way then the other, eyes working from middle ground to further out. If necessary, lower yourself to one knee and suck everything up like a vacuum cleaner, all senses at full throttle. It was the scout's creed, a reversal of the well-known saying, but for a man scouting—who carried the safety of his whole section on his shoulders—so true: *Don't Do Something, Just Stand There*. Patience ... the ability to wait a second or two longer. Fools rush in, scouts wait a little longer. Ferrier was now on one knee and beginning to lift his Armalite, eyes probing through vegetation that cut visibility to no more than 4 or 5 metres. The scout suddenly became aware that he already was standing in the outer pits of a bunker system.

Freeze. Watch. One second ... two seconds ... movement ... sounds. Suddenly black-clad figures rising from the under-growth. The scout jerked the rifle up and leant forward, breathed in quickly and squeezed the trigger all in one fluid movement.

Braaat! Braaat!

The Ferret hit the ground after putting a short burst to his front and right flank.

Braaaat!

The closest machine-gunner to the forward contact was Bluey Twaits, who nearly choked on his chewing gum as he dived into a firing position—across the ashes of a cold camp fire—and pulled the M60 back into his shoulder. Twaits gave the bush to the front and right of Ferrier 50 rounds, then snapped on a 100-round link belt. Deak was frantically assessing information coming back from his scout. Complicating matters for the platoon commander was the fact that there was now incoming fire—the VC was maintaining contact and returning fire with automatic weapons. The platoon went into a regular contact drill: M60 to the high ground with remaining flanks covered and tail-end Charlies covering back down the creek line.

'How many, how many?' Deak shouted to his forward section.

'Five, six, and maybe a light machine-gun,' shouted Mulby, who was commanding the forward section.

John Lea-Smith was up next to Deak, and the two quickly figured this was a 'suck in'—the enemy would break contact and try and pull the Aussies forward. To the men in Mulby's section, the bunker system looked enormous: Mulby's first assessment was 'possibly company size'.

Mick Deak got on the radio and started to order up artillery, at the same time telling his men to move back.

'We're not going to try and assault this lot. They're dug in—bunkers, the whole lot.'

The first spotting round of artillery dropped 300 metres to the front. Deak walked the next spotting round forward, bracketing the enemy position, then called fire for effect, putting 36 shells into the bunker system. The platoon pulled back, and artillery further pounded the enemy position. Recce made its way back down the creek line, scouting for a harbour before dark. It was likely that Delta Company would move up at first light and follow the enemy. Deak figured he would sort that out later with the company commander; right now it was time to break contact, prop and lay-up.

After-contact plays hell with a soldier's nerves: every sense is notched up ten points. The smokers are dying for a smoke, the non-smokers have chewed their gum flavourless, breathing is short and sharp, everyone wants water for parched mouths. There is a critical need for silence, even when moving through bush that crackles and snaps with every foot-fall. The darkness under the double-canopy throws up shadows that with each movement send adrenaline coursing through the body.

Contact!

Blue Mulby's section and Bernie Smith's lead men saw four more enemy stand and dart across their front. Every weapon in Recce's forward section opened up with a wall of automatic fire.

'Five—five of the bastards!' Ferrier and Smith both yelled back as the first wave of automatic fire from the enemy came back, cutting across the platoon at just above knee-level. The men from Recce were already hugging the ground, burrowing into the hard dirt.

Crack, crack, crack, crack!

The sound of the enemy rounds passing overhead continued for several seconds.

Hug the ground, hug the ground.

Silence, apart from panting and the occasional expletive from men peering through the trees. The silence went on until Mick Deak called out, 'Anyone hit?'

Negative responses all round.

For a brief moment the silence returned to the jungle on the side of the mountain. But there was the pulsating of blood rushing around behind the eyes, inside the ear, and the sphincter was clenched to prevent something embarrassing happening. Eyes focused on the branches and leaves of the interesting bush in front of you. Look through it and past it to another bush. No green leaves; all is black and white. There is a grating sound, like sandpaper being pushed over wood. It's coming from close by. It's coming out of your mouth. It's you, breathing. Your mouth is so dry, it would just burn up if you threw a match in. You make a slow movement with your free hand down to your water bottle. Then a shout from behind—it's Deak. His voice is hoarse from that same dryness.

'Okay, up and sweep. Go now!'

The men moved forward in an extended line. Mulby was the first to spot the dead Vietcong. He knelt and examined the corpse after pulling clear the American-made Garand rifle.

'We got a KIA here, and it's a sheila!' he called out. He was shocked to find himself looking down at a beautiful young woman who moments earlier had been trying to kill him.

Deak was speaking to Delta Company HQ, seeking instructions on disposal of the dead enemy. He came over to Blue's section. 'Do the right thing and bury her.' Three soldiers dug in with their entrenching tools and lowered the dead woman into a shallow grave. One man placed a sprig of leaves on the dirt. Recce settled down for the night. Some of the men slept, others stared into the dark until first light.

Morning came with a promise of more heat to fry the men on the Long Hais, and Delta Company requested Recce platoon move back to the bunker system from the previous day's assault. The men from Delta already had their hands full, finding tracks left by at least 100 enemy.

'Well, Delta'll be shitting bricks for the rest of the day,' Mick Deak grunted as Recce approached the bunker system. There were 50 bunkers with connecting trenches and all had been concealed with those huge quilts of sewn leaves, identical to those in the Nui Thi Vai.

Strange things as well as Bad Things happen in war—behaviour, sights and sounds that are nothing special in themselves, but in the context of battles, brutality and death, become truly bizarre. Later that night the Vietcong were determined to have a meal of hot rice and fish, and they decided to do so just 200 metres from Recon Platoon across an impassable ravine. Each digger was on his back, feet propped against a boulder or a large tree stump to prevent rolling into the deep gully, watching the flickering light from the enemy's fire.

'You've gotta be bloody jokin',' said signaller 'Jacka' Aitken, echoing what every other exhausted man was thinking: in the middle of a huge operation directed against him, Charlie was brewing up at night over a camp fire.

'Bloody Nogs don't think we're up here. They reckon we've shot through, and they think the rest of the battalion can't see them,' whispered Mick Deak, taking the radio from his signaller. Deak had a hushed conversation with Battalion HQ and called up a mortar mission. It wasn't long before the first rounds came in, dropping short of the flickering camp fire. The fire's light vanished and Deak corrected the fall of the bombs—just as the flames reappeared. The light vanished again. Deak waited until what seemed like a cover was pulled from the camp fire, then called for another bombardment. The mortar rounds *crump*-ed across the ridge line. Minutes passed, then the fire reappeared once more. By now most of the platoon was grinning, sniggering and snorting like a bunch of men watching a football match.

'For Christ's sake, let the bastards have their meal,' said Mulby. 'Let's get some bloody sleep.'

Those who weren't already asleep from fatigue watched the fire glow on until past midnight.

THUNDER ALLEY

Flinders Ranges, 2000

We are sweating like crazy in the heat out here, but the purity of the air, the silence in the Ranges and the beauty is almost spiritual. It tops up your soul.

There's still the bugs and insects to annoy everyone, though. We have some great, scary bugs in Australia that chew you, chomp you and sting like hell. We are lucky there's no leeches in the Ranges. There's no double-pincered 'RTA' bug: one bite from that bastard and you're on a plane 'Returning to Australia'.

Scorpions . . . you think you've seen big scorpions? Try the lower slopes of Nui Nghe or near the Rung Sat in the Wet. They invented scorpions in those bloody places. They were black and yellow and scuttled around with claws extended like front-end loaders. Grown men shook at the sight of the full-grown Vietnamese scorpion. And everywhere was leech country. How many ways can you kill a leech? Squeeze it, stick a match up its rear-end and turn it inside out, toss salt on it or pass a Zippo over your own skin, watch the leech drop off and its anti-coagulant cause the blood to gush out of the hole it left behind. Get a leech down the eye of his dick and watch a soldier weep.

Blood suckers? There are none better or more powerful than Anopheles the Mighty Mosquito, airborne serial killer. He was a tiny bugger with a black-and-white-striped body, and he zoomed in like a Kamikaze pilot. He stuck his tube in your arm and took an almighty drink—and at the same time he'd transfuse a dozen different diseases that drove you mad, made you sweat to death or turned your brain to cheese.

Just one more bug that made Vietnam famous: the golden orb spider. Eight legs, big as a dinner plate, webs that would stop an APC in its tracks strung between rubber trees . . . walk into one of those and live the nightmare forever.

Vietcong? Stuff the Vietcong. It was the bugs that had you jumping out of your skin. And we haven't even discussed ants and snakes yet . . .

CONFIDENTIAL INTSUM: 14 August 1966—To harass or destroy large enemy concentrations deep in the jungle, giant eight-engine B52 jet bombers fly regular missions from Guam, 2400 miles away, and drop a wide variety of non-nuclear bombs that can obliterate an entire camp within seconds or penetrate the deepest bunkers and tunnels where the Vietcong are hiding.

Reconnaissance Platoon came back down off the Long Hais after being 'forgotten' and left out two days longer than anyone else. It was still February, and the Tiger Battalion had lost 10 KIA and 27 wounded in one month. For the Battalion Commanding Officer, John 'Wingy' Warr, it must have been a nightmare relived. Warr wasn't called 'Wingy' for nothing. He had joined the Army in 1944, served in Japan and with the 3rd Battalion (3RAR) in Korea before taking command of the 5th Battalion. It was during his service as a platoon commander in Korea that Warr, along with five of his men, had been blown up by a landmine. He was wounded by shrapnel in that explosion, and one of his arms was now partly paralysed—hence the affectionate nickname.

Warr had been instructed to bring his battalion back to Nui Dat. Sixth Battalion had also been recalled to the Task Force base. The reason for the 'reoccupation' was that intelligence indicated that the enemy's 275 Regiment had moved to within 16 clicks of the 'Dat.

But in February I had real problems of my own.

'You are a total dickhead!' Blue Mulby was shouting at me.

'You're a strobe, Dogs, you know that? Long periods of dullness with flashes of brilliance.' Suave Harve had his face next to mine. 'Right now you are really dull.'

Mick Deak was glaring at me. 'You do have your bad days, don't you, Dogs? No-one could be so totally stupid.'

Last was Bernie. 'Were you just completely pissed when you bought these, or are you taking the piss out of us?'

I was looking at the collection of long-playing records in Bernie's hands. I'd made a mess of things, and let the boys down. The day before, I'd arrived back from my week in Taipei on R and R leave. The men had given me a shopping list of LPs of their favourite artists and the money to buy a collection—Johnny Rivers, The Supremes, The Rolling Stones, The Four Seasons. I had dutifully flicked through the albums at the first record store I hit and grabbed an armful before getting drunk for the next four days.

Only now it wasn't the sounds of Johnny Rivers coming from the expensive stereos most of the men had already bought—it was the wail of a Chinese opera.

'That's right, Dogs, every LP is a Chinese opera!' Mulby was glaring at me, ready to inflict serious bodily injury. 'You've been bloody had.'

Not me, mate, I thought, *it was your money, not mine.*

I'd had a great time, and the one record I'd bought sounded just fine.

Mick looked at his four Supremes LP covers—he was a Supremes freak—and then back at me. 'Didn't you play 'em first?'

'And every tune is the damned same, for God's sake,' Bernie was at me again.

I went on the defensive. 'That's probably because the Chinks only ever made one opera in their entire history. Well, that's the last time I buy records for you fuckin' ungrateful lot!'

I sat in my tent, depressed, and sorted out the money I had to pay back, with Mulby's words ringing in my ears: 'Last bloody time! You're not wrong.'

Blue relented on his rage against his Chinese Johnny Rivers to suggest we go over to the B Company wet mess and have a drink. I went, and soon wished I hadn't: the bar was like a cemetery. A place I had previously visited and known as full of drink and cheer was a now a tin shed for the broken and dispirited. Mulby and I walked back in the dark not saying a word.

That same week two things happened: Mulby was promoted to Acting Sergeant of Recce Platoon, and John Lea-Smith moved across to Bravo Company as the acting CSM, temporarily replacing one of the many NCOs they had lost in the massive mine blast on the Long Hais. We saddled up next day and climbed aboard APCs to go on patrol. Deak had spread his map and indicated a large, dark green patch to the west.

'It may not be so dark and green when we get there,' he suggested. 'It's been pattern-bombed by a B52 air strike . . . we are doing a BDA.'

'What's a BDA?' asked Bob Searle, the new commander of Blue's section.

'Bomb Damage Assessment. How many trees knocked down and holes in the ground, maybe count dead VC,' Deak shrugged. 'It may be rough travellin'.'

The Reconnaissance Platoon men were basically grunts. Grunts were infantrymen who grunted and whinged everywhere they went. The grunt was the frontline soldier, the combatant. I always figured if I went into the Army I wanted to be a soldier, up the sharp end, closing with the enemy—whoever the enemy was going to be when I was 19 years old. I didn't join the Army to prop up a desk. I wanted adventure.

I must have been barking mad. The jungles of Vietnam were a

hothouse teeming with everything that slithered, crawled, jumped or sprang out from the closest bush. Not some Noggie booby-trap, but a cigarette-butt-size piece of slime that twisted and extended its neck, sniffing for animal heat—the Vietnam leech, that found you, latched on and then literally hooked in. During the last two patrols I had become aware of the damage these bastards could do. They got up under the trouser leg and silently went for you with a suction mouth that siphoned the blood out. They could get under your bush hat, and the first indication they were there would be blood trickling down into your eyes. The bastards got into your pants, even up under your eyelid. The bite marks festered, and you could lose your damn leg if the poison the leech left behind went through your blood stream.

We weren't in leech country now, but this was a nasty alternative. Down on my hands and knees, every part of my webbing and backpack entangled in a mesh of roots, vines and smashed foliage, I couldn't believe anyone would volunteer to be here, doing this, with another two days or more of it in front of me. I was now seeing, at stomach level, the effect of pattern bombing. The 500-lb bombs from the B52 Stratofortres had come down in thick forest and detonated in a long string of huge explosions. The men in the B52 would have had absolutely no comprehension of the hell they created on the ground. I'd heard that B52s were programmed to drop their load according to target coordinates loaded on a tape in the control console; or maybe a marker beacon was dropped first, sending the 'drop now' signal to the plane. In any event, the aircrew could have been reading *Playboy* when the bays opened and the bombs fell.

From where we were crawling, the effect was the destruction of every living thing above ground: every tree was flattened, with the smaller ones broken like toothpicks. It seemed that not a single leaf was left, everything had been blown away as if in a tornado. The resulting landscape resembled the aftermath of a firestorm or a hurricane.

Men crawled, tripped, stumbled, fell. We stopped to catch our breath. I turned to Deak.

'How come we got this shit job?' I asked. 'Aren't we supposed to be doing reconnaissance? Are we the Damage Police now?'

'Listen, Dogs, I'm as stuffed as you. The idea is to let the CO and the Yanks know how effective the bombing is.'

Mulby hissed at me through the entanglement. 'Keep your bloody voice down—every Nog for a mile around'll hear you.'

I tripped and fell, stood, became trapped in hanging vines, and fell on my arse again.

'A mile away? Give it up, Mulby, there wouldn't be a Nog within a hundred miles of this place—shit, it's the end of world as we know it. And what are we going to report when we get back? "Well, sir, we found a lot of trees that have fallen down and someone's been digging huge holes in the ground. Could be a lot of bombs may have fallen on the place." Jesus, if Deak asks for one of these again, we should shoot ourselves.'

We spent hours scrambling in a half-crouch or climbing across masses of trees that looked as if they'd been hit by a tidal wave. The bomb craters were so deep we couldn't walk down into them, so we struggled around their rims like ants, fighting for a purchase in dirt, muck and shattered roots. We were looking for bodies as well as making notes on the BDA.

You gotta be jokin', right? There's going to be any part of a human left in all this lot?

No sooner had the thought come and passed than Kenny Scaysbrook, one of Bernie's diggers, propped and pointed to the bottom of crater where parts of a man—or men—were scattered and burnt by the detonations. Scaysey squatted and peered down at the carnage, then at me.

'Tell you right now, I'm not going down there to work out how many there were, so don't even think about it.'

'Righto,' I hissed, 'keep movin' and let's get the hell outta this place.'

This was an aspect of the Vietnam War none of us felt comfortable about, like burning the huts on Long Son. There was a feeling of senseless destruction that had nothing to do with fighting for this country's freedom. But I quickly stopped myself thinking such things: the worst thing a soldier could do was try and rationalise.

I slumped for a moment on the side of a mound of dirt thrown up by a bomb blast. I lifted my arm and wiped my brow, then put my hand down again. Something, whatever it was, was watching me. I felt my scalp prickle for a moment and stared back at it. It had emerged from the bowels of the Earth, as long as my index finger, two claws extended and twitching in front of its head. The head was arrow-shaped, with two black eyes that gazed up at me; the body was similar to that of a swollen walnut, bright red with a dozen black hairs that stood upright. I counted four legs. It resembled a small crayfish, but the moment I saw it I knew it was the 'RTA' bug, the most revolting of all the things that slithered, scuttled or crawled in this godforsaken place. My hand was resting inches from it. I slowly drew it away. The claws twitched and moved up and down. Where else but Vietnam would a creature like this call home a place that had been bombed back to the Stone Age? It lived underground and made its unsuspecting and revolting appearance when some poor digger was hacking away at the Earth to excavate his weapon pit. It was almost as if getting below ground, away from the enemy, only drove you down towards something just as deadly. Only after an explosion had disturbed its underground existence would something like this come up for air. Its bite was said to be near-fatal. Was that another Vietnam deadly insect myth? I didn't care. I stood and grunted, slamming my rifle butt down. Its back arched and it died.

We sat back on our cots at Nui Dat and sucked on cans of beer. It was forbidden to drink beer in the lines, but like every other digger at the 'Dat, I couldn't care less.

'Know what "illegal" is, Dogs?' Bernie Smith winked at me. 'It's a sick bird.'

Bernie was trying to lighten the mood in his tent. He was leaving for Australia the next day. His time was up and he was going home.

Suave Harve jumped in. 'Here's one for you, Bernie. Minnie Mouse laid charges against Pluto for telling everyone she was crazy. Pluto beat the charges: he says in court, "I didn't say she was crazy, I said she was fucking Goofy." '

'That the best you can do, Harve?' Bernie was looking around his tent, capturing in his mind's eye things he would never see again.

The furniture was knocked together from old mortar boxes and shell cases, and the floor of the tent was banged together from duckboards. Everything in the soldier's small world was scrounged to make life bearable, and these small possessions were precious as gold. Bernie was proudly attached to his clothes 'cupboard'—a few planks of wood nailed together to hang clothes in. He was now staring at the vacant space where it had stood, then he glanced across the tent to where it now stood.

'Heck, somebody moved my dressing table . . . '

I laughed, and then thought how pitiful we had become; but we were also as tight as brothers whose world had shrunk to the basics of surviving.

'I'll miss you,' Bernie said between slugs on his can. 'I'll miss all the shit you got me into, but most of all I'll miss all the major shit you got me out of.'

UNCOMMON VALOUR

Flinders Ranges, 2000

Two men sit on the high ground, another two down near a spring, and a group is settled under a great gum tree. There is that eternal silence out here, broken only by the odd murmur of conversation. You walk around from group to group talking quietly, no loud conversation. It's like that in the Flinders, you said, everyone speaks in hushed tones. We are old soldiers, exchanging yarns like the old diggers from World War II who meet on Anzac Day in pubs and clubs and RSLs, gibbering on, comfortable in the bosom of mateship formed in the war years. We had fathers and grand-fathers in the RSL, and some Vietnam vets went to the RSLs when they came home.

One man pours coffee and begins to smoke. He tells us how he was given a cool greeting at his RSL, but not as bad as Ringo.

Ringo was a machine-gunner. He patrolled with his M60 tucked up under his arm and walked like a duck with splayed feet. We knew Ringo as one of the most popular blokes in 2RAR. When he grinned what you saw were two enormous front fangs—and Ringo grinned a lot. The last day we saw him in Vietnam was when he hobbled away from a chopper pad at a Fire Base up in Long Khan Province. His grin that day was a grimace and his eyes were almost standing out on stalks.

'You can stick this place right up your bloody arse,' said the gunner, who had run into a deadfall in a real heavy contact and smashed his knee badly. Contacts in those days were all really heavy because the TET Offensive had started and blokes were dying all over the place. A lot of us thought, this time we're gone, the Nogs are going to win this war.

Anyway, Ringo gets Medivaced out and says, 'There's no way in the bloody world I'm going back out there—three days, three bloody days we've had contacts with NVA.'

If any man in the world needed some support from old diggers when he came home it was Ringo. It would have been the late 1960s or early '70s that Ringo rocked up to his RSL club in a small town in the Blue Mountains, just outside Sydney. The poor bastard gets in the club and sits down to drink with a couple of World War II blokes. What do they say to him?

'You lost that one, didn't you, mate?'

Ringo knows he's getting pissed on by these guys, but he holds it in. They go at him again about how they won their Big One but we lost our Police Action. Ringo gets up to go.

'I don't need this shit,' he tells them.

They tell him not to bother to come back. That did it. Every atom of hate and bitterness in him exploded.

'Stick your RSL up your arse!' he yelled as he stormed out.

Pity that sort of thing had to happen in an RSL. But you'd never believe it: it was the late 1980s and we caught up with Ringo. He was the president of that RSL.

CONFIDENTIAL INTSUM: October 1966—Probable enemy reaction in the Nui Thi Vais is that the VC will seek to avoid contact with friendly troops.

Mick Deak walked from the 36th Evacuation Hospital in Vung Tau with mixed feelings about the war. He had commanded Recce through no fewer than 30 patrols in six months, and he was worn out. It was the bonding and unity of his men that had, on many occasions, kept him going and alert to his command— that and the small issue of staying alive.

But the sight of Lieutenant Jack Carruthers in hospital had been a sobering one; frighteningly real. You see dead enemy, you see dead soldiers, and then you see near-dead platoon commanders. Carruthers was the only man Deak knew who could stand on his head and drink a bottle of champagne. Deak was a punter, and immediately saw a quid in Carruthers's freakish gift. It wasn't long before Deak, a capable drinker himself, was able to con every American officer in every Officers' Club he visited with his upside-down drinking mate into taking a bet on something they believed was impossible. As 'manager and bookmaker', Deak quickly made big bucks out of the champagne stunt.

Now Carruthers was a dying man: shrapnel had entered his brain, and there were Deep Serious looks all round when Deak inquired of the surgeons about his wounded mates.

Bruce McQualter was also wounded in the head and was dying. Back at Nui Dat, Mick Deak was finding things a struggle in the Officers' Mess. Battalion Commander Warr made a valiant effort to keep morale up—and morale in the 5th Battalion had always been high—but there was an increasing number of vacancies at the dinner table.

Officers and other ranks alike viewed Deak as a man who operated out on the edge. Not for a moment was he careless; quite the opposite. He was super-efficient, capable, even courageous, but he was also a maverick, a larrikin and a loner. What few soldiers knew was that he was a platoon commander who cared passionately for his men: their safety and wellbeing were paramount, and he went to extraordinary lengths to minimise risk. Typical of this was his use of supporting fire in contact: Deak would call in 1000 air strikes if that would lessen the likelihood of the wounding or death of his men.

It may well have been some of those traits which saw him awarded the Military Cross.

During Operation Queanbeyan in October 1966 on the Nui Thi Vais, Deak was leading his Anti-Tank Platoon ahead of

Battalion Headquarters (BHQ) when they were cresting the north-west spur. Suddenly three shots rang out and Deak's scout saw a lone VC bolt. Deak knew an ambush was in the offing, and no sooner had he thought that than the BHQ behind him came under a hail of gunfire. For BHQ the situation was desperate: the Vietcong held the high ground and had blocked the only escape route from a ravine.

Deak slipped up onto the high ground unnoticed. Now the VC were between Deak's Anti-Tank Platoon and the BHQ. The platoon leader noticed that the VC were well concealed by a rockfall, and were gradually zeroing in on the BHQ group.

Colonel Warr ordered Deak to flush out the enemy. It was an instruction many commanders have given to many subordinates in many wars: 'to flush out' the enemy meant advancing, sometimes in the face of withering fire, and in face-to-face combat, to kill or be killed. On the rocky incline, Deak had a platoon of men who were totally exhausted after a 1300-foot climb lugging full packs and belts of ammunition. Now the objective was to move down over boulder-strewn terrain and take on a concealed enemy. Time was critical, as the BHQ group was struggling to save the life of one of their seriously wounded officers.

Deak told his men to drop their backpacks, then gave hurried instructions to his section commander, Norm Womal, to make the first move of a difficult fire-and-movement advance on the enemy. Deak would arrange cover while Womal took his men from boulder to boulder to try and surprise the Vietcong.

Sweating and gasping and moving from rock to boulder, Womal and his men had nearly completed the dash when a bullet ripped into Womal's throat. Deak could only watch in frustration as his wounded section commander fell out of view into a position horribly exposed to direct enemy fire. Bleeding profusely, Womal directed his men into fire positions before collapsing. Deak knew he had to get his section commander out as well as deal with the VC.

Meanwhile, BHQ had called in a small Sioux chopper from 161 Recce to evacuate the wounded Regimental Signals Officer, Captain Brian Ledan. While the pilot, Bob Askew, risked his life and his machine to lift Ledan out, platoon medic Peter Fraser (a National Serviceman) and platoon sergeant Ray 'Skinny' Calvert crawled to within speaking distance of the wounded Womal. Suddenly Fraser darted forward and threw himself next to the wounded man. Bullets were now raining down on the group, shattering fragments of rock and sending up fountains of earth. Deak watched as Fraser battled to save the life of his wounded mate by shielding him from fire and frantically trying to stop the flow of blood. It was one of the most courageous, compassionate and moving actions Deak had ever seen.

The platoon poured machine-gun fire onto the Vietcong, who were now directing all of their fire at Deak, the man they recognised as the platoon commander. Every time Deak yelled an order or instruction, he attracted a hail of bullets. Ray Calvert managed to get Norm Womal onto a stretcher and the rescue party man-handled their load around boulders and through undergrowth to the safety of battalion doctor Tony White. White's initial examination of Womal confirmed that most of the major blood vessels in his throat were torn through. A few minutes later he died.

Mick Deak went back on patrol—back to fighting the war—but there remained the vision of nearly four hours of blood and fire on the Nui Thi Vai. Months later, leaving the 36th Evacuation Hospital, he was still thinking about life and death, about dead friends Tich Tomas, Norm Womal and Jack Carruthers. But there was more than that on Deak's mind. He was wondering what it was that made men go beyond the call of duty as combatants. What made Peter Fraser, in the face of enormous danger, try to save a friend? And Ray Calvert had thought little of his own safety when getting Womal out. Another question: what prompted Womal to continue leading his men with part of his throat blown away?

In the cold sterility of the official recommendations for bravery—which saw Deak awarded the Military Cross, Fraser the Military Medal, and Womal the MID (Mentioned In Dispatches, Posthumously)—it read as if a few blokes had simply fought like hell and done brave things on a mountain. But Deak had to admit that he saw virtually *every* man on the Nui Thi Vais fight ferociously and act with total unselfishness and bravery.

Jesus, how about Bob Askew in that flying plastic bubble called a chopper? And the medical officer, Tony White—he was always there when men were dying.

In the end, the answer was probably quite uncomplicated: it was just something you knew you had to do. Leadership. Bravery. Medals for valour beyond the call of duty . . . imponderables.

PATIENCE AND THE RED

Flinders Ranges, 2000

Beautiful country near Hannigan Gap. Here the vegetation is amazingly varied, and we spend time poking about while you point out the unusual: mistletoe, parasitic plants that attach to gums, tobacco bush, and the spindly 'Dead Finish'—the one shrub that hangs on in the worst drought right through to the dead finish. Here also are sleepy lizards, blue tongues and skinks, and—high on the ridge—wild goats. Shoot the bastards!

We sit and smoke and talk about things that happened to you that you've never been able to speak of. Not Bad Things, but bizarre things that defied logic. Sure, everything in Vietnam defied logic, but some stuff is so way out you wouldn't even bring it up with friends and relatives.

You talk about your second tour of Vietnam and how you went on a night ambush down near Xuyen Moc. You were in thick bush at a triple track junction, and you suddenly recognised the place from your first tour. There had been an almighty fight down here, and up to 20 VC were killed and buried near that junction. Nothing unusual about this: after a couple of years in Vietnam you were always revisiting Bad Places where horrible things had happened. You were sitting that night watching the killing ground in front of the ambush location when three huge monitor lizards came out of the jungle. Through the greenish flaring of the starlight scope you saw them lurch forward with that lizard gait, tongues flicking, picking up scent, and they started digging in the sand. Jesus, they were pulling up bits of body almost two years old. This was the stuff of horror films—lizards stalking off into the jungle carrying bits of dead people.

Then there was the incredible story from the Regimental Medical Officer, Major Peter Byrne, who told of the digger who stuck his head around a tree: a VC bullet entered one side of his forehead, zapped around the front of his head and burst out the other side. You'd think that'd kill a bloke for sure, right? Not according to the RMO who 'tidied him up' after he was dusted off and sent him on to the US 93rd Evacuation Hospital, where the neurosurgeons fixed up the front part of his brain. RMO Byrne got a call from the CSM of the digger's company a while later: the CSM asked if Byrne could do the same for some other soldiers. It turns out the wounded soldier had been a real aggro smart-arse before he was shot in the head, but now was a quiet bloke with a great attitude. Yep, the bullet had lobotomised him—and made him a better man.

You can laugh about that, but what wasn't so funny was the day we rode through the village outside Vung Tau and there were all these young Vietnamese kids looking up at us while they dragged on cigarettes. In the middle of the group was one small girl of about five, with blond hair and blue eyes. Angelic . . . and what the hell was she doing there? Who was she? Just another Vietnamese waif, the product of a union between a white soldier and a Vietnamese woman. Where is she now?

CONFIDENTIAL INTSUM: July 1966—There can be little doubt the communists are bringing in more materials and men. A US military official disclosed Hanoi is now infiltrating at least 5500 troops per month and the tempo could conceivably rise.

Mick Deak stood and lifted his head, almost air-scenting like a field dog. The platoon commander wasn't smelling anything; he was sensing something.

Recce had patrolled quietly for the past few hours, checking tracks and trails for enemy movement. It was a tedious task, making notes and cross-checking with maps: more pieces in the jigsaw of intelligence. The VC were thought to be advancing in numbers from the east towards the ATF base, according to latest Intel. Like all intelligence, this was part fact, part fiction. There was no question the enemy were out there in numbers, from platoon to company size; maybe even a battalion of up to 500. As to their intentions, however, who knew? They could have been on a training jaunt so far as Recce was concerned, or they could have been massing to form a mega-unit for a grand assault.

Forward scouts Page and Ferrier had alternated in front of my section and Blue Mulby's. Stop, start, creep forward. Listen for sounds, those give-away sounds—chopping, talking or the crackle of breaking bush. At track and trail junctions we would stop in silence for 10 minutes. If we were bounced by enemy, or we bounced them, let everything go at once—shoot and tear-arse out to a pre-designated RV a kilometre or more away.

Deak was nudging his signaller, Jacka Aitken, to grab the radio and come with him.

The two men melted away among clumps of bamboo without a word to the rest of us. It was fairly typical of Deak to go off and do his own thing, carry out his own one-man reconnaissance.

The truth was that this time Deak, a master map-reader, wasn't certain of his Locstat. His doubts had emerged as he was 'bedding down' his DF (Defensive Fire) coordinates for the night. Deak was always conscientious about correct map-reading, and now he wasn't sure where he was; he needed a visual check of nearby trails to confirm to himself that he was on the money.

As he worked away from the rest of the platoon, Deak thought about his eight months in-country and about his paranoia. Had he really developed a sixth sense since he came to Vietnam? Was the prickle he was feeling now an indication he was very close to the enemy? Too close? He could always pick up the smell of the

Vietcong—their hair, their body smell—but could he detect their presence by premonition? At this moment, and for minutes before, he had a premonition that they were very close.

He and Aitken reached an ox-cart track. It was the one Deak had been looking for, and he went to ground and pulled out his picto and topographical maps to confirm his Locstat. At the same time he felt a coldness wash over him.

They are close. Do not go out on that track. Lay down flat.

Deak noticed Jacka Aitken was shrugging his pack. The young Nasho was getting impatient, and nodded to Deak. 'Can we go now?'

Deak placed a finger over his lips and rolled his eyes out towards the track.

They're here. Very, very close. Not a sound. No voices. They're getting closer.

He looked back at Aitken.

Quiet. Wait.

The two men rolled onto their stomachs and waited. Five minutes felt like an hour. Ten minutes passed, laden with sweat and quiet breathing. This was Recce's job: long spells of patrolling with nothing, just squatting and waiting. Patience was one of the keys to survival as a Reconnaissance group—patience, and listening to that small inner voice. But what if—

There were always the 'what if's, Deak thought to himself while the patrol headed back to its RV for the night stop . . . and then another ambush on another track. It wasn't actual incidents—contact and an exchange of fire with the enemy, or even a landmine blast—that stuck with a soldier and stayed locked in the mind, replaying when he tried to sleep. It was always the 'what if's.

Think back to the fight on the Long Hais—what if the platoon had gone into that bunker system 12 hours earlier? There could easily have been 100 enemy soldiers in there. Deak would have seen his men chopped to pieces. He would have called arty in to compare with the Battle of Long Tan. But on a mountainside, with no APCs charging in like the cavalry and no way to effectively Casevac, Deak was certain the platoon would have been wiped out.

I was at the Grand Hotel in Vung Tau during an R and C break when I met my first US Army deserter. His name was Red. He was tall and lanky with long red hair. We fell into talking and I stupidly asked him why he was called Red.

'Well, buddy, if I was an Aussie you'd call me "Blue", right?'

I then launched into an explanation of why Aussies with red hair were called Blue, bald blokes were called Curly, and short and tall guys were Shorty and Lofty, respectively. Red became serious when I asked him why he had shot through during a break in Saigon and was now in Vung Tau.

'Had a gutful of the war. Didn't want to be here in the first place. There's a group of us living together down here now, behind the Ganh Rai mountains.' Red nodded his head and indicated the range of hills we had practised on when we were training for Recce with the SAS men. 'Got us a bunch of shacks; we fish, comb the beach and come in to Vungas every now and then on our Harleys.'

I liked Red straight away, and the fact he had deserted didn't seem to bother me too much. I could understand why he did it—I knew GIs by the platoon-load were opting out of the war. I'd heard some had shot through to Thailand and gone native; or never returned from R and R in Hong Kong or Taipei; or had even gone totally feral and were hiding out in small highland villages. These men almost qualified for Missing In Action; certainly, they would be MIAs when the war finished. What I couldn't figure was how come they weren't picked up by the MPs or White Mice in Vung Tau.

'Money and contacts, buddy. The only thing we can't do, and we probably never will be able to do, is go back stateside. We've condemned ourselves to living here for the rest of our days.'

Red gazed off across the bar for a while then spoke again.

'But it's better being alive here than going home in a body bag. This war sucks, you gotta agree. There's not a fucker in this country, other than Charlie, who knows what the hell he's doing here.'

We talked on for a while, and I started wondering if Red was full of garbage and not a deserter at all. He finished his drink, said goodbye, and headed for the main entrance of the Grand. I quietly followed him—and watched him climb onto a gleaming Harley. He spotted me and waved with a grin as he gunned the big bike into the traffic.

MARATHON MEN

Flinders Ranges, 2000

A bush track outside Oratunga Station and two men are sweating and grunting beneath a big Land Rover. They bang at the exhaust, muttering, until one realises he was in Vietnam the same year as the other—same battalion, same company, same platoon.

'You gotta be jokin', right? I bought a new Monaro when I came home.'

'Yeah? Me too. Canary yellow, two black stripes down the bonnet.'

'No shit? Mine was blue . . . with two black stripes.'

Everyone in Vietnam had a dream car waiting when they came home.

Your car fanatic was Ribs. He came from a place outside Lithgow in New South Wales, hoon territory in the early '60s—and to hear him tell it, everyone up there was infected with the Bathurst 500 bug. Rib's dream was the ultimate car: a 1964 EH Holden, worked over with a shaved head, a set of extractors and a straight-through exhaust system. Ribs, whose most noticeable feature was his prominent rib cage, went on for bloody hours about this car and what he was going to do to it: block the back suspension and cut the springs on the front, lower the thing to within an inch of the ground and armour-plate the bottom. He was going to slam on seven-inch-wide wheels—chrome, of course—then tear out the column shift and anchor in a four-on-the-floor.

But the big thing was colour: seven coats of metallic blue. This was going to be the hottest-looking machine in Australia. Ribs needed money, and Vietnam was a godsend: can't spend, gotta save.

Ribs walked through the war talking nothing but The Car. At night he'd whisper about how bloody great it was going to be and how every cent of his money was going back to the four mates in the workshop in Lithgow. Most of us counted down to the girl back home and how we were going to work her over; Ribs was counting down to the blue rocket and the sexy tachometer fixed to the dash.

He took all the misery of the war and grunted through until we landed back on Australian soil, then he was gone in a cloud of dust and small pebbles, headed for that Lithgow workshop.

It must have been two weeks later, he was back at Ingleburn Army camp. He was driving some clapped-out old Falcon.

'Ribs, Ribs, where's the bloody dream machine?'

Ribs looked miles away and mumbled, 'Back home in the shed.'

You watched him and waited. 'Yeah, right . . . ?' you said finally.

Ribs was quiet for a while then added, sort of dreamily, 'It was beautiful, mate, beautiful. Drove it out on the big sweeper on the Lithgow road and rolled it five times. It's a fucking write-off.'

Everyone in Vietnam needed a dream car to come back to.

CONFIDENTIAL INTSUM: January 1967—NVA soldiers sent to fight in the South quickly discover life is filled with hardships. The need to continually move is a drain on the energy of troops. NVA troops suffer from disease, hunger and exhaustion.

The four APCs were just inside the rubber near Binh Ba, and were getting a fair rock-and-roll up as part of a deception plan the Special Air Service had dreamed up. The lead machine, with Blue Mulby's section on top and inside, rumbled towards the end of the tree line. Behind, in the other three, were Mick Deak and the other two Recce sections. Mulby's APC slowed as it reached the end of the old plantation and the rubber tappers' road, and suddenly its back lowered. At the same time our three carriers revved their engines. The SAS patrol—men loaded up, and faces black and green with camouflage cream—ran down the back ramp of Mulby's carrier and in an instant disappeared into the thick bush. The rear ramp was pulled up and the carrier accelerated away. Any VC in the area would have been deceived by the rolling deployment, with the lead carrier's gear change and the drop in revs concealed by our revving motor.

It was a variation on another trick, where all the carriers ground to a halt and Recce and the SAS men dismounted and went walkabout. Returning an hour later, only Recce got back on board while the SAS patrol was quietly moving away, and still moving by the time we headed back to Nui Dat. There was no way we would ever know if the ruse worked, but it made the war interesting.

It was late in the day on a road heading south to the 'Dat. This was farmland: patchworks of paddy, open paddock, the occasional clump of thatched huts, or homes constructed from compressed kerosene tins. This was peaceful, pastoral Vietnam, the heart of the Phuoc Tuy food basket. These people in their conical straw hats, women with babies strapped to their backs and children holding a shielding hand to their forehead as we rumbled by, were the ones we were fighting for. Freedom was an abstract thing. I knew freedom as part of my life in Australia, but I had no concept of the lack of freedom. I was walking around the jungle, presumably to ensure freedom and a way of life for those people living in the compressed kerosene-can houses. But what of those other people—those dressed in black and khaki, those fighting for freedom? Their concept of freedom was a lot more intense: to fight and to rid their country of invaders, foreigners—us.

The APCs had got up to a fair stick, throwing clouds of dust behind them. Men were clinging to anything they could hang on to and we had wrapped sweat-rags around our mouths to prevent swallowing the choking red dust. Even in this semi-safe zone you watched the fields and those lounging outside their homes.

Never switch off.

Suddenly Mulby yelled and pointed into a paddy field. The sight was appalling: an old cow with a huge chunk of shrapnel hanging from its rump.

'For God's sake, do something to put it out of its misery,' the crew commander yelled at us.

Mulby jerked his M16 up to his shoulder and fired. The shot failed to hit a vital spot and ripped at the animal's underbelly. The carriers were still moving.

'Call yourself a rifleman?' I yelled at him. 'You couldn't hit a bull in the arse with a handful of wheat.'

I had to put my money where my mouth was—for personal esteem as well as the cow's welfare—so I raised the Slaughter-matic. Allowing for the tilt and rock of the APC I snapped off one shot. Blood spurted from the cow's neck and it dropped to the ground. I was the most surprised man on the APC.

The carrier commander spun around. 'You shot for the jugular so it would die quickly, right? Why not his brain?'

'Cows only have small brains—same size as Suave Harve's.'

Mulby grinned. 'That was arse, Kearney, pure arse. You couldn't do that again if your life depended on it.'

About 6 kilometres south-east of the ATF base was Dat Do, a medium-sized town of several thousand souls and of strategic importance because of its location in central Phuoc Tuy. On a topographical map, just half a click to Dat Do's north is a feature shaped much like a horseshoe: an extinct volcano with the southern part of its caldera blown away. No military commander could ignore using this natural defensive and offensive feature, and on 6 March 1967 at 0700 hours the operation to take over The Horseshoe was launched.

This was part of an ATF masterplan. First, establish a permanent presence of at least a company-sized infantry unit on The Horseshoe. Second, place an artillery battery inside the crater in order to extend artillery range in the province by at least 5000 metres (the only permanent artillery fire base was at Nui Dat). Third, build a huge barbed-wire fence from The Horseshoe east of Dat Do and straight down to the South China Sea. Inside this fence will be seeded 20,000 anti-personnel mines.

By any yardstick this was a major military development for the Australian command: it would prohibit huge numbers of enemy moving freely across southern Phuoc Tuy, from the jungles and badlands in the east to the populated food-producing centres in the west. The 100-yard-wide minefield, with protective barbed-wire fences on either side, would be covered by South Vietnamese troops—who would patrol to prevent the VC stealing mines, as well as manning outposts along the fence line—and by machine-guns on The Horseshoe.

Immediately there were misgivings about the plan, the main one being that patrolling would not work, as the VC were active at night. Permanent guard posts were the answer, but there was still the question of reliability with respect to the local military forces. Every man, from the grunt to the senior echelons, knew the likely cost in death and wounding if the mines were lifted—and used against us.

Reconnaissance Platoon was under the command of the hard-hit Bravo Company, which on its first night hunkered down into an ambush on the main approach to The Horseshoe. In the early hours of the morning 25 Vietcong decided to recce the Australians' latest position. It was a fatal move for four of them, who were chopped up by machine-gun. The Vietcong desperately tried to recover their wounded, and probed B Company until well after 0230 hours.

We moved onto the south-west corner of The Horseshoe's rim and constructed a bunker pit for a .50 calibre machine-gun.

'The job is this,' said Blue Mulby a day or two later. 'No great shakes, we're to walk in front of the bulldozers while they clear the slopes of The Horseshoe before the wire goes up.'

Suave Harve, myself and gunner Bluey Twaits looked at the Acting Sergeant and made funny noises.

'To do what?' I asked.

'Look out for unexploded shells, buried bombs, booby-traps, all that shit. Because if it goes off, Dogs, it'll damage the machinery.'

Ken Scaysbrook shook his head. 'Sorta like human mine detectors, Blue, we go *beep beep* if we see a mine . . . '

'And *bang bang* if we see a booby-trap,' I chipped in. 'Sounds foolproof . . . '

Mulby could detect a Dogs-style debate coming on. 'Just use your initiative, Dogs.'

The Dat Do populace did not take kindly to plans for a minefield, or to the 6pm curfew we had now imposed on working in the paddy fields around the new Aussie base.

I watched a group of farmers lead their water buffalo home, struggling to beat the clock. We fired a flare into the air on curfew; anyone outside the village after that was considered fair game. As a result, the Vietnamese farmers were finding that they had to crank up their slow lifestyle.

I sat in the bunker on The Horseshoe and thought, *they've been farming this land for 1000 years, who the hell are we to come in and tell them to go home at dusk? And how would they know the time, anyway? Most can't afford a block of soap, never mind a bloody watch.*

No sooner had we settled into patrols around the new base than Wingy Warr sent us out to Xuyen Moc. This was the last outpost, a village manned by friendlies in the far east of Phuc Tuy province, not unlike the lonely fort surrounded by 'redskins' on the plains of the old American West.

'No problem here either, troops,' said Mulby as we walked down to the APCs. 'Goes like this: we sit in the trim vanes (or splash ramps) and watch for mines as we go down the road.'

Suave Harve looked at me and I looked back at him. 'These bastards are working on the best way to reduce numbers,' he commented. 'Ride in the fucking splash ramp?'

The trim vanes made up the front wooden flap on a carrier. When the vehicle entered water—APCs could motor across streams and rivers—the ramp dropped down to prevent water flowing up and over the driver. You could sit behind the ramp and watch the road flashing beneath the carrier—which is what we did on one of the most notoriously mined roads in the province for 17 kilometres to Xuyen Moc. We clanked and squeaked and generally held our breath all the way along Route 23 into the VC territory of the province's far east. The road was cleared by man and machine, but it was hours before the howl and thump of the carrier ride cleared from the ears and head. That night at Xuyen Moc: set an ambush. Early next day: walk back to The Horseshoe.

I had felt exhausted many a day in Vietnam during the past eight months, but the trek-cum-patrol back to The Horseshoe was one of the toughest hikes any of us had done in the war. On the topographical map the distance was 15 grid squares—15 kilometres. We shouldered our main packs and made ourselves as comfortable as possible for a patrol that would cover almost all types of terrain—high and low ground, moderate jungle, open grasslands and bamboo in sandy soil . . . mine country. It was dry heat, slightly overcast, and in less than an hour every man in Recce was saturated, his green uniform turning black as the perspiration poured out by the bucket-load.

The platoon spaced out or closed up, depending on the ground. I watched Pagey in front of me, studied him for hours until I knew every crease in his shirt and every detail of his pack. I watched his small stove as it swung backwards and forwards on his main pack. Pagey had nearly won the Stove Competition. A quirky feature of the war was a competition to see who could make the best stove for personal cooking. This simply involved taking an empty ration can and puncturing and shaping it so that it gave the most effective heat for cooking. A civilian observing this stupidity would consider the participant mad. To the grunt it was a small diversion; a moment's humour. You used a can-opener to open the sides to allow ventilation, and curved back the top to create a ring on which to stand a can of food. The Hexamine block or small C4 pebble sat in the bottom of the tin, and the better it flared the faster the cooking. But what mattered wasn't so much the effectiveness of the heating as what the thing looked like when the artisan had completed his handiwork. Pagey's was a beauty, I had to admit—better than mine.

At times like this a soldier's mind drifted . . . mine drifted to my backyard back home and the 1938 Vauxhall that the cops had ordered to stay there until it was roadworthy again. The wallopers had found me driving along the footpath and collared me. One look at the relic my stepfather had forked out £30 for, and the vehicle was given the thumbs down. The cops said the brakes were shot, I claimed they weren't: they did slow me down even if they didn't stop me first time. But the black Vauxhall was off the road and that was final.

I was going to turn that 'Vauxhy' into a hot rod. Rip off the front fenders and chop the roof and look like James Dean in *Rebel*

Without A Cause. It'd be rusted a bit when I got back but, tramping the rice paddys of Vietnam, I figured I could turn the old bomb into a great set of wheels.

Five clicks, and we collapsed on the edge of dry paddy and thick undergrowth. Deak had worked out bearings that took us near Route 23, the road we'd come up on in the APCs. But this 'walk' back was in fact a recce—we were watching, observing, making notes on track movement and examining deserted enemy camps. Right now the enemy was forgotten; we were gasping to get our wind back. Physically we were exhausted; each man felt his mental faculties evaporating in the day's heat. This was a dangerous time, and passing the 10,000-metre mark I felt the ache in my shoulders from my 60-pound pack begin to spread to my lower back. The pain was reaching agonising proportions. Another stop, and each man hunched over his knees, barely a word spoken. Twaits, Wollner and Riley, lugging the big M60s and belts of link ammo, were panting and going red in the face.

Water, get water in. We've got to drink.

My smoke tasted like camel shit, so I butted and buried it.

The landscape began to open up to working paddys, and the fence and military posts around Dat Do finally appeared just as the sun began to dip. Vietnam had some of the most beautiful sunsets in the world—they could actually stop you in your tracks, and we were glad this one did.

Deak set us in a lay-up while he contacted battalion command. Minutes later Mulby came down the line. 'Sorry, you poor bastards, we've been told to set an ambush.'

No-one spoke; not a man groaned at the sheer injustice of it all. We were being asked to stay awake all night after the punishment of a marathon route march.

Jesus, that's not asking much, is it?

We lay in ambush that night, and I reckon everyone manning the machine-guns went to sleep. Frankly, no-one gave a stuff.

From Mick Deak down to tail-end Charlie, every man in Recce was now reaching an all-time low. Patrolling and ambushing day and night had stripped away all reserves of energy, and there was a real risk that our lack of alertness could be fatal.

Next morning outside Dat Do, Mick Deak sent my section on surveillance. 'Check the locals and try not to be seen, Dogs,' Deak said, chinographing a rough route for me to follow on my map.

We had walked for a click when I told Bob Godfrey, 'Stuff it, take a break and brew up.'

Bob squatted near me and began munching crackers. I smoked, watching the locals in the paddys going about their business. A child was riding on the back of a massive water buffalo.

'Bob, how is it those kids treat the buffaloes like pets, but the bloody things get aggressive with us round-eyes if we go near them?'

He thought for a minute then said, 'It's your smell, mate, they hate your smell.'

'Bullshit. They can't have any sense of smell living in those villages.'

'No, no, no,' Bob lit up an after-lunch smoke. 'We eat meat, Nogs eat fish, the buffalo can smell meat coming out of you and thinks you're a predator—wants to stamp the living shit out of you. Got it?'

I thought, *Bob's a clever bugger, I never would have thought of that.*

I reached over for my pack, but instead my hand sank into something soft and squishy. I knew in a flash what it was. For the first time in the war I felt I was going to snap. Bitterness, frustration, anger, hatred, suppressed resentment—the whole lot came up like lava in a volcano. I sprang to my feet and screamed out at the peasants.

'Fuck you and all your fucking relatives, build a bloody shit pit if you can't afford toilets!'

'You still don't understand Asians, do you Dogs?' Bob was back to his philosophical self. 'It's their way of fertilising the ground. Two birds with one stone—they fertilise and dump their shit.'

I was now pouring my hot brew all over my hands to get the mess off. Insult and injury—I'd been shat on by the locals *and* lost my hot brew. I was still gasping from my outburst; even the chuckles from the men hadn't rubbed off. I normally joined in on any joke, but not now. I wondered if I was starting to crack.

'It's too unhealthy around here. Barney, and you, too, Bob, dump your brews, we're pissing off. I'm asking Deak for a Purple Heart after this lot.'

WAR WEARY

Flinders Ranges, 2000

Ian Fargher, who owns the sheep station, comes out this afternoon and puts a spread on for us veterans. It's the classic Australian barbecue—steaks that hang over the edge of the plate, sausages, and lashings of fried onions. Piles of chops and potatoes, diced, sliced and served up with bowls of salad. Then there are huge chunks of homemade bread and a special sauce to pour over it all. It brings tears to our eyes.

Food.

In the war it wasn't as if we were fed a Third World diet—we were certainly more nourished than the diggers who fought in the two Big Ones—but there were things you missed. And one of those was simply eating a meal in comfort and security. It sounds stupid, but try eating a pasty-coloured egg omelette out of a can, all the time waiting for Charlie to wander in and interrupt your lunch. But some of the blokes could eat absolutely anywhere: you once wolfed down a tin of ham and lima beans—God, that was shocking stuff—while bodies were being dug up for identification and a document search. Was it that you were just too hungry to wait, or more that you were so familiar with gruesome sights and smells you just didn't give a toss?

We packed and carried everything to eat when we were going into the 'j', but at times you looked at the prospects for dinner—biscuits, cheese, bacon and beans in a can, and curry powder—and thought, stuff it. You had three cigarettes instead. Your weight dropped, your condition deteriorated and your stomach shrank.

Back at Nui Dat we always had a company barbie after an operation. They backed a trailer full of ice and beer into that little area with stools and tables knocked together by the Assault Pioneers. The cooks had acquired a pile of steaks and spuds, and we settled back into a little bit of Australia for an hour, fanging away on steak and sauce wrapped in a freshly baked roll. Amazing how such a commonplace occurrence—like this here today—could mean so much to a soldier.

But what about all the poisons? You know, that stuff that came out of the skies, sprayed over thousands of acres; settled down on the Vietnamese veggie gardens, filtered down into the soil and eventually reached the water table. On it went into the creeks and streams. We drank the water and ate the veggies, and those insidious toxins found their way into our blood systems.

Years later we realised that maybe fresh food was the one thing we should never have eaten in Vietnam.

CONFIDENTIAL INTSUM: January 1967—Both the level and intensity of VC-initiated activity increased during the reported period. Enemy attention was directed against ARVN and PF units . . .

The Reconnaissance Platoon split into three groups for a patrol east of the big new mine fence now well under construction running south from Dat Do. The 5th and 6th Battalions were still conducting major Search and Destroy operations east of Nui Dat, as the main enemy threat was believed to be to the east and northeast—the jungle areas around Xuyen Moc, Thua Tich and further out near the Mao Tao Secret Zone. These were terrible places— the thickest forests, the biggest enemy bunker complexes, and low mountains that showed as dark, menacing patches on our maps. The NVA used these zones as training and staging areas: to go in, Allied Forces needed significant numbers and heavy backup.

'Search and Destroy' was the term used to describe a precise, almost surgical military operation where Australian soldiers hunted down and killed the enemy. But the reality wasn't quite that neat: the Australians and the VC wandered around the same jungle looking for each other. When they bumped into each other, the best team on the day won. To date, our team had been doing the winning.

Contact with the enemy usually lasted no more than a matter of seconds, and there was no indication of how many VC the Recce Platoon killed or wounded. But those seconds seemed like hours. Mick Deak described contact as always feeling like slow motion: in an instant you see the expression on each of your men's faces—eyes wide, mouth open, and a burst of high energy.

We stopped for a break and I caught a whiff of rotting vegetation. Smells and Vietnam. Everything in this place had a smell. When the monsoon came the country was purified. You knew the daily downpour was on its way because you could smell it; carried on a slight breeze, it tingled the nostrils. Nui Dat was the stale stink from the urine pipes, the 'piss-a-phones'; the almost gagging stench from the six thunderboxes; and the fogging machines during the weekly spray around the tents to kill the mosquitoes. That same insecticide was dumped on the ATF base by the Hercules: it came down in an invisible cloud and stung your eyes. Then there was the smell of the villages, a putrid concoction of buffalo dung, fish heads and cooked rice—the same smell we'd detected a mile offshore from Vung Tau back when we were arriving in-country. That seemed like a century ago now.

Mick Deak came back from relieving himself in the jungle and watched us eating. He wore a mischievous look on his face while he splashed water from his water bottle over his hands and face. Officers: all manners and cleanliness. He winked, hauled open his pack, and dragged out what looked like a sandbag. He upturned it and spilled the contents on the ground. Another grin, then he whispered, 'Tucker time, men.'

Mulby and I looked at the bright shining cans of mussels and crabmeat, the jars of pickles, sardines and oysters that lay before us. Deak just grinned on like a fool. 'Spread 'em among the diggers, men.'

I was stunned. 'Skip, that's Officers' Mess stuff . . . '

'Yeah, I picked it up before we came out.' He took on a mock pained expression. 'I pay mess fees, you know, Dogs. We get privileges, but we have to pay for them. What's wrong with bringing some of this stuff out bush? Don't want those bastards back there fanging it all . . . how do you feel about pâté, Dogs?'

The Reconnaissance Platoon RV'd late in the afternoon and we all climbed back onto the APCs. Our destination was soft, sandy tracks not far from Phouc Loi, 1500 metres south of Dat Do on Route 44. I sat on the back of the rear carrier with my section and watched the scrubby paddy fields whiz by. A group of Vietnamese soldiers appeared on the side of the road. The ARVN men were generally a happy lot: they looked small, almost childlike in their hand-me-down US uniforms, and most had grins permanently fixed on their faces. They were always puffing on cigarettes, and carried their rifles on their shoulders as if they were out on a deer-hunting party. One young soldier gave me a wave and I saw that he wore rubber thongs instead of boots. We swung off the road and into a paddy in the general direction of our night location. Covering our rear, I continued to watch the ARVN patrol make its way along the main road, and then *crump!*—an orange flash and black smoke and a man tumbling through the air before crashing down in the dry paddy.

'Stop the tracks, *stop the tracks!*' the APC commander wasn't listening and I jabbed him in the head with my rifle butt.

I yelled at the carrier commander, 'Tell my boss an ARVN bloke's been blown up on the road. We're getting off.'

We dismounted and I started barking instructions. 'Blue, take the gun to the right with Bob. Pagey, take the left with Barney and Max. Little Mac, with me.' I waved both arms to get an extended line to move up to the blast site.

'Slow down, it ain't a race.' Everything was moving quickly now, and the anxiety rate was rising—*mines again*.

I suddenly realised I'd forgotten my rifle. I shouted to my men, 'Go to ground. I've left my rifle on the carrier. Won't be a tick.'

By this time Blue Mulby and Deak had reached me, along with Bob Searle's section.

'Forget something, Dogs?' Mulby was looking past me, fighting to keep a straight face.

'Root your boot, Mulby, if I hadn't seen the poor bastard blown up, you'd still be hoofing it over the paddy.'

Mick Deak took control and spread the platoon in a defensive perimeter, at the same time calling for a dustoff chopper.

'Don't any of you blokes go walkabout—there could be more mines,' Blue Mulby stated the obvious as we took up fire positions.

At that moment I had to blink to believe what I was seeing. The young Vietnamese soldier in thongs walked calmly along the side road—which he certainly knew was mined—into the paddy, which also had to be mined, then towards his wounded friend. He bent, hoisted his wounded comrade onto his shoulder, then walked back to the road, where he lowered the bleeding man to the ground. We watched, then applauded.

'Unbloodybelievable,' said Twaits, who was on his knees clapping.

The dustoff chopper came clattering in near the APCs, and we cleared a route to the wounded man. Blue Mulby came over to me.

'He's had the shit blown out of him and not one word of complaint, Dogs, not a single grizzle. Just wants to know if he's still got his balls. I told him he had but there's a helluva lot more missing—he ain't gonna make it.'

We patrolled into the scrub and located the foot track. Deak gave field signals to prop and ambush. One M60 machine-gun faced south and the other, Bob Searle's—carried by Dave Wollner—faced north. We were spread both sides of the well-used foot trail with machine-guns pointing outwards at both ends. Anyone using the track would walk smack into a 100-round belt. This was different from a normal ambush, and it was a Recce speciality. Every man was armed to the teeth with a full comple-ment of automatic weapons, from M60s to automatic SLRs and M16 Armalites.

I couldn't erase the image of the wounded ARVN soldier from my mind as I sat on gun sentry that night. The starlight reflected from the road, and I saw the flash and heard the *crump* again. Then I saw the young man walk calmly in to recover his mate.

In a few months I'd be gone from this war, hopefully with all my bits and pieces intact. Those young Vietnamese would still be here, possibly fighting on for years. Fighting and dying. Bravery was an everyday occurrence with the Vietnamese soldier. We derided him, but there was absolutely no question about his courage. And there was no debate about the VC, either. Those bastards kept coming at us day and night in the face of over-whelming odds.

I felt suddenly chronically fatigued. A great weariness washed over me—the energy gushed down through my legs to my feet, then into the track's sandy soil. I wanted to go home. I wanted out. I wanted to kill any VC that was in the way of me or my mates, and I wanted to leave this place forever.

Peasants, farmers, ARVN, Vietcong, North Vietnamese Army . . . who's against us and who's for us? I don't care about what's right and wrong any more. I'm too fucked up . . .

Since Operation Hardihood—the push that began the securing of Phuoc Tuy and laid the foundation for the building of the ATF base—the war had been wearing us down, taking another year off our lives with every week in-country. I felt weak, scared and alone. Would I be up to another fight, another day or another week in the jungle? I'd seen the same weariness in the face of every man in the battalion. The words from week one in Vietnam came back: *They didn't tell us it was going to be this bad . . .*

March 18, 1967 and the North Vietnamese, along with local Vietcong, were ready to mount another mass attack against the Australians and the South Vietnamese in southern Phuoc Tuy. The combined force, which rendezvoused on the eastern side of the Song Rai River, numbered about 1500—a combination of NVA regular soldiers from the 275 Regiment and the Regional D445 VC Battalion. This was, in essence, a mix of experienced troops trained in full-on combat tactics and VC trained to fight and hold ground guerilla-style.

The thrust of the attack was an outpost defended by 38 Provincial Force soldiers at a tiny military camp called Lo Gom, about six clicks south of The Horseshoe. Provincial Force members were peasants by day, soldiers by night. Part of the bigger picture was for the enemy to strike a psychological blow against the Australians building the fence. Probe parties, VC sappers, heavy weapons units and NVA assault groups concealed themselves in the jungle around the Song Rai. At the same time, the Reconnaissance Platoon was tasked to ambush and patrol two clicks out from the area where the mine fence was being constructed.

RECON'S LAST STAND

Flinders Ranges, 2000

Dawn near Breakfast Time Creek. The camp fire is a splash of grey ash, most men are still snoring in their swags. A man sits smoking by himself. He wants to talk about something; for two days he's talked about a lot of things—unloaded nearly 30 years.

He finishes his cigarette and lights another from the butt.

'My wife says I smoke too much. She's noticed a lot over the years, like how the smallest thing can make me angry. She always walks behind me from restaurants, to apologise to everyone for my unusual behaviour.

'I've got a son, in his thirties now, from my first marriage. When I left to go to war he was a six-week-old lump in my arms. When I came home from Vietnam he was just walking. Thirty years on from Vietnam and I'm wondering what's happened to him, where is he today? What's happened to relationships—the wife, the son, the close friends?'

He is letting loose a tear. Yesterday he was saying how after he came home he couldn't stop grinding his teeth and drinking all the time. Back to the job as a sales rep with the food company where, as a Vietnam vet, he was regarded as an oddity. Other guys settled in, why couldn't he?

'I often have these storms in my head, connected with flashes and images that always seem to be fire, smoke . . . and there's the sound of a woman screaming a long way off. She's been screaming for 30 years, and I can't stop her.

'I created a perimeter and became a victim bombarded by paranoia. You know, *Don't come inside my wire.*

'I told myself I was sick, I had this baffling illness . . . I shrank inside myself . . .' We tell him he is not a victim. He was—he is—a warrior. A gentle, peaceful, caring warrior.

CONFIDENTIAL INTSUM: June 1966—All companies and platoons must use correct procedure to pilots to bring helicopters into a landing zone (LZ).

Charlie and Bravo Companies had worked hard constructing 4 kilometres of mine fence in nine days. It was soul-destroying work, hammering in steel stakes and rolling out barbed-wire. Soldiers used to patrolling and combat wore special gloves, swung 'dollys' to drive the steel stakes into the ground, and slaved for hours in the sun. Close behind came the engineers, laying and setting the M16 mines.

Reconnaissance Platoon was tasked with patrolling by day and ambushing tracks by night 2000 metres from the work parties. There was a good reason for this: the VC were probing the fence at night and also trying to lift the mines and re-lay them so we'd walk on them. The enemy followed a series of foot tracks in towards the fence, and these tracks were our night ambush sites.

On the late afternoon of 18 March, Mick Deak checked his maps and we set off for a track junction 1500 metres from the town of Dat Do and a nearby creek called Suoi Ba Tung. Nearing the ambush site, Deak signalled for us to prop and we studied the ground—disused paddy field, scrubby bush on both sides. The two tracks met in a V junction. It was here we would set a triangular ambush. Deak considered this form of ambush excellent for covering two tracks. A machine-gun was placed at the two base points of the triangle, and another gun at the apex. The base of the triangle ran parallel to the track, the killing ground. The rear gun covered the other track. Deak, Mulby, medic Peter Fraser and radio men Jacka Aitken and Tex Western, the battalion signaller attached to Recce, sat in the middle while the other sections formed the three sides of the triangle. The ambush team bristled with automatic weapons and M79 grenade launchers, which broke in the middle like a shotgun and fired a 40mm bomb. As fast as the soldier could reload from a bandolier around his neck he could fire the M79, with its distinctive 'dupe' sound, and when the bomb exploded it killed anyone within 5 metres.

Blue Twaits laid his M60 down on the sandy soil and settled back beneath the undergrowth. His support—or number two on the gun—John 'Blah' Williams readied his link belts to couple onto the 50-round belt on Twaits's weapon if the ambush was sprung. Suave Harve, the section commander, settled in next.

To their left, lying in the increasing afternoon shadows, were Recce men 'Butch' Moroney and 'Blue' Edwards. On the right point of the triangle, facing east, were gunner 'Blue' Wollner, Gary 'Background' Nottage—a digger who was neither seen nor heard, always in the background—and section commander Bob Searle. Round the flank and linking into my section were Denis Mills, Ken Scaysbrook and Bill Evans, through to our gunner, Blue Riley, and on to Barney Gambold and Max Campbell.

Having done scores of ambushes in Vietnam, it was a familiar routine: every man settled quickly and quietly. It was necessary to be settled in the ambush position just on sundown so your eyes had time to adapt to the changing light. In the jungle the light disappeared instantly, but in open country with low scrub, dusk came and went gradually. The terrain out here was sandy, reflecting light; there was no moonrise yet, and very soon we were looking into semi-dark. We could sleep, one man dozing while one lay awake, but invariably each man hovered in a sort of twilight zone, unaware at times whether he was awake or asleep. The ambush was fast and lethal. The idea was to throw everything at anyone in the killing ground—a wall of fire cutting the enemy down.

'Shoot low, aim for the legs,' Deak had repeated time and again. 'Make them drop in the killing ground . . . for good.'

I rolled onto my back and studied the stars through loops of bamboo. I was trying to work out why the saucepan was upside down. There was no Southern Cross here but it was a beautiful night—

Thump, thump, thump, thump . . . Craaaack! craaaak!

The crash of Twaits's M60 going into overdrive almost blew me off the ground.

The red-headed machine-gunner had his hat down low over his eyes and he tugged it lower to cut out reflective light as four Vietcong appeared, jogging along the track. Twaits was able to discern, as he pulled the M60 back into his shoulder, that these men were ready for action and obviously alert, with weapons held at waist height swinging left and right. The gunner nudged his number two, Blah Williams, gave the thumbs down, then pulled the M60 butt in tightly to his shoulder and squeezed the trigger, holding it back for a sustained burst. Red tracers were streaming down the foot track, ricocheting into the darkness and arcing lazily back to ground.

'Incoming or outgoing, Dogs?' Little Mac was straining to look up towards the left gun. 'Are we copping it?'

I hissed for him to shut up, so he wouldn't draw fire by speaking. But I was wasting my time: as soon as our M60 stopped there was the distinct *bapbapbapbap* of an AK-47 returning fire, then a much louder burst of fire from the enemy, followed by a volley of the green tracer bullets they used.

The enemy had hit the ground and rolled in a counter-ambush measure, and one had levelled a Browning Automatic Rifle (BAR) at Twaits's M60 muzzle flashes, almost emptying a magazine. The stream of bullets raced across the ground and through our left gun position. The bullets tore into Blue Twaits's leg, almost filleting the flesh and smashing through the bones. Twaits rolled and writhed in pain. He had not been able to sustain his fire because the link ammunition got snagged in grass.

I pulled up my Slaughtermatic and prepared for the usual silence after an ambush.

Braaaat! Braaat, Crack, crack, craaaak!

The trees above us shuddered and whipped as enemy fire swept across the top of our position.

'Fuck, that's bloody Nog fire!' Barny Gambold and Little Mac grunted at the same time.

Deak was now yelling at the top of his voice, 'Harve, Harve, get the gun going, *give it back to the bastards!*'

Blue Mulby was on his knees, knowing well that something was wrong—the enemy had regrouped and were now sending a hail of bullets into what they thought was the Australian position. *These bastards know what they're doing, and there's more than four of the fuckers, too.*

The low trees around the ambush site were now flickering as if a strobe light had been switched onto them. Muzzle flashes from small arms fire and terrifying bursts from automatic weapons lit up the scrub opposite our ambush site. Their green tracer and our red tracer bullets together looked like a dozen sets of traffic lights winking on and off.

Mulby crawled forward at the same time Blue Wollner and Background Nottage swung their M60 around from the right flank to cover the trees where the enemy were directing fire from. The Reconnaissance ambush had now developed into a full-on firefight. Mulby reached the track and began to crawl towards Twaits's gun position.

Remember, you're trained for this, he told himself. *You are responsible for your men. You're the platoon sergeant, get it together.*

Mulby saw section commander Suave Harve pulling at his

wounded gunner, at the same time placing his body between Twaits and the enemy fire.

Mulby was now level with the gun group. 'Get that bloody gun going, Harve.'

Blah Williams had already crawled past the wounded Twaits and Harve to reach the M60. Harve was panting with exertion, frantically pulling shell dressings apart to wrap around his mate's shattered leg. Immediate Action (IA) is a drill a soldier follows when his weapon jams or is empty—a protocol that takes the soldier from a rifle or M60 not firing, for one reason or another, to a gun firing in the fastest possible time. Williams lifted the gun cover then flipped up the feed plate, swept it clean and dragged on another belt of link ammunition, slammed down the cover, recocked, squeezed the trigger. Another stream of 7.62 was soon shredding the trees across the track.

It was during the firing that I heard a sound that made my blood freeze—a soldier screaming in pain. It was a wailing, a howling that reached a crescendo. Then another sound just as terrifying—the shouts and commands of Vietcong officers, obviously planning a counter-attack.

'Fuck, this is bloody big, mate,' I shoved Little Mac and yelled to Blue Riley, 'Watch our arses, it's coming from everywhere. We could get hit from the back.' Riley knew his job, he could swing to the right or left flank if necessary to support the other two M60s. That was the beauty of the triangular ambush.

I may be a fumbler and a bumbler at times, but come the time for action I surprised myself how coolly I could assess situations and act. Maybe it was training, maybe it was something deep in me.

I seized the M79 grenade launcher from Little Mac and slammed in the first round. I aimed it like a mortar tube and pulled the trigger. *Dupe,* the round zoomed out and over into the far trees. I broke the launcher and shoved in another bomb.

'That's bloody mine, give it back,' Little Mac tried to grab his beloved weapon from me.

'Fuck off for a minute, I'm just showing you where I want them, right?'

Deak was on the radio calling up gun support from The Horseshoe while his sergeant, Blue Mulby, assessed the size of the enemy. Mulby was now crawling and rolling parallel with the track, figuring where most of the enemy fire was coming from. The stream of sporadic gunfire was above knee height—if each man hugged the ground and ate dirt at this stage no more casualties would be inflicted. But right now we had to get effective fire back into the low trees where the VC were massing.

This is bigger than a platoon of Nogs, it's got to be company size—50 to 100, maybe. And they've got real heavy weapons—and they're not breaking off. They're going to try and roll us up from the sides.

Mulby made his decision and then stood up and ran back to me.

'Dogs, Dogs, '79 over there into the trees. *Now!*'

I stared at the big platoon sergeant *standing* 10 foot tall in front of me for a second. 'What the fuck are you doing standing up in the middle of a shitfight?' I yelled.

'Shut up and get those friggin' grenades going.'

Little Mac grabbed his M79 back and tipped bombs from his bandolier between the two of us, then in quick succession sent a barrage up and over our bamboo thicket into the trees. The shed-load of grenade rounds only brought another wall of fire from the Vietcong and more shouts.

Suddenly there were bursts of automatic fire from the far flanks. The VC had spread out, and their commander's shouts were closer now.

They really know what they're doing—we could be fucked here.

'Watch the flanks, they're going to try and roll us up. *Watch the bloody flanks!*'

I'd never heard Deak sound this concerned before, and I began to feel a prickle down my neck.

There's 21 of us here, how many are going to get out?

Deak was now working furiously to raise a fire mission and get 105 rounds to hammer the VC position. He would normally have broken contact straight after the ambush, RV'd and come back to do a search, but he was now desperately wrestling with a situation where he had a man badly wounded and could not break from the enemy, who looked as if they were preparing for an assault.

By the book, by the book and get fire support in. Everything you can get, right now.

As Deak feared, the Vietcong began a pincer movement on both flanks of the Recce platoon. First hit was Bob Searle. Gunner Wollner opened up with a sheet of fire to his right flank. It is basic tactics in a usual contact to hold back machine-gun fire until the last minute, thereby depriving the enemy of knowledge of machine-gun positions until they can be used to cut down the enemy.

The attack on the Recce platoon intensified. From the forward enemy position across the ambush killing ground, fire was still coming in at Blah Williams in Twaits's gun position. They were trying to roll up Searle's section from the other flank.

I lobbed the last of the 40mm bombs over the bamboo and expected the VC to appear on the secondary track to my rear at any moment.

We are going to get done over, but we've got enough ammo to last two hours.

Recce always carried double the regular front-line ammunition requirements for just this sort of attack.

Whoosh, CRUMP. Whoosh, CRUMP.

The two largest shells used in the Vietnam War were the big navy guns and the 175mm rounds fired from the US Army 'Heavyweights'. Both were available in a serious, sustained enemy contact. Deak had managed to muster naval gunfire from a destroyer in the South China Sea and the 175s at Nui Dat. He also called up the next biggest, the 155 mobile guns, as well as 105 howitzers, based at The Horseshoe.

When massive artillery fire came in 20 minutes after the ambush was triggered, its power almost lifted us off the ground. The flashes from the shells as they struck several hundred metres away turned night into day. There were *whirrr* and *wooz* sounds as massive chunks of shrapnel spun over our heads. Deak had already laid DFs, and was now 'walking' the wall of thunder towards the enemy. I heard him yelling, 'Drop 100, drop 100 . . . drop 50!' into the radio handset. I flinched: this action wasn't without very serious risk to us poor bastards crouched under nothing more than clumps of bamboo.

Deak knew that within minutes the VC would call their own mortar support down on us, so he opted for a withdrawal under fire. He mustered his three section leaders. 'Dogs, Harve, Bob— in here, men, we're bugging out.'

Now a sudden silence. Twenty men shuffled like beggars away from the ambush. Just the sound of boots in sand. It was deadly quiet. Twaits was wrapped up in a plastic hootchie supported by four Recce men. He was as silent as the night was black.

Mulby was encouraging the men to keep quiet and vigilant as he caught up to me. Suddenly another barrage of artillery and naval shells came over like a roaring train.

Blam, blam, blam.

More strobe flashes from small arms back at the ambush location. 'I reckon bloody Mick Deak has gone for the all-time record,'

I commented. 'That must be the most shit ever called in by a Second Lieutenant. What next, a B52 strike?'

I looked behind. We were now 300 metres from the enemy, and were beginning to stand out in the reflected light from the dry paddy. 'We're stuck out here like dogshit, Blue. Bloody Nogs are gonna blast us any minute.'

No sooner had the words left my mouth than our old ambush location exploded in a series of orange flashes. At the same time green tracers streamed into the very places we were lying five minutes before. The enemy was using 60mm mortar to pound our position.

'Down, down, down now,' Deak whispered urgent instructions and we threw ourselves behind the paddy's earth bunds. I rammed my shoulder in and pushed the rifle over the top. All the other men did the same. Deak was talking to the dustoff chopper, which could be heard as a low hum, then a drone that increased and receded on the horizon.

'No, fuck it, *our* west, not *your* west.'

Deak was going frantic on the radio trying to get the Casevac in. 'Yeah, it's Victor Charlie with heavy weapons but we've got their heads down.' Crackle and more inquiries from the chopper pilot. 'I'm checking arty fire now. Come in and I'll put some light on the ground for you . . . do it right now, no incoming small arms fire. You're clear.'

While Deak battles to get the chopper down and Twaits out, we lie with weapons pointing back at the low bush. Those bastards are going to brass us *and* the Huey if they can.

Next moment Deak is standing next to me. 'Dogs, gimme your Zippo. Quick, man.'

I look up at my platoon commander. 'Don't you think a smoke's a bit risky now, Skipper?'

'Gimme your lighter, I know you've got a bloody Zippo.'

Deak snatches my cigarette lighter and scuttles away into the dark.

Mulby was next. 'Okay, chopper's coming down. Everyone eyes front and ready to open up if there's one sniff of a bloody Nog.'

The clatter grows louder and I roll over and look back to see Deak standing in an open rice paddy, arms outstretched and a lighted Zippo in each hand.

Mulby is kneeling next to me, mouth open, staring at his leader standing like a man ready for crucifixion as the wash from the rotor blades whips up sand and grit around him. Next second the pilot flicks on his spotlight.

I feel like I want to shit. My mouth is dry and in my mind's eye I can see a stream of bullets hit the helicopter and flames and men falling in a hail of enemy fire. Deak stands like a dancer on stage with a brilliant white light on him. The picture of courage is totally unreal.

'Get him on, get him on. Come on, fuckin' move!' Mulby is screaming above the noise. For a moment I watch Mulby and think, *I love that big ugly bastard.*

As Twaits is pushed onto the inside deck of the chopper, he swings around to the door gunner. 'You RAAF blokes took your time . . . can't navigate yet, uh?'

The American gunner looked down at the wounded Australian. 'Not easy at night, buddy, and we ain't the RAAF.'

'Come on, get goin'!' Mulby hustles the Recce men across the paddy in a half-stagger and stumble. We crash into the thick growth, every man wheezing, coughing and spitting. Deak gets back on the radio and calls for more fire to block our withdrawal.

Braa-up, braaup.

Deak spun around. ' . . . the hell was that?'

'Dogs farted,' Little Mac said, struggling to keep a straight face.

There was a series of giggles and coughs and snorts that quickly became a collective hysterical laugh.

'Shut up, the war's still on, you blokes.' Deak went back to his radio.

The action had lasted $3^1/_2$ hours and exhaustion swiftly overtook most men, who collapsed into sleep. Anyone who snored had the hell booted out of him. I slumped, my pulse still racing. I wondered if I'd hallucinated the whole event.

DAY OF TEARS

Flinders Ranges, 2000

Here is a place called Secret Creek. What is spoken in Secret Creek never comes back. No-one will ever hear the confessions, the admissions, the apologies and the soul-speak uttered up here. These things are laid to rest with the spirits of the landscape.

You are talking now about the last day, when we all scrambled aboard the big Chinook helicopter at Luscombe Field and left the war zone. The loadmaster didn't lift the rear ramp, so when the machine turned south you could see the Nui Dat rubber fading to brown. Out west the Warbies were retreating in a sort of serene blue. You wanted to curse out loud at those mountains. The rice paddys flashed in the sun, a thousand bomb craters full of water strung out like shining pearls . . . and then the swamps of the Rung Sat, a beautiful emerald.

The men were slumped forward, not a word was spoken. Not enough energy for elation, no relief in the clattering and shaking Chinook; just disbelief and numbness at being alive. The faces of two men appeared in front of you, grinning and talking. They have been left behind but only in spirit, because their bodies were flown back to Australia for burial in their home towns months ago.

You recalled the death of one of them, his expression of shock, then dullness. The jab of pain and guilt came when you thought of his mother, his father, his brothers and sisters, and the indescribable pain the loss of a soldier can cause. You felt the survivor's guilt, which is very common—not that that was an atom of consolation. You ground your teeth at the insanity, the word often used to describe war. It was absolutely true. Was it like that in the World Wars, too?

In Secret Creek you've gone quiet. But listen, you should carry no guilt for some politician in Canberra who made the decision to send men like you to the Vietnam War. You were an Australian soldier, and at all times you were honourable in the service of your country.

CONFIDENTIAL INTSUM: September 1966—President Johnson said our quarrel is not with the people of North Vietnam . . . we are more than eager to let North Vietnam live in peace if they will let South Vietnam do the same. North Vietnam cannot succeed in the conquest of South Vietnam.

First light over the paddy found a bunch of men bleary-eyed and exhausted, staring out at the ambush site. First thought: *do you think we've got a minute to brew up? If there's one thing in the world right now that can put everything back into perspective, it's a bloody cup of coffee and a cigarette.*

'Dingo's brekkie, this morning, Dogs, just a piss and a look around.' Philosophical Bob Godfrey had read my thoughts while lying on his stomach looking at me. In those few minutes of sunrise I noticed how much we stank: a collective odour of sweat and dried-out fear. There was a crackle of radio transmission, then the howl and squeak of APCs approaching from the north. The cavalry had arrived.

Deak called a quick briefing, then we saddled up and moved out to the carriers. Every man in Recce was struggling to find some shred of normality, to find his way back to soldiering mode.

The night before . . . what the hell had happened the night before?

I sat on top of the lead machine and was the first to dismount at the ambush site. A quick look back at the paddy and I saw a vision of a man standing with Zippo lighters in his outstretched hands beneath a hovering chopper. Two minutes wandering around the ambush position and there was Little Mac insisting he have his grenade launcher back.

Deak strode up to me. 'The safest place to walk today is on the tracks. The Nogs could well have booby-trapped both sides of the trail, so stick to the middle, Dogs, and you'll be all right. Space out and stagger your blokes as you move up.'

Thirty yards on and Pagey gave me thumbs down. He pointed to an object ahead, a mass of blood and cloth. I knelt and examined it—a muslin cloth filled with damp rice that the VC carried around their waist. They ate from it on the move, like I'd bite into a chocolate bar or a fig slice while patrolling.

I didn't feel too good following the trail of the wounded enemy, who had obviously fled at high speed. I felt like a hunter quietly pursuing a wounded quarry. All around were shattered trees and massive craters. The stillness was playing hell with my already-shot nerves; I knew we were all running on our last the drop of adrenaline. Blue Mulby was now up with me, stepping in front of me with his typical chicken-emu stalk. I suddenly exploded. 'Fuck off, Blue—we don't need you sticking your big head in.'

The platoon sergeant spun around, glaring, 'What's with you, Dogs . . . ?'

I grabbed him. I was beyond rational thought. I was angry, exhausted and one of my best mates was pissing me off.

'Get back to fuckin' platoon HQ where you belong. If there's anything to find, my blokes'll do the finding.'

Mulby stepped back and I thought we were about to get into a punch-up in the middle of the war zone.

Really bright move, Dogs.

'Shut up, hey, bloody shut up and look over here,' scout Page defused the moment with more evidence of blood, bandages, and jerry cans of water—an obvious sign that a lot of men had retreated at full stick.

We took a break, had a smoke and I was able to get a brew going. My guts were still churning, like everyone else's. Fatigue swamped me again. We tended to think we were getting on top of things in Phuoc Tuy; patrolling, ambushing, securing sectors, dominating in the air and plastering the enemy with artillery. But still they were here—in huge numbers. Last night, I recalled, we had very nearly been wiped out. We were nearly overrun, and most certainly would have been blown away by VC mortars if Deak hadn't given us the word to piss off. The curious aspect to the Vietnam War was that we were fighting an enemy we never really saw. We heard words shouted in Vietnamese, we caught fleeting flashes of black or green uniforms, but the only time you got a good look at an elusive VC was when he or she was dead at your feet. Warfare of this nature sucked the energy out of you. *Fighting in shadows, that's what we did.* And we weren't winning this war. We had won every fight and taken territory by day . . . and Charlie was taking it back at night. Kill a hundred . . . and another thousand replace them.

It was a 1000-strong NVA force that hit Lo Gom that night. A small force of 28 peasant soldiers, supported by a handful of Australian advisers and soldiers, fought for their lives against rocket, mortar and massive ground assault. The NVA soldiers of the 275 Regiment were stopped by well-prepared machine-gun positions and belts of barbed-wire, as well as arty support from Nui Dat and The Horseshoe. It was another enemy failure—they ran, retreated along the south coast with bloody noses—only to be pounded by American destroyers cruising off the south coast. The 6th Battalion gave chase and recovered scores of backpacks and weapons during the operational sweep through the jungle and bamboo north-east. We discussed the battle and took no comfort from the fact that we may have bloodied a few noses ourselves: there was little doubt that the enemy we ambushed were part of the main force in the Lo Gom assault, possibly probing north of the hamlet.

The 5th Battalion's Bravo Company went back to mine fence work—more heat, dust and danger, preparing wire as the engineers followed, laying the lethal jumping jacks. Recce platoon moved out onto normal patrolling and ambushing to shield Bravo Company. I moved into a bamboo thicket for Mick Deak's briefing and had no sooner squatted on the ground when there was a bang in the distance.

Bob Searle looked at Deak. 'That was a bloody jumping jack.'

'Fuck, someone's copped it.' Mulby was on his feet. 'Listen in for dustoff and get details,' he said to signaller Jacka Aitken.

The details were: one Bravo man dead, two wounded.

Massive depression. Anger eating away, again. Bravo Company blown up *again*. I sat and smoked and thought.

How the hell is anyone from this place ever going to live a normal life when they get home? If they get home. Punch a clock, shop in a deli, talk to normal people about normal things. You couldn't. There are things happening here you wouldn't—couldn't—ever speak of again.

7 April and another butt-busting walk through the weeds. We joined Bravo Company near the mine fence for a night harbour. Lieutenant Kerry Rinkin was one of the most likeable guys I'd met. A National Serviceman, Rinkin won me over straight away when he turned up with a grin and fresh eggs and we fried up.

Deak was quiet, I noticed, going through mood swings in the past two days. He was angry, frustrated and had a very low opinion of whoever laid the minefield. 'I'm bloody telling you, this mine fence is the most stupid idea the Army's ever had. No cover, no protection to stop Charlie getting in and taking those fucking horrible things to blow the shit out of us.'

Nods all round, agreement. Silence. Rinkin bid us goodbye as we set off for another patrol.

Kerry Rinkin went back to his platoon and stepped up on a rice paddy bund to brief his men. After the O Group, the young officer stepped back off the bund onto a jumping jack.

It was 1100 hours and I was trying to catch a few rays of sun through the bamboo when I heard the dustoff chopper in full throttle. Jacka Aitken could barely whisper the words, 'NOTICAS, it's that new looey, Rinkin, he's listed as fatal.'

I stood and told my section I needed a crap. I crept away some distance and squatted. I began to sob, and the sobs soon turned to a flood of tears. I pushed my hands over my face and hung my head. I couldn't stop shaking. Like every man in the Tiger Battalion, spiritually, physically, psychologically I was now well and truly in the red.

Early April, and 7th Battalion Tracking Team Commander Chris O'Neil made his way along the dirt road towards Reconnaissance Platoon's tents. O'Neil, a Malaya–Borneo campaigner, was the leader of the first Australian Tracking Team attached to a battalion going to war. They were part of the 7th Battalion's Advance Party, arriving ahead of the main body by about two weeks. Walking behind O'Neil were Norm Cameron and Tom Blackhurst, with black Labrador war dogs Cassius and Justin. The men located the Recce tents and introduced themselves.

O'Neil's first impression was one of shock—the men he greeted looked as if they were physically disintegrating. Some were sitting on sandbag blast walls, others lounged in chairs, smoking. All were rake-thin and had the 1000-yard stare.

Chris O'Neil was still getting to grips with the trip to Nui Dat: a long ride on a Hercules transporter from Australia, then a wobbly flight by Caribou to Luscombe Field before climbing into a Land Rover for the short run up to the 5th Battalion. He was still absorbing the sights and sounds of the ATF base, but he was almost speechless at the state of the Recce men who had done more than a year in Vietnam.

O'Neil recalled how in Malaya–Borneo, five months of bush work had caused huge weight loss and stripped the physical condition from soldiers. But these men here looked as if they had done 10 months on ration packs. More, there was a flaky abstractness about them. It was clear that they were shattered by what they had seen and done. Until they loosened up, their conversation was limited to one- or two-word comments. But one thing was certain: they were happy to meet the Trackers.

Suddenly O'Neil was distracted by snorting and snuffling noises coming from a nearby weapon pit. A squealing pig emerged, ears flicking and snout twitching. It was painted with tiger stripes, and it took a second for the penny to clunk home. The 7th Battalion, known as 'Porky's People', had adopted a pig as its mascot—much the same as 5th Battalion had taken a tiger. Recce had decided on a big hello with a pig Mick Deak had bought in Hoa Long.

I sat in my tent after the pig greeting—denying I had painted those stripes on it—and fumbled with my final packing.

One of the Tracking Team men was asking me what Vietnam was like. I was trying to tell him, but it was impossible. How could you scoop up and explain what had happened during the past 12 months? Even for me, when I tried to spin back to week one, day one, when we had sat in this rubber in the rain and watched the flash and bang as that storm broke over us, it was impossible to believe we had later helped establish an ATF base here. I was feeling numb—and another sensation: guilt. I felt guilty that we were leaving, and that this soldier standing here in front of me was staying, soon to experience what we had gone through. I could think of only one thing to say, hopelessly inadequate as it was.

Be careful.

I made a brew over my pathetic little cutdown-can stove.

Probably one of the last coffees I'll make in Vietnam, I thought, squeezing in brown condensed milk.

The final words I heard that day were from a Tracking Team soldier as he walked past my tent. I wondered if he meant me to hear what he said.

'I reckon all these blokes have gone insane.'

COMING OUT

Flinders Ranges, 1996

The insidious and corrosive nature of post-traumatic stress disorder was such that a few—maybe only those close and intimate with veterans—recognised that men were falling to pieces and self-destructing in the years after the Vietnam War.

I was one of those who travelled 100 miles of bad road. I had been caught on a jag that had me spinning out: mood swings, anger, anti-social behaviour, unfocused hatred. Most of this was fuelled and fired by drinking and drunken rage. Two marriages had gone, I had lost contact with a son and was now sitting on the banks of a creek celebrating 20 postwar years of hopeless life.

Not far from me was a dead tree, bent and busted, leaning at a crazy angle. Certainly some sort of metaphor. Beneath that tree I could just make out tiny shoots of green, at least a dozen, that were now reaching up, almost as if they were trying to replace the perished and departed hanging above.

What brought me to this place was my role in an innovative new scheme to rehabilitate young men and women at risk: those who had done drugs, boosted cars, were in trouble with the law, and seemed headed for terminal burn-out. The one man they needed to talk about wasted life was me, so I became a volunteer on Operation Flinders. My military training, after two tours of Vietnam and subsequent postings as an instructor, meant that I had a lot to offer in a bush-oriented program. I was also now a prison manager with the Correctional Services Department, so I knew the workings of the young criminal mind.

The program, which took kids out into the Flinders Ranges hiking, camping and abseiling, had been a phenomenal success. The isolation and spirit of the Ranges had a calming and rebirthing effect. Operation Flinders refocused young lives onto good things.

Could it work for veterans? Men like me?

It was maybe a 'road to Damascus' experience, maybe a belated wake-up call, but at that moment I resolved to go the way of the budding green shoots: to be a better man, be a role model for vets who were hitting the wall by the hundred. The simple plan was to bring vets into the bush; the fees paid by the Veterans Affairs Department would be funnelled back into Operation Flinders.

So an experiment was born, called 'Trojans' Trek'. It started in 1997, and the following three programs have seen nearly 50 men take the Trek to a new life. On the Trek they would walk tall and uphold the ideals of those original warriors, the Trojans. No shrinks, no combat gear, no booze or drugs, and no fighting. I also forbade spitting on the ground.

The Vietnam veteran was 'traumypnotised': he needed a snap of the fingers in front of his face. He needed to shed guilt, and had to believe that one day he would say he was proud of what he was. The Trek's philosophy was: that day has come. He also had to communicate with other people once more—and the best person for that was a fellow vet. The place where all this would happen was right here, where I was sitting looking at that regenerating tree: the Flinders Ranges. Five days' walking and camping on the Oratunga and Moolooloo stations.

Flinders Ranges, 2000

The men make their way down the trail towards Oratunga Station, where their vehicles are waiting. After five days in the Flinders there is a relaxed banter. We are all still wheezing and sweating from the walk, but we have stopped looking at our feet. We've even shaken out of the patrol file we took up on day one. Many have scoured out the fears and paranoia they have carried for years. We found the Mouse Shit Box, that compartment in the mind where we will now shunt all the things that don't matter: life's inconsequentials—the criticism that doesn't count, the occasional seepage of self-loathing that has to be discarded. There's a lot more worth hanging onto nowadays, and the secret is discerning what counts—like throwing sand on a sieve, the good stuff goes through and the rubbish gets caught in the filter.

We went to Vietnam as 20-somethings, we came back almost 50-year-old relics. There were things we had seen and heard and felt that made us shrink into ourselves. A little help would have gone a long way. Why didn't good things happen to make us feel good again? Well, that's just the way it went; it's history, stop whingeing. You've gone on fighting a war inside your guts for 30 years or more. We've been talking about all this for the past five days, and you've seen that we really are good people—not soldiers from a 'dirty war', as some have called us. You need to remember that.

You say to us today that we've been emotionally wounded and immobilised by fear, guilt and remorse. We've had enormous burdens to carry. But we have faced life's greatest fears in and after the war, and it is time now to recognise that as Vietnam veterans we are—like everyone else—unique and fallible human beings. Accept all this, you say, and we will become gentle warriors—who take no shit!

You also tell us to remember, until the end of our days, that there are veterans out there who will always help us, no matter what comes our way.

Anzac Day 1991, and Mary and Olga—'Tich' Tomas's sisters—ushered me into a church pew in Nannup, Western Australia. It was a service for the man I had called a friend. I sat down, thinking about the days when as a young man Tich had come to this small place of worship. Each pew had a small silver plaque with a name of a deceased parishioner engraved on it. I glanced down to see which one I was sitting in, and sat bolt upright with a chill when I saw the name: *Kearney*. My old mate must have had this one waiting for me.

Not far from the centre of town was a small park, and in the centre of the lawned area was a life-size statue of the man I had come to know, and missed so much. Tich Tomas was in a squatting position with a rifle across his legs. He was wearing a helmet, and the sculptor, a Vietnamese, had captured the likeness of his face almost perfectly. I wondered about the local Vietnamese community that had commissioned the work, and the gratitude they felt at the young National Serviceman's sacrifice. I felt a lump in my throat when Tich's brothers, Frank and Brian, told me about the day they heard of his death. They were both on their way down to the farm's dairy when they saw the police car coming up the long driveway to the main house. The car stopped and the local police officer got out and said, 'I've got some bad news, boys.'

The young men waited and listened, then Brian said, 'No milking today, Frank. We'd better go and see Mum and Dad.'

But there was one more facet to the Tich Tomas story. It had surfaced the night before the memorial service.

'What time was it when Tich got killed?' Olga asked me.

I was nonplussed for a moment. 'That's a bit hard, Olga, but I can work through it. It was almost dark when the Skipper told me he had gone, so I suppose 'bout six or seven o'clock.'

The Tomas family was sitting at the table—sisters Olga and Mary, brothers Frank and Brian, and Brian's wife Frances. The only personal possession that ever came home after their loved one's death was a broken watch, but that wasn't what this conversation was about.

Olga looked at me, misty-eyed. 'Tich was killed at 7pm on

8 July 1966 in South Vietnam,' she said quietly. 'Here on the farm at 9pm his dog Shadow started howling and went out on the hill. Shadow howled till midnight. He went off his food, and about two weeks later just vanished. Shadow never came home after Tich died.'

I could guess what the family was thinking: *almost as if Tich came and took him away.*

The End

EPILOGUE

Many men from Reconnaissance Platoon went back to normal lives upon their return from the war. There have been reunions over the years, and many veterans attended—others seem to have vanished into the ether, wanting to put the Vietnam experience behind them. Some of the key players in the Recce story are still with us today. Others are not.

Robert 'Dogs' Kearney stayed in the Army and returned to Vietnam as a Platoon Sergeant with 3RAR in 1971. He served in a number of units on return from his second tour, including 2 Commando Company and the Army Parachute Training School. He retired from service and became manager of B Division at South Australia's Yatala Labour Prison. In 1996 he was awarded the Exemplary Conduct medal for courage and leadership during the worst riot in the prison's history. He is now a project manager and training officer with the South Australian Emergency Services Unit.

Michael 'Skipper' Deak (Von Berg) was awarded the Military Cross and remained in the Army, where he served with the Special Air Service Regiment at Swanbourne, Western Australia. He retired from the Army to a successful career in the corporate sector. He now lives in Adelaide.

William 'Suave Harve' Harvey also went on to serve a second tour of duty in Vietnam. He became a parachute jump instructor and, after 20 years' service, retired and now runs a small business in Nelson Bay, NSW.

John Lea-Smith remained in the Army after Vietnam and later served in Papua New Guinea, along with other postings. He retired from the Army as a Major and has since run several successful businesses in Victoria.

John 'Blue' Mulby returned to Vietnam as a Sergeant Patrol Commander with 1 Squadron, SAS, and completed a second tour of duty which involved attachment to US Navy SEAL teams.

He remained in the Army and became the Regimental Sergeant Major (RSM) of the SAS. Severely injured in a training exercise, he is now retired and living in Perth.

Bernie 'Smithy' Smith rejoined 5RAR after his first tour of Vietnam and returned to the war for a second tour of duty with 5RAR. Smith was killed in a mine incident near Hoa Long on 9 March 1969.

Anthony 'Blue' Twaits had his lower leg amputated after being wounded in the Recon ambush but remained in the Army for several years. He lives in Hobart and still attends Reconnaissance reunions.

Fifth Battalion, the Royal Australian Regiment, was the first unit composed of regular soldiers and National Servicemen committed to operations in South Vietnam. The 'Tiger' Battalion, as 5RAR was known, was the leading element of the First ATF tasked with clearing Phuoc Tuy of Vietcong and NVA, who had dominated the province since 1945. Along with 6RAR, also a combination of regulars and National Servicemen, 5RAR established the ATF base at Nui Dat, which went on to become the centre of Australian operations until the 1972 withdrawal.

During the tour of duty described in this book, 5RAR suffered the loss of 25 killed in action or died of wounds, and 79 wounded in action. Members of the 5th Battalion received a total of 32 awards for bravery and service.

Reconnaissance Platoon, 5th Battalion—1966–67
Mick 'Deakey' Deak Von Berg M.C. (platoon commander)
John Lea-Smith (platoon sergeant)
John 'Blue' Mulby (section commander, acting sergeant)
William 'Suave Harve' Harvey (section commander)
Robert 'Dogs' Kearney (section commander)

Robert 'Bob' Searle (section commander)
Peter 'Doc' Fraser M.M. (medic)
Dudley 'Jacka' Aitken
Glenn 'Moose' Benham
Walter 'Jock' Brannan
Maxwell 'Max' Campbell
Trevor 'Taffy' Cheeseman
John 'Bluey' Edwards
Robert 'Bob' Egan
William 'Bill' Evans
Ray 'Ferret' Ferrier
Barney 'Barney' Gambold
Robert 'Bob' Godfrey
John 'Little Mac' McLaren
Dennis 'Millsy' Mills
Darryl 'Butch' Moroney
Garry 'Background' Nottage
Wayne 'Pagey' Page
Daniel 'Blue' Riley
John 'Scalesy' Scales
Ken 'Scasey' Scaysbrook
Anthony 'Blue' Twaits (WIA)
John 'Blah' Williams
David 'Blue' Wollner
Bernard 'Bernie' Smith (section commander—deceased)
David 'Tex' Western (signaller—deceased).

APPENDIX

Executive Summary: Trojans' Trek

From 20–24 August 1998, the Operation Flinders Foundation Inc. and the Vietnam Veterans' Counselling Service (South Australia) conducted a joint initiative in the northern Flinders Ranges. Named Trojans' Trek, its aim was to provide—in that remote setting and via structured activities—an enjoyable and challenging experience for up to 16 participating Vietnam veterans. Planned outcomes centred around enhanced self-insight and self-image, improved social confidence, and the provision of impetus for the development of constructive lifestyle coping strategies.

Results were very encouraging. All who completed the program regarded it an unqualified success, meeting or exceeding their expectations. Respondents and their partners who were surveyed reported that the program resulted in significant improvements to personal and social functioning.

Doug Knuckey
Consultant Psychologist
Operation Flinders Foundation Inc.

Feedback on Trojans' Trek (TT)

Dogs,

I trust you won't mind me taking the liberty, but I thought a quick note of thanks may be in order. As a broken down old 'grunt' who had perhaps lost his way, and who hadn't enjoyed himself so much in years, I wanted you to know that Trojans' Trek was possibly the best thing I've done since getting out of the Army.

Indeed, it was an experience that I can say I wouldn't have missed for the world. The only real downside was that it had to end. It went back to everything that was good about my Army life—and left out the crap.

I must confess, in the beginning I was extremely dubious and rather sceptical: I had visions of blokes running around the bush playing tin soldiers . . . led by a group of would-be NCOs that should have known better. I'm very glad to say I was totally wrong. Indeed it was the NCOs who made it . . . If I had to do it all over again, I'd happily have Dogs Kearney as my platoon sergeant any time.

Best regards,
Ron (TT participant).

To Trojans' Trek Organisers,
Trojans' Trek is a credit to all those involved in putting the program together. As a direct result of participating in TT, the health care professionals I've seen, and my wife and family have all noted a marked improvement in my health and outlook. Thank you to anyone who had anything to do with the program.

TT participant.

Dear Bob,
Please find enclosed an evaluation of Trojans' Trek. The evaluation found that the project was an outstanding success. It exceeded the expectations of the participants in all ways and was judged by the partners as having significantly positive effects on the personal and social functions in the relationship.

I have presented a copy of the evaluation to the Vietnam Veterans' Counselling Service, who is forwarding it to Canberra for the information of their senior management group . . .

John Shepherd
Executive Director
Operation Flinders Foundation Inc.

Dear Bob

To create a first-time program that generates as much positive feedback as Trojans' Trek—from both participants and partners—is a marvellous achievement.

From all reports you have created a working model that can be used in any remote or wilderness region. I understand there are plans to organise more treks.

For me the most telling aspect was all 13 respondents said the program met, or exceeded, their expectations and that half of the group reported they had achieved a measure of peace . . .

Alec Mathieson
Chairman
Operation Flinders Foundation Inc.

ABOUT THE AUTHORS

PETER HARAN joined the Army in 1966 and first served in Vietnam during 1967–68 with 2nd Battalion Royal Australian Regiment, attached to a combat tracking team. As one of the first Australian dog handlers, he wrote of his experiences with tracking dog Caesar in the highly successful book *Trackers: The Untold Story of the Australian Dogs of War* (New Holland, 2000). After two years as a dog trainer with the Army's Tracking Unit in Sydney, Peter served a second tour in Vietnam as an infantry section commander with 3rd Battalion in 1971. He left the Army in 1972, and is now a journalist with the Adelaide *Sunday Mail*.

ROBERT KEARNEY joined the Army in 1963 and was a member of Airborne Platoon with 1st Battalion before his first tour of Vietnam with 5th Battalion, where he was a section commander with Reconnaissance Platoon. His second tour of duty was with 3rd Battalion as rifle company platoon sergeant. Bob went on to serve as an instructor at the Army's Jungle Training Centre, 2 Commando Company, and was later a training officer at Officer Cadet School, Portsea, Victoria. After his full-time military service, Bob joined the Correctional Services Department and later became a prison manager. He was awarded the Correctional Services Exemplary Conduct Medal for courage and leadership as a hostage negotiator during a 1996 prison riot. Today he is a training consultant, working with the South Australian Country Fire Service and the State Emergency Service volunteers. He is also a company commanding officer with the Army Reserve 10/27th Battalion, based in Adelaide.

GLOSSARY

GENERAL

1, 2, 3, etc, RAR: Battalions of the Royal Australian Regiment (Infantry).

1ATF: First Australian Task Force, based at Nui Dat.

1ALSG: First Australian Logistics Support Group, based at Vung Tau.

2IC: Second-in-command.

ARVN: Army of the Republic of Vietnam.

break contact: Disengage from contact with the enemy.

Casevac: Casualty evacuation.

Charlie: Vietcong, also known as Victor Charlie or VC.

click: 1000 metres, 1 kilometre.

CO: Commanding Officer, the commander of the battalion (not to be confused with the OC, who commands a company within the battalion).

DF: Defensive Fire, a predesignated and planned fire mission to be called upon if attacked or counter-attacked.

digger: Australian soldier.

dustoff: Evacuation of the wounded.

FSB: Fire support base, established as an artillery fire base in the field to allow for greater range during operations.

harbour: A tactically laid-out platoon or company position, usually adopted at night to allow for all-round protection from enemy attack.

grunt: Affectionate term for an infantry soldier.

H and I: Harassment and Interdiction, fire from the artillery at selected likely enemy rendezvous points.

INTSUM: Intelligence Summary briefing sheets issued by the Task Force.

KIA: Killed in action.

lay-up: Hide, observe and listen for any enemy activity while resting.

LO: Liaison Officer.

Locstat: Location statement: map reference indicating a position on the ground.

Looey: Lieutenant.

LZ: Landing Zone for helicopters.

Medivac: Medical evacuation from the field through illness.

MIA: Missing in action.

MID: Mentioned in Dispatches. The Victoria Cross was the only medal for heroism that could be awarded posthumously. Those killed while performing a heroic deed—if not awarded the medal—were generally MID. The MID is also recognition for an exceptionally good job.

Mortrep: Mortar report (on enemy fire).

MP: Military Police, empowered to police all military members.

Nasho: National Serviceman.

NCO: Non-commissioned officer.

Nog: Derogatory term used by Australian troops to describe the enemy. American equivalent: **Gook.**

NVA: North Vietnamese Army regular troops.

OC: Officer commanding a major unit, such as a rifle company.

O Group: Orders Group, the Army's method and sequence of briefing individuals and groups to ensure that no critical information is missed.

Papasan, mamasan, babysan: Father, mother, baby.

PF: Provincial Force: South Vietnamese troops from within a particular province.

Piquet: Sentry duty.

POW: Prisoner of war.

prop: To stop (when on patrol).

punji pit: Pit containing sharpened stakes.

recce: Reconnaissance to survey or probe an area for enemy presence.

re-entrant: A gully or creek line running from high ground to low.

RF: Regional Force: South Vietnamese troops from within a particular region.

RP: Regimental Police: soldiers within the battalion empowered by the CO to police members of that battalion only.

RPG: Rocket Propelled Grenade fired from a shoulder launcher.

RSL: Returned Services League.

RV: Rendezvous point where soldiers met during patrols or after action.

sapper: A soldier in the Royal Australian Engineers Corps (RAE).

SAS: Special Air Service.

Sitrep: Situation report.

slick: A group of helicopters.

TAOR: Tactical area of responsibility.

the 'j': The jungle.

tracer: A round or bullet with a red or green glow at the rear to enable soldiers to see its trajectory.

VC: Vietcong. (See Charlie)

web belt: A belt from which a soldier hangs water bottles and ammunition pouches.

WIA: Wounded in action.

Zippo: Cigarette lighter, ubiquitous in the war.

WEAPONRY

.50 calibre: Heavy machine-gun.

AK-47: Soviet or Chinese 7.62mm automatic assault rifle used by VC and NVA forces.

Armalite: Lightweight 5.56mm US automatic rifle, which became standard issue to American forces. Also known as the AR-15, and later the M16 rifle.

bandolier: A shoulder-carried ammunition pouch.

banister: Anti-personnel artillery or tank round containing flechette or chopped steel rod.

CBU: Cluster Bomb Unit: a single bomb containing hundreds of smaller bombs that are armed and released during flight.

Claymore mine: Command-detonated explosive device loaded with C4 explosive and 700 small steel balls used to defend a position or ambush enemy.

Colt AR-15: See **Armalite**.

howitzer, or 105: Artillery piece used by Australians as heavy fire support weapon. Fired a 105mm shell.

jumping jack: See **M16 AP mine**.

M16 AP mine: Also known as 'jumping jack', an anti-personnel fragmentation mine.

M60 7.62mm belt-fed: General purpose machine-gun (GPMG) with a cyclic rate of 550 rounds per minute; issued at section level (three per platoon).

M79: Infantry section weapon that fired a 40mm high-explosive grenade.

Owen machine carbine: Australian-produced 9mm submachine-gun.

RPG: Rocket-propelled grenade carried by the enemy, fired from a shoulder-supported launcher.

SLR: 7.62mm semi-automatic self-loading rifle, the standard infantry weapon issued to Australian troops.

TRANSPORT

APC: Armoured Personnel Carrier: used as a troop carrier and fitted with heavy calibre machine-guns. Also known as **tracks** or just **carriers**.

B52, or B52 Stratofortress: Heavy US strategic bomber.

bird dog: Small fixed-wing reconnaissance aircraft used for spotting for ground-attack aircraft.

Caribou: Twin-engined light transport aircraft.

Chinook: Large twin-rotor helicopter (CH-47).

Hercules C-130: Long-range heavy transport aircraft with four engines.

Huey: Iroquois helicopter, Bell model UH-1H: used as a multipurpose aircraft in Vietnam.

Iroquois: See **Huey**.

Lamboretta: Three-wheeled motorbike used as a taxi.

LCM: Landing Craft Medium: used for beach landings of troops, stores and equipment.

Sioux: A light utility helicopter.

For further information on the authors of *Crossfire*, *Trackers*, unpublished photographs, a tribute to National Servicemen and Trojans' Trek, visit the website **www.vietnam-crossfire.com**. This site also links to the official 5th Battalion website.